I0797812

lonely planet

EPIC VAN TRIPS *of* EUROPE

Explore Europe's Most Beautiful Routes to Travel by Campervan

Astrid Duvillard and Alexandra Lam

CONTENTS

INTRODUCTION

Adopted in the 1960s by young Europeans trying to reach Kathmandu via the Hippie Trail, the camper van is now the subject of a new craze, spurred by the need to spend more time in the great oudoors after the confinements of the pandemic. A growing desire for simpler travel and getting back to nature are also major factors behind the boom in van travel – a way of life for some; a short break for others. There are a thousand types of adventure possible when you decide to travel this way. Solo, as a couple, with family or friends, in your own vehicle – fitted out with care or in a more rudimentary fashion – or at the wheel of a brand-new camper rented from one of the agencies springing up all over Europe.

This type of nomadic travel has its own special quirks. You need to have a taste for the unexpected and be ready to enjoy the moment. The great thing about the camper van is that you can improvise a stopover at any time and savour the experience: admire a sunset over the Baltic Sea, enjoy a cup of hot chocolate in an Austrian cafe after a rainy day, take the time to meet other itinerant travellers and extend the moment by sharing dinner on a Spanish beach. The other distinctive feature of this means of transport is the minimalism that inevitably imposes itself. Learning how to reconcile the discovery of new lands with the daily routine of life in a very small space, where every object must have its place, is a real challenge but also rewarding.

Europe is big and ripe for exploration – ideal for a change of scenery. When you travel with a little house on wheels, however, it's also easy to feel right at home everywhere. In this book, Astrid (www.histoiresdetongs.com) and Alexandra (www.issia.fr) present 50 itineraries covering one end of the continent to the other, taking you on the most beautiful European roads. With them as your guides, you'll tour the mythical Dolomites in Italy, discover the golden cliffs of the Algarve, answer the call of the far north in Norway, feel the magic of nature in Iceland and contemplate wild landscapes on an escape to Scotland – all must-do drives. Other more remote, but just as memorable, journeys will take you to the furthest reaches of the continent, to the shores of the Black Sea, to the heart of the Balkans, to the hot springs of Hungary and up into the Swiss mountains. There are a wealth of destinations to discover.

HOW TO USE THIS BOOK

Organised into four geographical sections, these 50 stories are accompanied by a road map that includes all the information you need to embark on your own adventure. Depending on the mileage planned for each journey, the duration of the trip can range from a few days to several weeks. Many culinary specialities are also listed, as well as favourite places to spend the night, picnic, take pretty pictures, swim and so on.

To inspire you, or inspire you to create your own itineraries, the 'More Like This' sections detail 150 similar escapades, grouped around a common theme or geographical area. More than just a means of transport, the camper van comes with a genuine travel philosophy, and once you've read the tips in the Practicalities section, all you have to do is start your engine and embrace freedom.

PRACTICALITIES

ADMINISTRATIVE FORMALITIES

• **Within Europe, only the United Kingdom** (England, Scotland, Wales, Northern Ireland) requires a passport when travelling around. For other European countries, a valid identity card is sufficient (some countries, such as Switzerland and Italy, even accept an identity card with extended validity: check your destination).

• **Apply for a health insurance card** (three weeks before departure; free of charge). It is valid in all 27 European Union (EU) countries, plus Iceland, Liechtenstein, Norway and Switzerland.

• **Check your bank card's withdrawal limit** and the amount of commission deducted on transactions, depending on the country. Make sure your phone's data is included in your package and valid for anywhere in Europe.

• **Make sure you don't carry any prohibited products** (beware of medicines), by consulting local regulations.

ON THE ROAD

• **Find out about the particularities of the Highway Code** of the countries you visit. Some require vignettes (prepaid road tax stickers you fix to your campervan's windscreen) for highway use (Austria, Slovenia, Slovakia, Switzerland, Bulgaria, Romania, Czech Republic, Hungary), while others have low-emission zones (Germany, the Netherlands, Spain, Belgium, UK, Scandinavia, Italy).

• **Running water** is not always potable: it's best to purify it by installing a filter in your water circuit if the vehicle is yours; or by using a flask or filtering straw, boiling it or exposing it to UV light with a special pen-lamp if it's a rental.

• **Take along pipe fittings and international adapters** for electrical outlets. Bring a set of four Truma lyres to connect your gas installation to cylinders in other countries. It's possible to refill cylinders in approved establishments.

• **Pack these essentials:** toolbox, duct tape, battery cables, rope, reflective vest, parking disc, safety triangle, and European accident report forms. If you're renting a van, check that this equipment is included.

TRAVEL WITH PEACE OF MIND

• **Camper van travel means dealing** with the weather. On hot days, park in the shade and stay hydrated. If it rains, plan indoor activities (and stay off muddy dirt roads). In winter don't forget chains, an ice scraper and big blankets.

• **Prevent dampness from setting in by** drying clothes and boiling water outside. Above all, ventilate your cabin.

• **For added comfort,** bring a sunshower, wedges for sleeping flat, a sun visor and a mosquito net. And if you've got room to squeeze in a bike, kayak or paddleboard into the van, you won't regret it.

• **Don't leave valuables in sight when parked** and, if possible, park in a busy place when you're away from your vehicle.

• **Road trip** expenses revolve around fuel, food, sightseeing, tolls, sometimes camping (for the comfort of a real shower) and maybe renting a vehicle. Add 10% contingency to your budget to cover all eventualities.

READ MORE

• **There are many ways** to find a place to park overnight. These include the park4night and iOverlander apps, the *Caravan & Camping* guide and the FFCC (Fédération des campeurs, caravaniers et camping-caristes) network.

• **Alternatively,** you can look for motorhome parks, surf Google Earth to see a suitable spot before you go or get friendly with local people and them ask about options for parking your van.

• **During the day,** in large conurbations, it's a good idea to park for free on the outskirts then take public transport or a bicycle to visit the city centre. Using a camper-friendly GPS (such as the Garmin CamperVan) can help you find parking easily.

SOUTHERN EUROPE

ON ANDALUCIAN SOIL

Explore the splendours of Andalucía, from fabulous cities like Granada, Córdoba and Seville to exceptional natural sites such as the Guadalquivir delta.

I pick up the converted van I've booked with a rental company in Málaga and set off without further ado on the vast east-west loop I've planned across Andalucía. My first objective: the Tabernas desert, not far from the southeastern tip of Spain. To reach it means taking the A7, which heads east along the coast. Interspersed with tunnels, the road crosses mountainous, arid landscapes, and in places overlooks the sea. This is the first time I've been behind the wheel of a van, other than my old LT35, and I have to admit I'm enjoying the ride. However, there's an unpleasant surprise in store – this Fiat Ducato van has no heating or water heater. Today's lesson: find out all you can about equipment and options when booking.

Arriving in Tabernas brings a complete change of scenery. This dry desert, with its palm trees, prickly pears and cactuses, is reminiscent of the American West. Many spaghetti westerns were filmed here (old sets remain, often integrated into amusement parks). After discovering the nearby Baños de Sierra Alhamilla oasis, famous for its thermal springs, I climb up the Mirador Desierto observation deck for a bird's-eye view of the sunset. Spending the night in the Tabernas desert is not allowed, so I find a spot right on its doorstep.

When I wake up, I take out my yoga mat to greet the sun under the aerial gaze of a peregrine falcon and then set off for Granada. The A92 skirts the Sierra Nevada Mountains to the

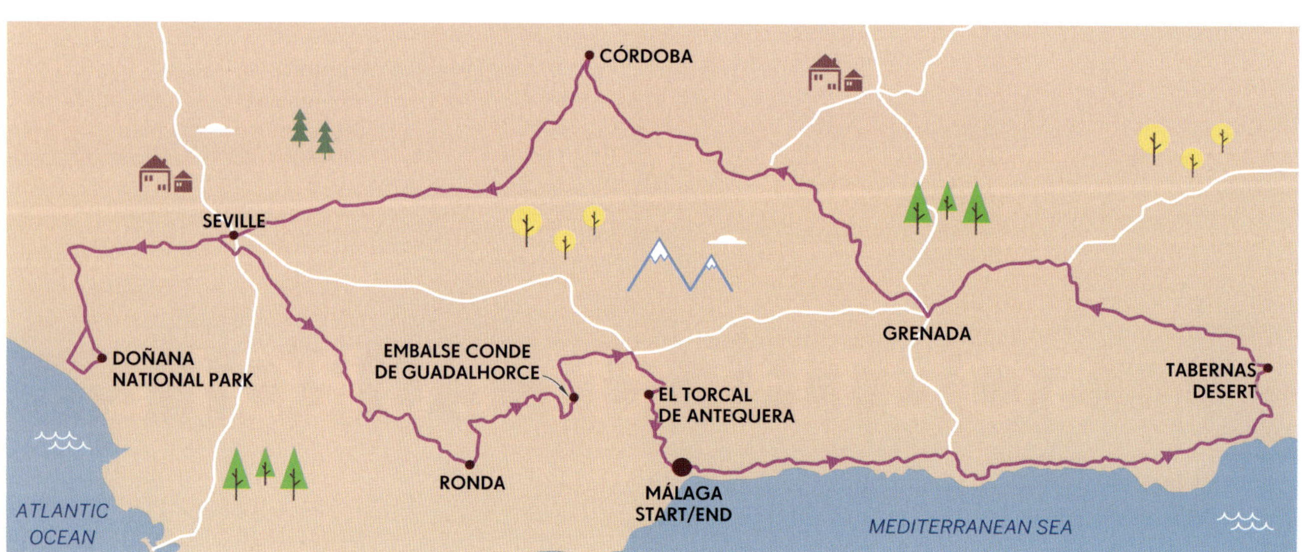

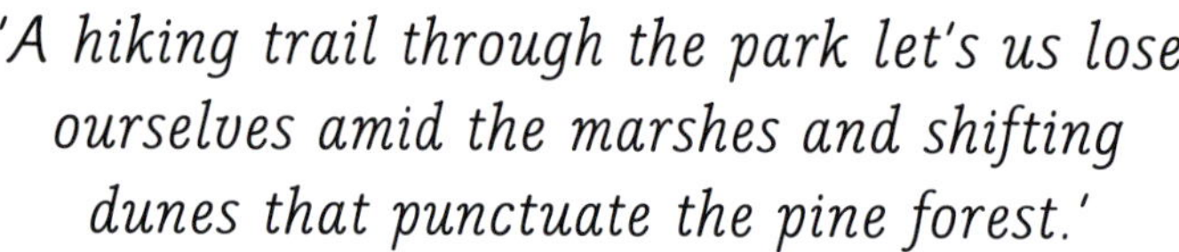

'A hiking trail through the park let's us lose ourselves amid the marshes and shifting dunes that punctuate the pine forest.'

north, and I look out of the window at the snow-capped peaks. I finally reach my destination and park the van. The Moorish citadel of the Alhambra occupies a prominent position on the Sabika plateau overlooking the city. Within its ramparts are the sumptuous Nasrid palaces, the beautiful summer gardens of the Generalife, imposing Christian churches and medieval towers. I wander the city's winding streets, contemplating its whitewashed gardens, the *cármenes*, before taking a break in a *tetería*, a Middle Eastern-style tea room.

After Granada, the next stopover is Córdoba, where I have a rendezvous with vanlife friends. Most of the sights here are centred around the Mezquita, a masterpiece of medieval Muslim architecture combining a former mosque with a cathedral. We stroll through the narrow streets to the bustling Plaza de la Corredera where it's a pleasure to mingle with the crowds enjoying tapas on the sunny square. At the end of the day, our procession rolls through meadows populated by sheep to reach our evening spot, El Hecho, near Guadalcázar, where we're grateful to the local community for providing picnic tables, barbecues, drinking water and a rubbish area. I even take the opportunity to do my laundry by hand and hang it on the tree branches while the red sunset gives the arid landscape an African flavour.

After a wonderfully quiet night, we get to spend the day in this little corner of paradise. As I travel alone most of the time, I appreciate these moments of conviviality all the more. Especially enjoyable is discovering the ingenious layouts of the other mobile homes parked near us. At the end of the day, we reach Seville, one of my favourite cities, with its extraordinary Mudéjar Alcázar (fortress-palace), its immense Gothic cathedral incorporating an 11th-century minaret (the Giralda), its courtyards bathed in the scent of orange trees and its flamenco clubs.

The following morning, we leave the city for Doñana National Park, in the heart of the Guadalquivir delta, 110km (68 miles) southwest of Seville. This vast wetland is a veritable oasis of biodiversity. We set up our vans on a large, dirt parking area on the edge of the reserve from where wooden walkways provide access to the beach. A hiking trail through the park let's us lose ourselves amid the marshes and shifting dunes that punctuate the pine forest. Along the way, we come across wild horses, fallow deer, various species of birds including pink flamingos – and an old animal carcass that's probably been eaten by an Iberian lynx. Not very reassuring. It's time for us to leave the park. We walk along the immense white-sand beach which offers another sublime sunset.

An early wake-up call means we're soon heading for Ronda along the A374, stopping for lunch at the foot of the town's gravity-defying Puente Nuevo bridge. Known as the place where bullfighting was invented, Ronda is built on a spectacular site, draped across the sides of the deep El Tajo Gorge.

After a stop 16km (10 miles) north in Setenil de las Bodegas, a small white village with cave dwellings, we set up camp at Embalse Conde de Guadalhorce, a beautiful turquoise-blue reservoir in magnificent natural surroundings. Unfortunately, next day we discover that the famous Caminito del Rey trail is closed, dashing my hopes of walking its vertiginous cliff-hugging

MINAS DE RIOTINTO

This former open-cast copper mine in the foothills of the Sierra Morena offers exceptional landscapes, tinted red, brown, green and blue by rocky materials. Streams turn reddish-brown, orange and green.

Opposite: Doñana National Park. Above, from left: Alhambra, Granada; Andalusian landscape. Page 11, from top: Torcal de Antequera; Plaza de España

footpath. Instead we set off in search of the panoramas from the Mirador de las Buitreras overlooking the Caminito del Rey. We continue towards Pico del Convento and exceptional vistas over the valley – before being chased off the summit by the viewpoint's namesake vultures.

I leave my friends and continue 46km (29 miles) east to El Torcal de Antequera nature reserve, with its strange limestone columns. Old memories come flooding back. I came here in my old LT35 and recall the steep climb up, praying the overheated engine would make it to the summit. I keep my fingers crossed that, unlike last time, I'll make the Ruta Amarilla, a circuit through the impressive karst landscape. **AL**

ROAD MAP

Start // Málaga
Finish // El Torcal de Antequera
Distance // 1171km (728 miles)
Recommended duration // 10-to-15 days
When to go // Avoid summer and its extreme heat
Culinary specialities // *Salmorejo* (cold tomato soup with breadcrumbs, hard-boiled egg and cured ham), *huevos a la flamenca* (eggs and vegetables cooked in a clay dish), *torta inglesa* (flaky pie with squash, cinnamon and powdered sugar)

THE PERFECT PHOTO SPOT

Description // Lookout over the Tabernas Valley
GPS coordinates // 37.01419, -2.418581
Light pollution // None
Access // Dirt road
Facilities // None
Parking // 4 places
Little extras // Magnificent site, Tabernas desert view

Opposite, clockwise from top: Van in the New Forest National Park, England; Bison in Białowieża National Park, Poland; Bear paw print, Kocevsko, Slovenia.

MORE LIKE THIS
MEETING THE ANIMALS

EUROPEAN BISON IN PODLASKIE (POLAND)

Animal lovers, head to Podlaskie in northeast Poland and park your camper in Białowiez National Park. Europe's last primary deciduous forest is also home to the European bison, the continent's largest mammal, weighing in at one ton. If they're not easy to spot in the wild, you can at least see the king of the forest in the Bison Reserve. Drive into the heart of the region to reach Narew National Park, the 'Polish Amazon'. Rent a kayak and cruise the Narew, one of Europe's only braided rivers, then follow the DK65 road to the Biebrza National Park, a vast wetland of marshes and peat bogs that's a birdwatcher's heaven, with hundreds of avian species, some of them rare. Finish your trip at Wigry National Park, where hills alternate with dozens of lakes – beaver territory.

Start // Białowiez National Park
Finish // Wigry National Park
Distance // 261km (162 miles)
More information // pologne.travel

THE BROWN BEARS OF KOČEVSKO FOREST (SLOVENIA)

In southeastern Slovenia lies a vast karst plateau, Kočevski Rog, cut by densely forested valleys and home to the country's largest population of brown bears, plus wolves and lynx. The tourist office has a variety of bear-spotting outings (evenings on the lookout, searching for footprints). Have lunch in your van by Lake Kočevski, then explore the Željnske Caves, inhabited since the Paleolithic era and featuring natural windows. Take forest road 917 through Kočevski Rog's beech and fir forest to the Roška Žaga clearing, the starting point for numerous hiking trails leading to small caves, chasms and hills, including Veliki Rog at 1099m (3606ft). Keep your eyes peeled for animal tracks – or even a bear. The forest was the headquarters of Tito's partisans during WWII, and known as Base 20.

Start // Kočevski Rog
Finish // Base 20
Distance // 53km (33 miles)
More information // kocevsko.com

ANIMALS ON THE LOOSE IN THE NEW FOREST NATIONAL PARK (ENGLAND)

After an overnight stop at Midgham Farm campsite, head deep into the New Forest National Park, known for its many free-roaming animals – cows, donkeys, pigs, sheep and, most famously, ponies. The New Forest pony breed is descended from wild animals, but the ones you see here today all have an owner. Explore the park's moors and forests by camper (animals are free to graze and roam, so be careful when driving), stopping to stride out on some of the hiking trails. Don't miss the observation platform at Bolderwood Deer Sanctuary, overlooking a large meadow where a herd of wild fallow deer gather for midday feeding. Round off your visit with the New Forest Wildlife Park.

Start/Finish // Midgham Farm
Distance // 100km (62 miles)
More information // new-forest-national-park.com

ALONG THE ISTRIAN COAST

Road trip between Croatia, Slovenia and Italy, focusing on the Istrian coastline and its pretty resort towns.

The sky is studded with stars and, sitting on large rocks just a few metres from the camper, we enjoy the silence. Camille, José and I gaze at the water stretching out before us in the moonlight. Several thousand kilometres of driving across Europe have brought us here, to Istria, a triangular peninsula in the northern Adriatic Sea, shared by Croatia, Slovenia and Italy. It's February, and over the next few days we'll be touring this region, a less popular tourist destination at this time of year, taking in deserted beaches and towns untouched by the hustle and bustle of summer.

Built on the eastern coast of Istria, Rijeka is an important Croatian town on Kvarner Bay, and my travelling companions and I are keen to visit its various, strikingly elegant neighbourhoods. From the wide pedestrian street of Korzo, lined with shops and cafe terraces, we reach the Baroque Cathedral of St Vitus, a white rotunda with an astonishingly massive silhouette. Other sites of interest include the Rječina River, which flows into a pretty marina, and the finely restored old stones of Trsat Castle, which bear witness to a local history dating back to antiquity. What's more, a number of crystal-clear pebble beaches stretch for miles around the city, making Rijeka an ideal holiday destination for vitamin D-starved tourists.

If we had come in search of sunshine though, we were in the wrong place. The rain stays with us all week, and the three of us, in my little T4, try to organise the drying of our clothes as best we can – without much success. The weather plays a crucial role on a camper van road trip, and can make comfort levels highly variable. Nevertheless, bad weather is an integral part of the adventure, so the only option is to make the best of it. On many occasions on this drive, with this weather, we're the only ones enjoying an unobstructed view of the open sea.

Istria's spit of land lies at the foot of the Dinaric Alps, and the interior of the peninsula is mountainous. We cross this rugged landscape in one go, following the E751 for 100km (62 miles) or so, to reach the western coast and Poreč, a superb fortified coastal town which we explore on foot. It's easy to fall under the spell of this place and its remarkable buildings, including the Euphrasian Basilica, a particularly well-preserved Byzantine jewel adorned with mosaics. The heart of this small town sits on a peninsula, decorated with houses and palaces with Romanesque, Venetian, Baroque and Gothic facades. We visit

'Bad weather is an integral part of the adventure, so the only option is to make the best of it.'

the marina too, another pleasant part of Poreč to stroll around, before we continue north.

Along the Gulf of Trieste, a strip of Slovenian land stretches between Croatia and Italy. We cross the border without difficulty and drive on to Piran, one of the region's most beautiful destinations, surrounded by ramparts. We park on the outskirts of town so we can get around more freely on foot. Life here revolves around Tartini Sq, lined with narrow, pastel-coloured houses. A few steps beyond and our wanderings bring us to the marina, which offers a fine view of the city and St George's Cathedral – its bell tower was inspired by that of St Mark's Basilica in Venice.

Koper is our second Slovenian coastal town, reached after driving 18km (11 miles) along a small secondary road. Tito Sq is Koper's nerve centre, home to a number of historic buildings including the Praetorian Palace, an imposing castle combining Renaissance and Venetian Gothic styles, now home to the town hall and tourist office. The narrow streets of the old town are well worth a visit. In this picturesque, colourful maze, strolling is the best way to spend your time. Finally, we emerge between the boats of the large marina – still trying to ignore the pouring rain.

It's the end of winter and bitterly cold so we don't regret having brought a whole stock of blankets, which we wrap up in as soon as night falls. Add to this a few ski hats, thick woollen scarves and warm fleece jackets, and you get a good idea of how we looked, coping the best we could with the weather. Fortunately for locals, we tend to stay away from urban centres, sparing the residents a parade of our eccentric clothing.

We extend our adventure to Italy, a country we know well and with which we've always had a special affinity. Just 22km (14 miles) across the border from Koper, Trieste opens its doors to us and we'll be ending this trip in style. We take in the refined architecture of the capital of Friuli-Venezia Giulia, whose perfect harmony strikes us as we go from square to palace. Among the many architectural highlights is gigantic Piazza Unità d'Italia, whose sumptuous buildings, surrounding the Fountain of the Four Continents, are a real eye-catcher. From this central square, we can see the Adriatic into which Trieste's Canal Grande flows a few streets away. This waterway is home to small boats moored beneath more majestic facades and, despite the never-ending downpours, our trio is definitely won over. **AD**

ISTRIA, A LAND OF EPICUREANS

Influenced by Croatian, Slovenian and Italian cuisine, Istria will delight the most discerning gourmets: truffles, *fuzi* (homemade pasta), fish and seafood are on the menu of many restaurants, and the olive oil is of the highest quality. On the wine side, *malvazija istarska*, a fruity white, is a must.

Opposite, clockwise from left: Istrian coastline; Koper marina, Slovenia; Trieste, Italy. Page 17: Port of Piran, Slovenia.

ROAD MAP

Start // Rijeka
Finish // Trieste
Distance // 202km (125 miles)
Recommended duration // 3-to-5 days
When to go // June or September for fewer crowds
Culinary specialities // *Gnocchi di pane* (stale bread dumplings that reflect the local 'no-waste' culture)

THE PERFECT PICNIC SPOT

Description // Parking with a sea view in Izola
GPS coordinates // 45.538998007931944, 13.665728860846587
Access // Easy, by road, parking limited to 12 hours during the day
Facilities // None
Visitor numbers // Less busy in low season; in high season, plan to arrive early
Little extras // Chat with fishers and walk to Izola's pretty beach.

Opposite, clockwise from top: Petrovac road, Montenegro; Galica coast, Spain; Bay of Kotor, Montenegro.

MORE LIKE THIS
BETWEEN LAND AND SEA

THE MANI PENINSULA (GREECE)

One of the joys of a van trip is finding waterfront spots where you can enjoy superb sunsets. On the west of the Mani Peninsula, the middle prong of Greece's Peloponnese, you're spoilt for choice. For a gentle start, park in Kardamýli, a charming seaside resort where you can recharge your batteries. The next day, take a walk along the long beach at Stoupa, before having lunch in Ágios Nikólaos, a coastal village with only a handful of streets but several tavernas where you can eat royally. Further south, regional capital Areópoli is an interesting stopover for travellers who like to wander among old ruins. For an end-of-the-world feeling, continue south towards the peninsula's tip. At the side of the road, a sign reading 'Last petrol station' sets the tone – from here on, make sure you have enough fuel. Round things off in Váthia, an intriguing abandoned village with tower-houses perched on a hill.

Start // Kardamýli
Finish // Váthia
Distance // 80km (50 miles)
More information // discovergreece.com

GALICIAN SHORES (SPAIN)

Open the windows and breathe in the salty air as you wind your way along the Galician coastline in northwest Spain. Park in Muxía to enjoy a variety of views of the open sea around the Virxe da Barca Sanctuary. Continue west to Finisterre, a town marked by the emotional arrival of many pilgrims, who end their Camino de Santiago slog here. The lighthouse on the cape, built on a rocky promontory, offers a unique atmosphere. Next stop, the vast dunes of Corrubedo and a heavenly lagoon, as well as a second body of water whose avian residents will delight birdwatchers. Still heading south, stop off to visit Pontevedra and the ancient buildings in its historic centre. Here, in the capital of the Rías Baixas region, on the banks of the Lérez River, you can sample delicious seafood before concluding your adventure in Baiona with a climb up to its castle for a panoramic view.

Start // Muxía
Finish // Baiona
Distance // 309km (192 miles)
More information // turismo.gal

MONTENEGRO'S COASTLINE

Begin your Montenegrin coast adventure in Kotor, a fortified city not to be missed. After exploring its historic old town and enjoying the pleasures of the beach, drive your van along the twists and turns of tarmac leading to Lovćen National Park. The Njegoš Mausoleum, resting place of a local prince-bishop, sits at the top of the mountain surrounded by expansive views of the rocky massif. Return to the seaside and stop in the village of Budva, a lively resort that is a good starting point for nature excursions. The next section takes you from beach to beach, heading due south – stretch your legs on Petrovac's, which is particularly beautiful. Last stop is Ulcinj, a renowned snorkelling location, where you can lounge on long Velika Plaža beach and visit a saltworks deep in the countryside, home to many species of birds.

Start // Kotor
Finish // Ulcinj
Distance // 150km (93 miles)
More information // montenegro.travel

FROM ROME TO THE CINQUE TERRE

Combine heritage highlights with nature stops on this drive from Italy's capital to the Ligurian Riviera.

U*n caffè per favore signore!*' Here I am at the counter of legendary Caffè Sant'Eustachio, in the middle of Italy's capital. I let myself be enveloped by the noise of the conversations, savouring the Italian intonations and observing the locals around me. This energising atmosphere is just what I was looking for at the start of my trip from Rome to the Cinque Terre.

The camper van is parked in Piazza Giuseppe Garibaldi, next to the Janiculum Hill and its breathtaking view over the city. I've walked to the historic centre, and after buying a few oranges and Tuscan spices at the Campo de' Fiori market, I amble over to the Pantheon, entering through the bronze doors under the monumental sixteen-column portico. Inside this millennia-old building, a spectacular beam of light falls from a circular opening in the middle of the dome. I hear a guide explain that on rainy days, the slight slope of the floor guides water drops towards small drainage holes hidden in the marble. A few streets away, tourists jostle to take their best selfie in front of the Trevi Fountain. I toss in a coin, make a wish and head for the capitol to see the statue of Romulus and Remus. Then it's the Forum, the Palatine and the Colosseum – so many places that get the imagination going. In the latter, I can almost hear the murmur of tens of thousands of spectators fervently following the gladiator fights.

It's with caution that I get back behind the wheel of my camper to leave the city – driving in Rome is rather stressful, so you have to be careful. Heading north, I reach the town of Bomarzo, some 90km (56 miles) away, and spend a peaceful night in a large car park there. The next day starts with a visit to the Parco dei Mostri (Park of the Monsters), an astonishing Renaissance garden where you can wander among dozens of enigmatic sculptures.

After this unusual sight, I set off again, in search of a pleasant place to have lunch. A spot by Lake Bolsena, 52km (32 miles) to the north, obliges. I pull over and go through the ritual step by step: open the gas bottle; turn on the hob; heat up the water; wait a few minutes; pour in the fresh pasta, bought the day

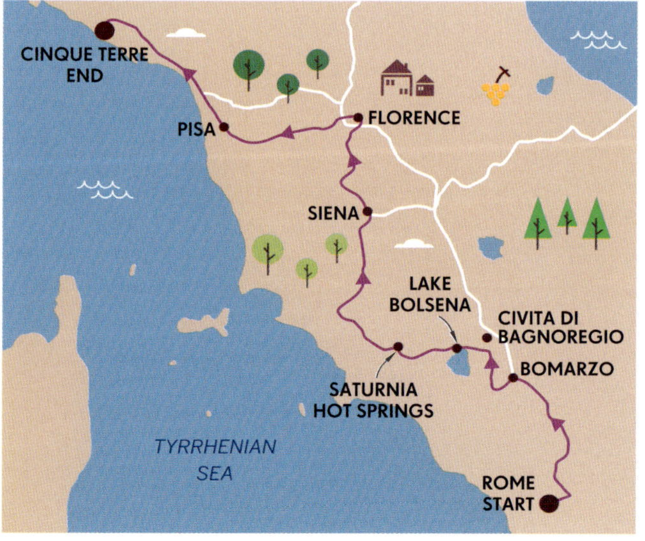

THE DYING VILLAGE

Perched atop a tufa-limestone promontory and accessible only by a pedestrian bridge, the small medieval town of Civita di Bagnoregio is nicknamed '*la città che muore*' (the dying city) because this village, one of Italy's most beautiful, has fallen victim to erosion, which is gradually nibbling away at the rock and sweeping away the houses.

'Following alley after alley, I eventually reach majestic, shell-shaped Piazza del Campo, then the striking cathedral, striped in black and white.'

before; serve. All the steps followed, I'm now ready for lunch in the middle of nature, right beside the lake's crystal-clear water.

While in Bomarzo, I'd met a family of motorhome owners, and we'd agreed to meet at the Saturnia hot springs, across the Lazio-Tuscany border, west of the lake. First impressions aren't great. The entrance to the car park is only suitable for vehicles no more than 2.1m (7ft) high, which effectively excludes my L2H2 van – but that's the price I sometimes have to pay to be able to stand upright inside the vehicle and enjoy all the comforts of a studio apartment. I find a spot a little further on and make my way to the spa. The sulphurous water, at 37°C (99°F), cascades down the sides of an old mill, creating small natural pools open for bathing. In some places, the current is powerful and provides an enjoyable massage effect. Afterwards I'm glad to be able to take a shower to get rid of the sulphur smell sticking to my skin.

The next morning, it's on to Siena via SP14. The rain is making itself heard on the camper's bodywork, but I'm reminded of the adage: 'Life isn't about waiting for the storm to pass, it's about learning to dance in the rain'. So, umbrella in hand, it's time to explore the city. Following alley after alley, I eventually reach majestic, shell-shaped Piazza del Campo, then the striking cathedral, striped in black and white.

Siena seen, I continue the drive on the SR222 towards Florence, cradle of the Renaissance. Having parked on the outskirts of the city, I jump on my bike and cycle to the Piazza San Marco to visit the Galleria dell'Accademia, where Michelangelo's *David* is on display. Then, after a stop at one of the oldest pharmacies in the world, hidden behind the Santa Maria Novella Church, it's on to the Piazza del Duomo, dominated by the iconic cathedral with its immense dome. To end the day on a high note, I cross the Arno River via the Ponte Vecchio, buy an ice cream at the Cantina del Gelato and enjoy it on Piazzale Michelangelo, an esplanade with a magnificent panoramic view of the city.

I'm now embarking on the last leg of my journey, which takes me to the sea. Following the Firenze-Pisa-Livorno road, I pass Pisa and its famous leaning tower, then, 90km (56 miles) to the north, the Cinque Terre National Park. Located on the rough coastline of the Ligurian Riviera, this region takes its name

Opposite: Siena. Below, from left: Colosseum in Rome; Riomaggiore, Cinque Terre, Italy. Page 23, from top: Trastevere street; Manarola, Cinque Terre, Italy.

from a succession of five ('*cinque*') colourful cliffside villages – Riomaggiore, Manarola, Corniglia, Vernazza and Monterosso – linked by a train and hiking trails. The whole area is a UNESCO World Heritage Site.

I follow the spectacular road along the coast until, at Riomaggiore, I find a place for the van on the side of provincial road 32. A dizzying descent leads me to a steep little port with colourfully painted buildings. The waves crash against the sea wall with a deafening roar. While in Cinque Terre, I travel from village to village, sometimes by train, sometimes following the hiking trails, which offer beautiful views of the attractive villages. Vernazza is perhaps the most picturesque. Elderly women chat in front of a convent. I lose myself in a maze of narrow streets and come to a square where a small church, upturned wooden boats and facades with peeling paint stand side by side. As the sea rushes into the port, I join the few tourists and villagers gazing out at the horizon. It's the end of the day and the sky is turning pink, a twilight that for me also marks the end of this Italian road trip. **AL**

ROAD MAP

Start // Rome
Finish // Cinque Terre
Distance // 605km (376 miles)
Recommended duration // 8-to-12 days
When to go // Outside summer and school holidays
Culinary specialities // Coffee, pasta, pesto, focaccia

THE PERFECT PICNIC SPOT

Description // Picnic and swim on Lake Bolsena.
GPS coordinates // 42.637801, 11.889072
Light pollution // None
Access // Easy, by road
Facilities // Children's playground
Parking // In addition to two parking spaces, there is ample parking along the lakeside path.
Little extras // Peaceful location with beautiful views and direct access to the lake.

Opposite: Cascata delle Marmore.

MORE LIKE THIS
ITALIAN WATERFALLS

CASCATA DELLE MARMORE

Explore the protected wetlands of Umbria's Parco Fluviale del Nera, home to the Cascata delle Marmore, at your own pace. There are plenty of trails to stretch your legs and the curious can also visit the Ferentillo Mummy Museum, housed in the crypt of the Santo Stefano Church. A few kilometres south, amid lush vegetation, is the Cascata delle Marmore itself. This artificial waterfall, built in 271 BCE, is 165m (541ft) high and drops over three levels. Leave your vehicle at the lower lookout car park, equip yourself with good shoes and a raincoat, and check the water release schedule. There are several walks in the park and over 600 steps to the upper lookout. After the waterfall, get out your paddle or take a dip in Lake Piediluco – for thrill-seekers, many agencies offer rafting and canyoning activities.

Start // Ferentillo
Finish // Lago di Piediluco
Distance // 28km (17 miles)
More information // cascatadellemarmore.info

CASCATE DEL DARDAGNA

This trip plunges you deep into nature, among the peaks and forests of the Parco Regionale del Corno alle Scale, in Emilia-Romagna. Park near the Madonna dell'Acero Sanctuary, and head off under the beech trees, following a signposted path that leads to the Dardagna Falls. Feel the spray refresh your face as you get closer. If you're feeling intrepid, push on to the sublime Lake Scaffaiolo to breathe in the mountain air. Back behind the wheel, extend your exploration of the region with a visit to the Neogothic Manservisi Castle. If you're not in a hurry, take a pastoral detour to Tresana, a timeless village of stone houses and hydrangea groves. Continue along the border with Tuscany and then cross it to the south to reach San Marcello Pistoiese, where you can test your balance on the suspension bridge.

Start // Santuario della Madonna dell'Acero
Finish // San Marcello Pistoiese
Distance // 71km (44 miles)
More information // cornoallescale.net

PARCO NAZIONALE DELL'ASPROMONTE

Travel the narrow, winding roads of Calabria's Aspromonte National Park by camper. Its 77,000 hectares are an arboreal paradise dotted with magnificent waterfalls, canyons and valleys. Let yourself be seduced by the hike to the Marmarico and Ferdinandea waterfalls, where you may well come face to face with a wildcat, Bonelli's eagle or peregrine falcon. Drive southeast towards the Salino Waterfall and the Byzantine church of San Nicodemo, before seeking out the falls of the Barvi stream, known as Mundu and Galasia and only accessible via an old mule track. Then pay a visit to the wonderful little Tre Limiti Waterfalls. Finally, park at the Menta dam and walk down the path to the Amendolea Waterfalls.

Start // Cascata del Marmarico
Finish // Cascate dell'Amendolea
Distance // 153km (95 miles)
More information // parconazionaleaspromonte.it

THE WEST COAST OF GREECE

While the Greek coastline is world-renowned for its wonderful beaches and unfailing sunshine, it's also where you can enjoy simple, authentic moments.

Greece has plenty to offer those who don't rush. Being quite laid-back myself, it's this sense of time stretching out that I appreciate most here. In the past, I've spent several months in Greece, and I'm delighted to be returning there in a van with José, my best co-driver. Arriving from Albania, the plan is to follow the west coast of the country to the south of the Peloponnese. We already know that we're going to be treating both our taste buds and our eyes.

Facing the island of Corfu, Igoumenitsa welcomes us. There's nothing exceptional about this port, apart from its seaside appeal, but we enjoy the fresh air as we stroll along the waterfront. We sit down in one of the many bars and sip the first *frappé* (iconic iced coffee) of many, before really embarking on our adventure. For 135km (84 miles) it's winding coastal roads to the island of Lefkada, accessed across a causeway. We take care to drive slowly, because in addition to the viewpoints that draw our attention, dogs, cows and a host of careless drivers escort us.

We take advantage of our visit to Lefkada Town, the capital of the island, to replenish our water supplies, as we're running low – we only carry two small cans so regularly have to find water fountains, although this is never a problem. We also do some shopping and buy *tyropita* (cheese puff pastries), *dolmadakia* (vine leaves stuffed with rice) and other delicacies. The town's colourful buildings are pretty enough, but it's the lagoon that really gets our attention: a colony of pink flamingos is parading in front of us. Busy fishing or sleeping on one leg, the birds are still, silent and graceful. The rest of the island features steep

cliffs, clear waters lapping sandy beaches and traditional coastal villages. The place is idyllic.

Gina, a Greek friend, is waiting for us in Patras, so we keep heading due south for 175km (109 miles) to make our rendezvous, threading our way along a cordon of tarmac, with the mountains stretching to the edge of the asphalt on one side, and the Ionian Sea stretching endlessly away on the other. We're delighted to cross the Rion-Antirion cable-stayed bridge, an earthquake-resistant engineering marvel linking mainland Greece to the vast Peloponnese Peninsula, which heralds our arrival in Patras. I really like the atmosphere of this student city, where I've already stayed several times. It has a large port, from which ferries set sail for Italy, but to enjoy the best view over the Gulf of Patras, it's best to climb up to the ruined castle, whose centuries-old stones have watched over the turquoise water since the 6th century. The staircase along Agiou Nikolaou street leading to the fortress is a must for visitors. In the evening, young people gather here for a drink, admiring the most beautiful sunset imaginable. My two companions and I do the same.

Gina then invites us to stay with her family in the small village of Kardamas, near Amaliada. We welcome her aboard the van and continue our slow progress southwards along the E55. With three of us up front, it's a bit cramped, which leads to a few acrobatics – the Transporter T4 model is all-purpose but not very roomy, but I'd gone for freedom of movement to comfort, a personal choice that I've never regretted.

Gina's parents, whom I know well, pull out all the stops to celebrate our reunion. The menu for the lunch we're welcomed with is the fruit of their labour: homemade bread toasted in the fireplace, feta cheese made from their sheep's milk, olives harvested from the garden and wine pressed by hand – a meal both simple and royal. To stretch our legs, we then head for Kourouta Beach, a popular spot for locals, packed with bars and restaurants. Naturally, we order large *frappés* and drink them on the terrace. The beach may be trendy, but there's an air of serenity as soon as you step onto the fine sand, away from the bars.

Much as we'd like to linger, time waits for no van and we need to push on. We warmly embrace Gina and her parents, thank them for their hospitality and leave laden with gifts: olive oil and bags of oranges. Route 9 takes us ever further south, in glorious sunshine, and we feel like we're on a route designed just for holiday-making, lined entirely with olive trees. There are also multiple opportunities to pull over at various beaches: Greece is a country where it's very easy to travel with a converted vehicle – there are few parking restrictions and most locals look on vanlifers kindly.

Some 170km (105 miles) from Kardamas, we reach Koroni, one of the most beautiful towns in the Peloponnese. The marina has a wonderful promenade, and under an electric blue sky speckled with cotton clouds, pleasure boats are reflected on the still

GREEK CUISINE

A gourmet destination, Greece offers a healthy and varied cuisine: feta (sheep's milk cheese), *spanakopita* (spinach puff pastry), *souvlaki* (meat skewers), *stifado* (stew) and *taramasalata* (fish roe dip) are among the tastiest dishes. This Mediterranean diet has many virtues, thanks to the antioxidants and omega-3s contained in the ubiquitous olive oil, herbs and vegetables.

Below: Agiou Nikolaou street steps, Patras. Above: Agios Ioannis monastery. Opposite: Koroni, towards Lefkada.
Page 29, from top: Rion-Antirion bridge; Egremni beach in Lefkada.

'We keep heading due south . . . threading our way along a cordon of tarmac, with the mountains on one side, and the Ionian Sea stretching endlessly on the other.'

surface of the water. Climbing up to the edge of the castle is the best way to fully appreciate the magic of the setting. From the top of the cliff, the ancient fortress extends its sprawling ramparts across the Gulf of Messenia, and several viewpoints allow you to gaze down onto azure coves. Beside the castle, a monastery crowned with white domes dominates the bay, and a few neatly arranged tombs are lined up below. A perfect place to rest in peace for eternity. **AD**

ROAD MAP

Start // Igoumenitsa
Finish // Koroni
Distance // 573km (356 miles)
Recommended duration // 5-to-7 days
When to go // All year, but beware of summer heat
Culinary speciality // *Frappé* (an iced coffee, usually sweetened, served in large glasses with or without milk)

THE PERFECT PHOTO SPOT

Description // The view from Koroni Castle
GPS coordinates // 36.7957978587447, 21.962396701301884
Access // Park in the town centre and walk up the hill.
Activities // Take a long stroll on the fortress' ramparts.
Visitor numbers // Very few off-season visitors
Little extras // Get here in plenty of time to watch the sun set.

Opposite: Timanfaya National Park, Lanzarote, Spain

MORE LIKE THIS
IN SEARCH OF SUN

CYPRUS

Touring Cyprus in a camper will leave you with unforgettable memories. Capital Nicosia is the starting point for this tour: take time to experience its historic heart and sample the local gastronomy before heading south along the A1 to Limassol. The medieval castle of Cyprus' second-largest city holds the keys to its past, so drop by before relaxing on the seafront. The next day, take your adventure to the southwest coast and Lara Beach, a wild stretch of sand that is home to sea turtles. Then retrace your steps until you reach Avdímou and follow the road into the wonderful Troodos Mountains where you can swap the steering wheel for hiking boots. Don't forget to visit the charming Byzantine churches along the way, before returning to the capital.

Start/Finish // Nicosia
Distance // 357km (222 miles)
More information // visitcyprus.com

CRETE (GREECE)

Cretan roads can prove quite an adventure, but one you won't regret. The seaside resort of Plakias is a good place to begin exploring the heavenly beaches of the surrounding area. After this dose of sunshine, drive a few kilometres west and stop off at Frangokastello, a massive castle built directly on the shore. Park at the entrance to the majestic Imbros Gorge and walk north along a steep road not made for anyone in a hurry. You'll arrive in Chania, where the old town, the fortress and the pretty harbour make for great photo opportunities. Next, let the E65 take you to Balos Beach, a turquoise lagoon on the Gramvoussa Peninsula, and programme your GPS for Elafonisi, a startlingly pink sandy beach at the western edge of Crete.

Start // Plakias
Finish // Elafonisi
Distance // 213km (132 miles)
More information // incrediblecrete.gr

LANZAROTE (SPAIN)

Whether you take the ferry from Cádiz or rent a van locally, chances are your road trip around Lanzarote will start in Arrecife. Departing from the capital of this Canary Island, get ready to explore a land of contrasts, between volcanic landscapes of black lava and long beaches. First stop, Teguise, for a wander through the historic old town. Then it's easy to make a loop to the north to discover Arrieta and its natural pools, Haría and its market, and Famara with its magnificent beach, the meeting place of local surfers – it's here that you'll find the best spots to sleep in a camper too. The logical continuation of this itinerary takes you to Timanfaya National Park, where you can admire the volcanic cones. With its superb beaches, the south of the island is not to be outdone. Take a swim on the picture-postcard-perfect Playa del Papagayo, before returning to Arrecife.

Start/Finish // Arrecife
Distance // 156km (97 miles)
More information // turismolanzarote.com

NORTHERN ITALIAN LAKES

A bucolic itinerary linking the lakes of northern Italy, lined with small ports and magnificent views, between the Alps and the Po Valley.

Setting off from the Alto Adige region, I head west with a promising itinerary – a tour of the lakes of northern Italy, enjoying their mild microclimate and sumptuous terraced gardens, planted with laurel, cypress and fruit trees.

I approach from the northern tip of Lake Garda, a blue jewel hemmed in by high mountains, sheer cliffs and forest. Once parked in Riva del Garda, I make my way to the foot of the clock tower, which has watched over the city since the 13th century. One after another, I discover the surrounding pastel-toned streets, then stroll along the pine-lined beach leading to the old fort. Before hitting the road again, I walk along the Sentiero del Ponale on the other side of town, a rock-cut path that leads to a wonderful viewpoint.

Then it's on to the scenic SS45, a bewitching ribbon of road that twists from village to village along Lake Garda. To the south, gentle hills covered with vineyards, olive groves and lemon trees take over from the mountains. For a spot of exercise, I take a break near a secluded stretch of water. When I return, I'm in for a nasty surprise – the van door is open and the barrel of the driver's lock is on the ground. A moment of panic because everything I own is in this vehicle. Fortunately, I seem to have returned just in time, scaring off the looters, because nothing has been taken.

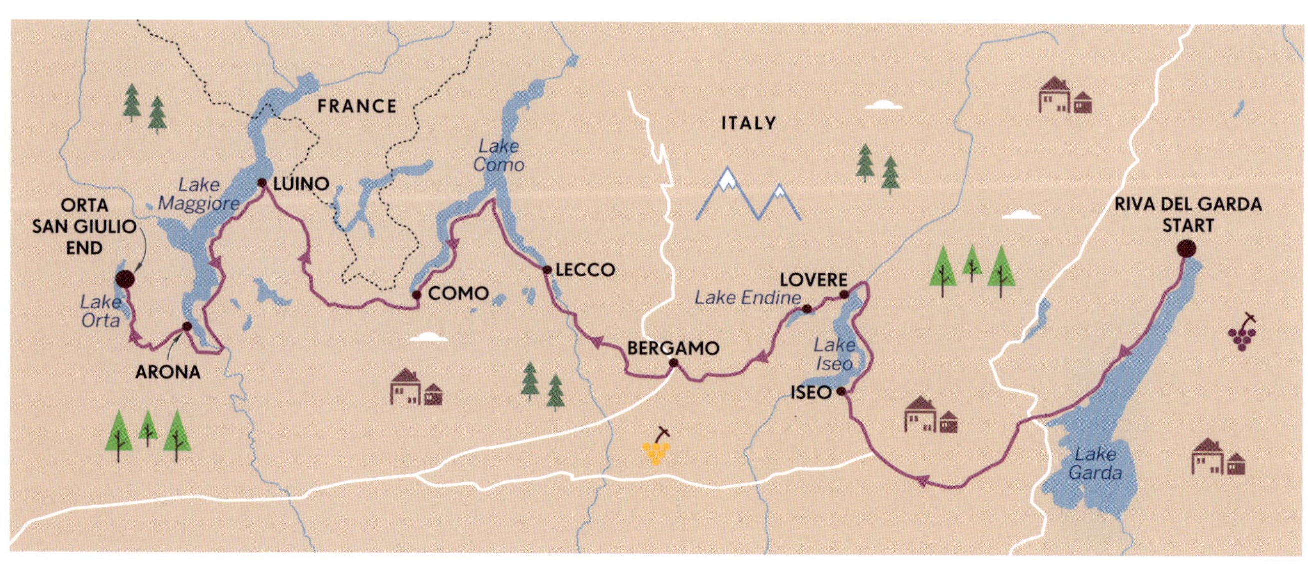

I continue on my way to Lake Iseo, nestled in a deep glacial valley 60km (37 miles) west of Lake Garda. Surrounded by green mountains and arcaded villas, it makes for a very picturesque pause. To recover from my scare, I park in a quiet spot, a stone's throw from the water, and slip under a blanket with a novel. Relaxed again, it's time to explore the colourful streets of Iseo in search of a cheap slice of pizza which I enjoy on the go – just what I need to get the region back in my good books. On my map, I've spotted a perfect parking area for the night, at the entrance to Lovere, at the northern edge of the lake, so I get back behind the wheel and drive along the shore on the SP510, admiring Monte Isola, Europe's largest lake island, a solitary peak enthroned in the middle of the water. I reach Lovere just as darkness is setting in.

Next morning, the first light wakes me from my dreams. The sky is fuchsia, the mountains amethyst. I walk down to the marina and along the deserted jetty, watching as, little by little, the town comes to life. I gulp down a cappuccino in a lively cafe and chat with my counter neighbours – moments of exchange that are always precious when travelling alone.

Small Lake Endine is only 10km (6 miles) away, but it provides a completely different atmosphere – just a few fishers can be seen on this wild-looking expanse, with its reed-covered banks. If I didn't have to refuel in Bergamo, I'd gladly stay longer in this peaceful place, but my food and water supplies are running low – in order to have more free space in the cabin, I use two water cans (rather than one bulky tank), each with a capacity of around 20L (4 gallons), which means I have to refill them regularly.

I arrive in Bergamo after covering almost 30km (19 miles) of the SS42. As usual, I park on the outskirts on a random street where parking is free. Autumn is coming to an end and there are few tourists in the Città Alta, the upper town, so I have Bergamo's staircases and funiculars largely to myself as I unlock the secrets of this charming city. Medieval, Baroque and Renaissance buildings sit harmoniously side by side. I pass through the imposing white marble San Giacomo Gateway to the ramparts – from the heights of these Venetian walls, the view extends over the whole of Lombardy. To make the moment even more delicious, I devour a *stracciatella* ice cream, a rich recipe with chocolate shavings that was invented right here.

Continuing on my way, I reach Lecco, 40km (25 miles) from Bergamo on the southeast arm of Lake Como, where a gloomy sky presages a turbulent night. When you live in a converted vehicle, daily life can be severely disrupted by the arrival of a storm. I have to look for a parking spot away from trees, where I can retreat as quickly as possible. Luckily, this storm doesn't last long, and after a few hours of half-sleep, I'm awake and ready to see what Lecco and its peaceful banks have to offer. Around the bell tower of the Basilica of San

© autofocus67 | Adobe Stock

GORGONZOLA

This creamy, blue-veined cow's milk cheese is emblematic of Lombardy and Piedmont. It's usually served in risotto, on pizza, with polenta or simply with a ripe pear.

Opposite: Riva del Garda. Above, clockwise from left: Lake Garda; Lake Orta; Gorgonzola. Page 35: Road along Lake Garda.

Nicolò, the buildings, in a palette of warm colours, appear neat and tidy. In the background, the vegetation remains sufficiently present to provide the city with a perfect balance between natural and urban.

After skirting Lake Como from the south, I reach Lake Maggiore, 50km (31 miles) west . Its geographical location, straddling the border between Italy and Switzerland, gives it a unique vibe. The cobbled, orange-coloured streets of Luino, where many buildings have been abandoned, are particularly photogenic. After a walk through the town, I take the SP69 along Maggiore's eastern side. Around Lavone, I leave the lake, heading south, with no clear goal in mind, ending up in Arona, on the western side of the lake where, after a night in a public car park, I head early to the local market. For a handful of euros, I leave with olives, vegetables, fresh bread and a large slice of gorgonzola.

An Italian friend urged me to visit Lake Orta, just 20km (12 miles) from Arona, so I set my GPS for Orta San Giulio. The friend was right. Piazza Mario Motta, a sublime square that encapsulates the soul of Orta, is well worth a visit, especially the unpretentious, elegant *palazzotto*, a small communal palace with arcades and frescoes of coats of arms. However, it's the view from the Sacro Monte d'Orta that really wins me over – from its summit, you can see the island of San Giulio. I decide to take a boat trip for a closer look at its Romanesque basilica, the real pearl of Lake Orta. **AD**

ROAD MAP

Start // Riva del Garda
Finish // Orta San Giulio
Distance // 407km (253 miles)
Recommended duration // 5-to-7 days
When to go // Spring or autumn for mild weather and fewer tourists
Culinary specialities // *Risotto al pesce persico* (risotto with perch, best eaten on the shores of Lake Como)

THE PERFECT PICNIC SPOT

Description // Near Piona Abbey in Olgiasca, overlooking Lake Como
GPS coordinates // 46.123720004639935, 9.330466658895501
Access // Easy, by road
Facilities // Toilets in Piona Abbey
Traffic // Very little, especially in the evening
Little extras // A rural stroll through the lovely village of Olgiasca.

Opposite: Lakeside in Sweden.

MORE LIKE THIS
FROM LAKE TO LAKE

IN THE HEART OF SWEDEN

Grab a kayak and enjoy vast stretches of blue water surrounded by lush green forests. Start 90km (56 miles) northeast of Gothenburg, in Vänersborg. From this unpretentious town, drive along Lake Vänern, the country's largest, to Karlstad, aka the Värmland Riviera. It's a great place for swimming, canoeing, boating and beach walking. To reach medieval Jönköping, opt for the picturesque Finnerödja route, and ogle the azure beauty that is small Lake Unden. You soon arrive at the wooded shores of Lake Vättern whose crystal-clear water is sure to inspire you to have a dip. Take a tour of the lake, then head for Örebro. After a visit to its castle, explore the shores of Lake Hjälmaren. Along the road to Eskilstuna (by the southern shore), hikers and cyclists will have a field day.

Start // Vänersborg
Finish // Eskilstuna
Distance // 729km (453 miles)
More information // visitsweden.com

JEWELS OF SLOVENIA

Begin at small Lake Planšarsko, close to the Austrian border, shaped like a heart and located in a green paradise. It's a quick circuit to walk, but you'll probably want to prolong the moment before taking the country road leading to justifiably famous Lake Bled. The setting here is idyllic – mountains surround Bled's blue expanse in the middle of which a pretty church sits enthroned on an island. It's difficult to find an overnight spot for a van in this Garden of Eden though, so continue your adventure southwest along the Sava River, where parking options are better. Not far away, Lake Bohinj offers another perfect backdrop. Here, the craggy Triglav Massif is reflected in the water's mirror-like surface. Finally, follow the winding road to Lake Divje, a tiny pearl fed by a deep karst spring – after heavy rains, the water gushes out like a geyser.

Start // Lake Planšarsko
Finish // Lake Divje
Distance // 160km (100 miles)
More information // slovenia.info

OHRID AND PRESPA LAKES (NORTHERN MACEDONIA)

The beautiful town of Ohrid, on the shores of its unmissable namesake lake, is well worth a visit outside the tourist season. Admire the panorama of the lake from the medieval fortress, before wandering the streets of the 'Jerusalem of the Balkans', with its many religious buildings. Drive along the shoreline to Trpeytsa, a resort with a small, family-friendly beach, then make a detour to St Naum Monastery, close to the Albanian border, before turning back to drive through Galitchitsa National Park. A winding road leads to a stunning view over Ohrid and Prespa lakes. On the other side of the mountains, the latter lake appeals to those who like peace and quiet and wildlife. Sleep at the water's edge before taking the R1308 to magnificent Dupeni Beach. Beyond that, it's Greece.

Start // Ohrid
Finish // Dupeni
Distance // 108km (67 miles)
More information // macedonia-timeless.com

MONTENEGRO TO ALBANIA

From wild landscapes to must-see towns, this itinerary is a condensed version of the Balkans.

Durmitor National Park, near the village of Žabljak, is the starting point for this road trip through two Balkan countries. My most faithful travelling companion and I have decided to make our way to Albania from Montenegro, and we can't wait to discover the mountainous and maritime landscapes this trip promises. A few towns will also punctuate the adventure, giving us the opportunity to stock up on supplies while learning more about local life and a culture we know little about.

José has control of the van. This gives me plenty of time to contemplate the lapis-lazuli-blue snake of the Tara River, unfurling below vertiginous cliffs – the P4 scenic route embraces these deep, wild gorges to our great delight. Soon we reach the Orthodox monastery of Dobrilovina, set in lush fields at the foot of the rocky massif. The tiny, picturesque building features a wooden bell tower with a sturdy frame. It's a perfect spot for a picnic in the sun, and we bring out our finest delicacies – canned corn, olives and rusks.

We continue along the river for another 50km (31 miles), before turning onto the E65 towards Podgorica. The capital, often shunned by tourists, was a flourishing Ottoman city for four centuries, but just a few vestiges remain in the old district of Staro Varos, the city having been destroyed during WWII. The many new buildings make it austere at first glance, and it's not until we reach the banks of the Moraca that we begin to find any charm. We linger a little longer and come across some real gems, such as the recently built and finely crafted Cathedral of the Resurrection of Christ.

We continue our descent southwards, but don't go far: Lake Shkodër (or Skadar) is only 20km (12 miles) away and we intend

CROSSING BORDERS

Border controls are not uncommon when driving a camper van. To avoid any tension, be conciliatory and smile. Beware of products being transported, which may be taxed or even prohibited: find out more beforehand on the diplomatie.gouv.fr website.

'On the roadway, goats, dogs, carts and bicycles are all obstacles to be avoided, not to mention the numerous potholes that plague distracted drivers.'

to spend the night on the shores of this peaceful lake, covered with water lilies and surrounded by mountains. At the end of an unpaved track, we find a spit of land on which we set our sights. Comfortably seated in the back of the T4, we watch the sun bow out over the peaks.

The lake marks the border with Albania, and we reach the checkpoint the next morning. The guard wants to inspect our house on wheels. A gas bottle, two cans of water and a foam mattress seemingly impress him. We make friends with the customs officer, who raises the barrier with a welcoming gesture.

We don't know much about Albania, so we're approaching it with no specific expectations, trying to free ourselves from any preconceptions. First stop is the town of Shkodër, at the southern tip of the eponymous lake. Albania's cultural capital is also its most European city. Parking is scarce, but we finally find somewhere, giving us just long enough to have lunch in the first bar we find. In a playful mood, and not understanding a word of Albanian, we order a dish at random: the waiter brings us two plates of spaghetti with grilled liver, so we've come to the right place. Having eaten our fill, we begin our tour of the lively

Above: © Astrid Duvillard, Opposite: © zm_photo | Adobe Stock

centre, with its clean, colourful streets. Orthodox churches rub shoulders with mosques; pedestrians with cyclists; one historic period with another. Shkodër is full of contrasts.

Next stop is the Adriatic Sea, an hour's drive away. On the roadway, goats, dogs, carts and bicycles are all obstacles to be avoided, not to mention the numerous potholes that plague distracted drivers. Various police checks slow our progress, but we don't mind – officers greet us in a friendly manner, before wishing us a good trip.

A little lost, we ask for directions and, not knowing how to say 'the sea' in Albanian, we try 'Adriatic?' Which means we find ourselves in – Adriatik, a perfectly lovely town but not on the coast. Amid hearty laughter from passers-by, we're escorted down the village's only street by a flock of sheep. Finally, we retrace our steps. The sea isn't actually far away and we park on the edge of Patok Lagoon. It's dark but the family who run the establishment we're staying at are delighted to receive visitors, showering us with attention: fruit, beers and the chance to watch a televised singing competition. In the morning, large bowls of coffee await us, as do big farewell kisses from the landlady. Along the water's edge, wooden cabins on stilts are linked by footbridges; there's an overwhelming serenity to the place. We continue along the nearby lagoon, in the Kune-Vain-Tale Reserve. Mountains and clouds are reflected in the water which is lined with reed beds, forests and dunes. We don't regret our detour.

Last stop is Tirana. As we approach the capital, the driving becomes more challenging, so we park as soon as we can and explore on foot. While the outskirts of the city are unattractive, the centre is pleasant and busy. Massive buildings adorn wide thoroughfares, like the impressive Pyramid (a former museum dedicated to the dictator Hoxha). But it's the immense Skanderbeg Sq, Tirana's central esplanade with its saffron-coloured facades and mix of old and new buildings (including the Et'hem Bey Mosque), which will be the highlight of our visit and a great way to round off this drive. **AD**

Opposite: View of Lake Shkodër. Above, from left: Tara river canyon; Dobrilovina monastery. Opposite, bottom: Village village on the Patok lagoon. Page 41, from top: Lake Shkodër; Skanderbeg square.

ROAD MAP

Start // Žabljak (Montenegro)
Finish // Tirana (Albania)
Distance // 389km (242 miles)
Recommended duration // 7-to-10 days
When to go // Spring or autumn, to avoid excessive heat (summer) or low temperatures (winter)
Culinary speciality // *Burek* or *börek* (puff pastry filled with meat, cheese or spinach – originally from Central Asia, it's widespread in the Balkans)

THE PERFECT SLEEP SPOT

Description // Car park with superb view of Patok Lagoon
GPS coordinates // 41.634911000931886, 19.590493348401605
Access // Easy, by road SH35
Facilities // Water, toilets and wi-fi in the many bars and restaurants in the area
Visitor numbers // A few tourists and locals, but large and very quiet
Little extras // Watch the sun set while sipping a drink overlooking the lagoon.

Opposite, clockwise from top: Mostar bridge, Bosnia-Herzegovina; Ubac canyon, Serbia; Mustapha Pasha mosque in Skopje, Northern Macedonia.

MORE LIKE THIS
THE BALKANS

BOSNIA-HERCEGOVINA

Little-known to tourists, Bosnia-Hercegovina is home to fasinating historic towns and glorious mountain landscapes. What's more, it's easy to travel around in a camper van. In Sarajevo, a capital at the crossroads of Ottoman and Austro-Hungarian influences, you're sure to fall in love with magnificent buildings such as the Gazi Husrev-beg Mosque, with the old quarter of Baščaršija, and the famous Latin Bridge, crossing the Miljacka River, near which Franz Ferdinand was murdered in 1914. Next up is Mostar, a city on a human scale with a Middle Eastern flavour. Not far away, don't miss the superb village of Počitelj, whose fortifications dominate the Neretva River. For some nature near Mostar, Kravica Waterfall is a refreshing spot, and more falls can be found in Una National Park.

Start // Sarajevo
Finish // Una National Park
Distance // 474km (295 miles)
More information // visitsarajevo.ba

SERBIA

It's said that time passes slowly in Novi Sad as you stroll along the Danube River. In this enchanting city in northern Serbia, linger around the Petrovaradin Fortress, with its view of Stari Grad, the picturesque old quarter. Then get behind the wheel and head for Belgrade, a lively capital with a rich cultural heritage. Its architecture is a highlight, starting with an imposing castle, built at the confluence of the Save and Danube rivers. Further south, Tara National Park will delight hikers on their way to various viewpoints, such as Banjska Stena, which offers a sublime panorama of the park's gorges. Some 130km (86 miles) separate this paradise from the Uvac Canyon, a grand nature reserve where a boat trip is a must. Finally, a stopover in Niš will allow history and architecture buffs to finish this trip with a smile.

Start // Novi Sad
Finish // Niš
Distance // 698km (434 miles)
More information // serbia.travel

NORTHERN MACEDONIA

In the heart of the Balkans, this republic has lots to offer adventure-seeking travellers. Begin in Skopje, a capital that contrasts historic vestiges (fortresses, caravanserais) with the austere architecture inherited from the former Yugoslavia. Just a handful of kilometres away, the Matka Canyon guarantees thrills for walkers, kayakers and climbers, while others opt for a boat trip. Heading southwest, stop off at Mavrovo National Park, with its many hiking trails. On the shores of the lake of the same name, encircled by mountains, spend a night in the camper near the ruins of a sunken church – only the steeple and upper section remain unsubmerged. Finish in Bitola, the country's second-largest city, with its fine architecture and pedestrian-only Shirok Sokak street.

Start // Skopje
Finish // Bitola
Distance // 234km (145 miles)
More information // macedonia-timeless.com

FROM THE NEAPOLITAN COAST TO PUGLIA

Drive across southern Italy, from the Mediterranean to the Adriatic, discovering archaeological and geological treasures on the way.

The vision of Vesuvius overlooking the city of Naples is suddenly revealed. Tonight, I plan to sleep next to the famous volcano. A great way to mark the start of my new adventure – a west-to-east crossing of Italy, from the Campania region to Puglia, taking in remarkable sites such as the ancient ruins of Pompeii, the splendid Amalfi Coast and the cave city of Matera.

I have a hard time on the Contrada Osservatorio, which twists its way to the top of the volcano. Other drivers are impatient with my slowness, but I remember the Italian proverb: *Chi va piano, va sano e va lontano* 'those who travel slowly, travel safely and far', so I let them pass and continue at my own pace, avoiding the eucalyptus branches that encroach on the road. Coaches coming down take blind corners by honking their horns at every bend to avoid a collision. As I gain altitude, the view clears. Ancient lava flows and volcanic rocks make their appearance. I arrive at the first car park but continue to a kiosk run by an old lady, Giovanna, who agrees to let me park outside her shop

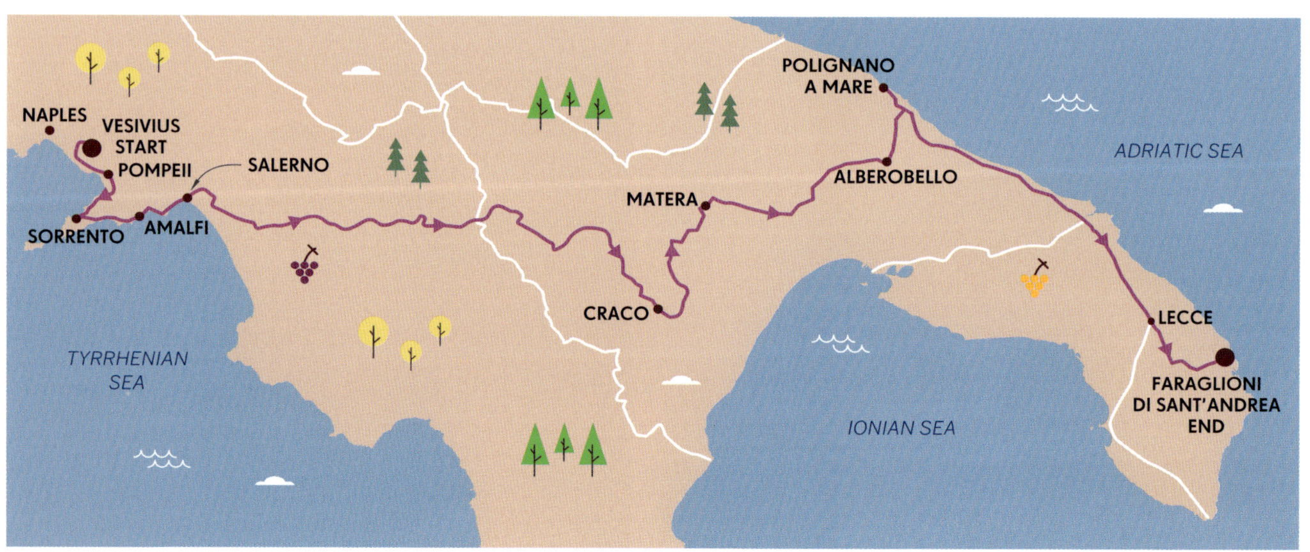

'As I gain altitude, the view clears. Ancient lava flows and volcanic rocks make their appearance.'

on condition that we buy something from her. I decide on a bruschetta, which I enjoy as the sun sets over the Bay of Naples, with the silhouette of the ancient volcano for company.

After a quiet night, with a partial view of Vesuvius through the window, I make an early start. It only takes a few minutes to reach the crater site where access to the summit is subject to a fee. The ascent is fairly fast but quite scary. The reward is a spectacular view of the volcano and the Neapolitan coast.

After this expedition, I hit the road again and drive down to the archaeological site of Pompeii, 24km (15 miles) to the south. For a change, I rent a pitch at the Spartacus Campsite, close to the ruins, allowing me to fill my water tank, charge my batteries and, above all, take my time wandering around the fascinating remains of Pompeii. I stroll the streets, imagining daily life of the inhabitants back in the 1st century CE, moving between baths, temples, forum and market.

Before leaving the region, it's detour time along the legendary Amalfi Coast, stretching from the Sorrento Peninsula to Salerno. From the first kilometre, I'm impressed by this Mediterranean scene, its beaches, blue waters, stylish villas and lemon trees. These landscapes are breathtakingly beautiful, but I have to keep my wits about me as some stretches are very narrow and crowded. The route takes me through a series of hairpin bends, and I realise just how useful power steering can be.

I'm now heading east, inland, to see the ghost village of Craco in the Basilicata region, the setting for several films (*Christ Stopped at Eboli* and the James Bond movie *Quantum of Solace*). Through the window, the scenery flashes by and the colours change. The rolling countryside is filled with olive groves. Craco finally appears. The village, victim of landslides and an

earthquake, has been abandoned for decades. Everything is closed and fenced off, so after taking a few photos, there's nothing to do but leave.

Next stop is Matera, a World Heritage Site known for its medieval rock churches and *sassi*, well-preserved cave houses. It's easy to get lost in this maze of staircases, alleys and dead ends carved into the rock and frozen in time. To escape the tourists, I take the camper to the Murgia Timone viewpoint for a wonderful view of the town and the Torrente ravine.

It's now time to head to Puglia, the heel of the Italian 'boot'. I start by discovering the picturesque architecture typical of this region in the village of Alberobello, famous for its numerous *trulli* – pretty little white houses with conical grey roofs. This tradition of dry-stone construction goes back thousands of years. Next is the Adriatic coast where I pull over for the night in a camper van park overlooking the sea at Polignano a Mare. This town of white facades, suspended above the Adriatic, reminds me of Bonifacio on Corsica. Polignano a Mare has a wealth of caves, the most famous of which, Grotta Palazzese, is home to a gourmet restaurant, but I prefer to buy two *panzerotti*, little pizza dough pasties, which I take to the beach. A tasty delight.

My itinerary is coming to an end. I skirt the coast and 20km (12 miles) south of Lecce – a dazzling Baroque town with palaces, quiet streets and churches – I stop at a very pretty bay: Faraglioni di Sant'Andrea. Legend has it that two women, bewitched by the beauty of this stretch of sea, threw themselves off the cliff. The gods, taking pity on them, decided to turn them into rocks so that they could admire these marvellous waters for eternity. The sea is still impossible to resist and I swim among the arches, caves and cliffs, savouring these moments of the *slow life*. **AL**

VALLONE DEI MULINI

Right in the centre of Sorrento, the Vallone dei Mulini is a deep ravine that was part of a series of gorges created by a volcanic eruption 35,000 years ago. The construction of Piazza Tasso in 1866 blocked access, but from a lookout you can see the remains of a mill, a sawmill and a washhouse, overgrown with lush vegetation.

Opposite, clockwise from left: Vesuvius crater; Polignano a Mare; Vallone dei Mulini. Above: Matera. Page 47, from top: Atrani, on the Amalfi coast; Trulli, Puglia.

ROAD MAP

Start // Parco Nazionale del Vesuvio
Finish // Faraglioni di Sant'Andrea
Distance // 598km (372 miles)
Recommended duration // 7-to-10 days
When to go // Spring and autumn
Culinary specialities // Bruschetta, *panzerotto* (savoury pie)

THE PERFECT SWIMMING SPOT

Description // By the sea, near Ostuni
GPS coordinates // 40.79753, 17.56638
Light pollution // None
Access // Sloping dirt road, slightly bumpy
Facilities // None
Parking // 10 spaces
Little extras // Flat spot with sea view close to the beautiful Quarto di Monte Beach. Rosa Marina Beach can be reached by bike in just a few minutes.

Opposite, from top: Troglodyte dwellings in Guadix, Spain; Frescoes in the Ivanovo monastery, Bulgaria.

MORE LIKE THIS
GOING UNDERGROUND

BASILICATA (ITALY)

Kick off this trip in the tiered streets of Pietragalla, home to the Parco dei Palmenti, a collection of underground huts with grass-covered roofs, reminiscent of Hobbit houses. Head south through the valleys to visit Potenza – don't miss San Gerardo Cathedral, an elegant Neoclassical edifice, and the town's two archaeological museums. Follow the E847 and then the SP37, a twisting road leading to the village of Brindisi Montagna. Dominated by a castle built on a rocky spur, it offers a majestic view of the mountains. Then backtrack and continue southwards, entering the steep terrain of the Gallipoli Cognato Regional Park. For a panoramic view, park at the foot of the Santa Maria Regina Coeli chapel, in the municipality of Castelmezzano, one of Italy's most beautiful and colourful cliff-side villages.

Start // Pietragalla
Finish // Castelmezzano
Distance // 75km (47 miles)
More information // visititaly.com

THE RUSE REGION (BULGARIA)

In northern Bulgaria, the attractive town of Ruse is nicknamed 'Little Vienna' because of its remarkable architecture – the bright red Opera House, adorned with white arches, is a fine example. Park on the banks of the Danube before heading south the next day to the village of Ivanovo, home to rock churches and chapels. Carved out of the cliffs, this monastic complex contains some well-preserved historical paintings. Nearby, explore the Rusenski Lom Nature Park, where the river of the same name meanders through craggy landscapes. Then get back behind the wheel and follow Route 501 to Koshov to explore new rock caves, then continue further south to Orlova Chuka Cave. Take a guided tour of this underground limestone cavern, at the entrance to which you can overnight in a large car park in the middle of nature.

Start // Ruse
Finish // Orlova Chuka Cave
Distance // 52km (32 miles)
More information // visitmybulgaria.com

AROUND GUADIX (SPAIN)

Soak up the Andalucian atmosphere among the whitewashed walls of Alcudia de Guadix. Climb to the San Gregorio Cross, which offers a view of the surrounding mountains, then drive on the A92 for 14km (9 miles) through cultivated fields until you reach Granada Geoparque, with its impressive yellow, orange and green rock formations. Continue your adventure in Guadix, a charming town with immaculate buildings – visit the Baroque cathedral and the ochre-tinted Alcazaba fortress. Enter a cave dwelling, crowned by a typical white chimney, before driving south along the curving Calle Nuestra Señora de la Paz, to enjoy exceptional views over badlands and ravines, including the Mirador del Fin del Mundo. Finally, head to Francisco Abellán Reservoir to find a spot to park your van by the turquoise water.

Start // Alcudia de Guadix
Finish // Francisco Abellán Reservoir
Distance // 47km (29 miles)
More information // spain.info

ROAD-TRIPPING AROUND ALICANTE

Cruise Spain's Costa Blanca, from rocky peaks to white sandy beaches, and from sporty hikes to strolls through pretty towns.

As spring draws to a close, I'm off in my camper to discover the Costa Blanca, in the province of Alicante, southeast Spain. Setting course for a section of the Mediterranean I know little about, the plan is to drive down the coast, stopping here and there to take in the lovely swimming spots and cycling opportunities.

My road trip starts in the extreme north of the province, in Dénia, a port built at the foot of a small hill topped by a ruined castle. After leaving the camper in one of the many car parks, I visit the Moorish fortress and then wander through the old town, including the picturesque and colourful Baix la Mar district. The central market provides ample opportunities to sample delicious specialities (including Dénia's famous red prawns), before discovering the charming white fishers' houses on the port. Various cycle paths invite me to get out my bike: on the advice of the tourist office, I set off on a 6km (4 mile) greenway between Dénia and El Verger, accompanied by the exquisite scent of orange blossom.

Next day, after a night near Marineta Casiana Beach, lulled by the sound of the waves, I sip orange juice with my feet in the sand before driving to Parc Natural del Montgó, named after the massif that separates the towns of Dénia and Xàbia. The destination is Cova Tallada sea cave. I park on the road and continue on foot along a lovely rocky path overlooking the water. After 1.5km (1 mile), a sign indicates the entrance to the cave, accessible only when the sea is calm. With its natural arches, translucent water and coral reefs, this is the perfect place for snorkelling.

I overnight in the picturesque town of Xàbia (the Plaça Suelos Nuevos is more than adequate for parking), then head south again to discover Granadella, one of the most beautiful bays on the Costa Blanca. You need to leave the car on the road to get down to the beach, which is surrounded by pines and cliffs. Swimsuit on, I slip my camper keys, phone and papers into a floating waterproof bag. It's a clever system for swimming without

'Soon the coast reveals a surprising limestone peak, 332m (1089ft) high, rising out of the sea: the Peñón de Ifach.'

leaving valuables on the shore – once filled and inflated, the bag remains on the surface of the water. The sun is at its zenith, the water turquoise and refreshing, lending itself to a long, relaxing afternoon here. I end the day on the Benissa ecological trail, which follows the Mediterranean between Cala Pinets and Cala La Calalga. A golden light tints the lovely little coves dotted with pine trees.

Soon, the coast reveals a surprising limestone peak, 332m (1089ft) high, rising out of the sea: the Peñón de Ifach, overlooking the seaside resort of Calpe and the water. It looks like a distant cousin of Rio de Janeiro's Sugarloaf Mountain. A hiking trail leads up to the rock. I tighten the laces of my shoes and begin the ascent. The route is easy at first, but requires you to be well equipped and not prone to vertigo – on some sections, the trail even looks like a *via ferrata*. The view from the top is truly breathtaking. Once back down, it's impossible to resist the call of the sea again. I plunge into the invigorating water, then settle down in the shade of the palm trees on the endless white-sand beach.

Back in the camper, I drive along the coast to Altea, an elegant white town crowned by a church whose blue-tiled dome gleams in the sun. I have fun losing myself in the old town's narrow streets, decorated with flowers. In stark contrast to the whitewashed walls of Altea, the famous multicoloured houses of La Vila Joiosa, 22km (14 miles) to the south, are painted in bright hues so as to be seen by sailors from their boats. This small village has preserved the pleasant feel of traditional fishing ports.

LAS FUENTES DEL ALGAR

About 12 km (7 miles) north of Altea, the Algar springs form a succession of waterfalls and pools of pure, clear water in which to cool off. They're in the middle of a remarkable nature reserve, ideal for a getaway, with footpaths and picnic area.

Opposite, clockwise from left: Peñón de Ifach; Altea; Dénia. Above, Las Fuentes del Algar. Page 53: Granadella.

I couldn't visit the province of Alicante without exploring its namesake capital: a dynamic seaside town, topped by a castle. The only problem is parking. I end up on the outskirts and use my bike to get to the centre, where I'm immediately seduced by the Barrio de Santa Cruz, a popular, lively, flower-filled district in the old town, at the foot of Mt Benacantil. Particularly enjoyable is the atmosphere of the central market, where I taste fresh, local produce before the climb up to Santa Barbara Castle, built in the 16th century. Then I pedal along the Esplanade d'Espagne, a long palm-lined avenue whose six million marble paving stones form tricoloured waves. I return to the camper to drop off some groceries. It's always a relief to find the vehicle intact after a few hours' absence – even if you take care to choose parking spots with positive reviews, you're not always safe from a nasty surprise.

My stay is drawing to a close, and I leave Alicante via the N332 to reach Torrevieja, 52km (32 miles) away, at the southern tip of the province. I've heard of the pink lagoon that borders the city but can't find any signs, so I park on Las Lavanderas Street and decide to follow the locals in their bathing suits. I'm intrigued to see them carrying containers of water. The walk crosses dunes before arriving at the edge of the famous lake, whose surprising colour is due to the presence of tiny pink bacteria in the water. It also has a high salt concentration which means you can float effortlessly. Once out, I finally understand the need for the water containers – patches of salt stick to my skin and itch terribly. How lucky I am to be travelling in a van – all I have to do is pull out my shower head and there I am, rinsing off on the sidewalk, under the amused gaze of passers-by. **AL**

ROAD MAP

Start // Dénia
Finish // Las Salinas de Torrevieja
Distance // 205km (127 miles)
Recommended duration // 7-to-10 days
When to go // Spring and late summer, excluding school holidays
Culinary specialities // *Turrón* (nougat), *paella de marisco* (seafood paella)

THE PERFECT PICNIC SPOT

Description // Los Limoneros is a very quiet location 300m (984ft) from the beach, in an orchard.
GPS coordinates // 38.145972, -0.638536
Light pollution // None
Access // Sandy track
Facilities // None
Parking // Numerous spaces
Little extras // Overnight stays finance the agro-ecological restoration of the site, the recovery of trees, the irrigation system and the planting of new trees. Reservations at spots.roadsurfer.com.

Opposite: Val d'Orcia, Italy.

MORE LIKE THIS ON YOUR BIKE

CYCLING IN THE NETHERLANDS

In the Netherlands, the bicycle is king. This flat country is criss-crossed with cycle paths of all sizes. Pack a bike in your camper (or rent one locally) to break up your itinerary with some two-wheeled fun. To get started, park in Dordrecht and set off on into the Biesbosch National Park: a cycle path (25-50km/16-31 miles round trip) will take you through the vast marshes, populated by beavers, of this huge freshwater delta. Then drive to Utrecht. This student city, one of the oldest in the Netherlands, is famous for its historic centre encircled by picturesque canals. From the city, bike to the splendid Kasteel de Haar, a Neogothic castle, or to the Utrechtse Heuvelrug National Park, ideal for forest bike rides. End your road trip in the capital, Amsterdam, from where a 37km (23 mile) cycling circuit leads to the Waterland region and its dykes, canals and emerald fields.

Start // Dordrecht
Finish // Amsterdam
Distance // 160km (100 miles)
More information // holland.com

THE WHITE ROADS OF TUSCANY (ITALY)

On this drive to Siena, you can follow the 209km (130 mile) L'Eroica cycle race route from the comfort of your camper, through the green hills of Chianti, the winding cypress-lined roads of Crete Senesi and the desert landscapes of Val d'Orcia. You'll pass through typical rural Tuscan villages like Murlo and Lucignano d'Asso, and wine towns like Montalcino and Radda di Chianti. Swap the van for a bike from time to time and create your own race route stages according to your interests and cycling ability. One option is the first part of the L'Eroica, which starts in Gaiole in Chianti and goes through vineyards for 20km (12 miles): it's fairly easy; only the climb to reach Castello di Brolio is steep.

Start/Finish // Gaiole in Chianti
Distance // 209km (130 miles)
More information // eroica.cc

ON THE TRAIL OF THE TOUR DE FRANCE IN DENMARK

Denmark is one of the world's leading cycling nations. Trace the route of the riders in the 2022 edition of the Tour de France, which began in the Danish capital. Saddle up and cycle Copenhagen, then drive to the town of Roskilde, on the edge of a fjord in the heart of Skjoldungernes Land National Park. Check out the UNESCO-listed cathedral, which contains 40 royal tombs. Continue on to Lejre, once an important Viking capital. Bike along the magnificent fjords of Inderbredning, Holbæk and Lamme. Drive south along the coast and in the port town of Kalundborg, visit the Church of Our Lady to admire its five impressive spires. For 50km (31 miles), follow the west coast to Korsør, then cross the Great Belt Bridge (the world's third-largest suspension bridge, rising 65m/213ft above the sea) to finish in Nyborg, the former Danish capital.

Start // Copenhagen
Finish // Nyborg
Distance // 180km (112 miles)
More information // letourcph.dk

ALL THE WAY AROUND SICILY

From Greek temples and Mt Etna to turquoise waters and Mediterranean scrub, take a journey rich in scenery and history.

Welcome to Sicily! A twenty-minute ferry ride has taken me and the camper from the port of Villa San Giovanni, on the tip of Calabria, to the port of Messina. To soak up the Sicilian atmosphere, and because the sun is shining on this spring morning, I turn on the radio, stick my elbow out the window and set off along the SS114 state road. The first stop on this trip, which will follow the island's coast from east to west, will be Taormina, 57km (35 miles) south of Messina, passing through several popular villages.

Taormina sits on a steep promontory that seems inaccessible by van, so I park by the town's cable car and use it to get to the village. Viewed from the cable car's cab, the gradient of the terrain is impressive. Taormina's treasures come into view, notably the Greek theatre and Piazza IX Aprile, which offer unobstructed views of the coast and nearby Mt Etna. I take a seat on a bench next to two friendly old locals and strike up a conversation in Italian. On their advice, I spend the afternoon in the Alcantara Gorge, half an hour's drive away. This place is an incredible work of geological art. The walls of the gorge have been sculpted by lava flows from Etna that cooled on contact with the icy waters of the river. I feel like I'm walking in the bowels of the Earth.

Using the Park4night app, I find the place where I'll be spending my next two nights – the car park of the Etna cable car at Nicolosi, at an altitude of 1900m (6234ft). To get there, I take the SP92 road, which is well maintained and gives a volcanic foretaste with its lunar landscape, caves and lava flows.

The ringing of the alarm clock snaps me out of my dreams. I draw the curtain, it's still dark. Perfect. I boil some water for my tea, which soon warms up the cabin. A quick wash, warm clothes and I'm outside just as the first light of day appears for breakfast at the top of the Silvestri Craters. The rest of the day is dedicated to a guided excursion to the summit of Mt Etna, an experience that comes with a hefty price tag, but which will remain an unforgettable memory.

Next up is Syracuse, a magical city and major metropolis in the ancient world. It's worth spending as much time as possible here, wandering among the Greek remains, admiring the Baroque cathedral and getting lost in the maze of alleyways on the small island of Ortygia, Syracuse's historical centre.

At Sicily's southern tip, I reach the Cavagrande del Cassibile Nature Reserve. The view of the Avola Canyon from the

© e55evu | Adobe Stock

MT ETNA LEGEND

The Greeks believed Hephaestus, god of blacksmiths, set up his forge on Mt Etna, where he worked with the Cyclops. In another legend, Hephaestus oversaw the punishment of the monster Typhon. When the god placed his head on the anvil, Typhon, agitated, caused Etna's eruptions.

'Taormina's . . . Greek theatre and Piazza IX Aprile . . . offer unobstructed views of the coast and nearby Mt Etna.'

viewpoint is spectacular, though the 30-minute descent under the sun and through the rocks is quite laborious. The reward is the natural pools at the bottom, heavenly with their crystalline waters. A 20km (12 mile) drive from the reserve is Noto, celebrated as the 'pearl of Sicilian Baroque architecture': the town was completely rebuilt in this style after an earthquake in 1693. I walk the streets, visit a few monuments – including the must-see San Nicolò Cathedral – and try a Sicilian speciality, a perfectly crisp ricotta *cannolo*, at Pasticceria Kennedy.

Then it's on to the Valley of the Temples, below Agrigento. One of the Mediterranean's major archaeological sites, the valley is home to the best-preserved Doric temples outside Greece. To make the most of it, aim to get there first thing in the morning.

Just 15km (9 miles) from Agrigento lies the awesome Scala dei Turchi (Staircase of the Turks), a white limestone cliff that plunges down into the sea via an immense series of natural steps. Unfortunately, due to the risk of collapse, access is forbidden so I make do with the view from the lookout on the SP68 road, then set up camp for the night in a large car park near the beautiful beach of Siculiana Marina.

The following morning it's the northwest of the island that is calling. Following the SS115 and then the SS119, I reach Segesta.

Opposite: Palermo cathedral. Above, from left: Valley of the Temples; Ancient theater at Taormina. Opposite, bottom: Road to Etna. Page 59: Tonnara di Scopello.

After visiting its unfinished Doric temple and 5th-century BCE theatre, in a marvellous location among the hills, you can take a break at the thermal springs – just park, cross the river and bask in this sulphurous hot bath in a natural setting. I extend this moment of relaxation with a 15-minute drive to the Faraglioni di Scopello beach, very photogenic thanks to its rocky peaks rising out of the water. If you're feeling active, head to nearby Zingaro Nature Reserve which offers numerous hiking trails leading to seven fish-filled coves. I take up residence in the car park on Macari Beach, a little beyond the reserve, where the view is captivating. The next day is devoted to exploring the Monte Cofano Nature Reserve, with its many pretty paths through the *maquis* (typical Mediterranean scrubland). A small open-air museum at the foot of the Mangiapane Grotto displays the living quarters of an ancient Sicilian farming family.

Journey's end is the Sicilian capital Palermo, an impressive blend of Byzantine, Arab and Baroque architecture. Its Arab-Norman cathedral, imposing Norman palace and Palatine chapel invite you to travel back in time. In the present, I stock up on *arancini* at the farmers' market – tasty fried rice balls stuffed with various ingredients.

It's time to set off again. Arriving at the ferry ticket office, I'm told there's a change of terminal and the ship is more than three hours late, so I'll have to be patient. The directions are confusing and, instead of queuing us up on a large esplanade as in most ports, the dockers divide us chaotically into different streets. Travellers crammed into cars become irritable. As for me, in my cosy little mobile home, I choose to relax with a hot meal and a good movie, comfortably stretched out in my bed and in no hurry to say goodbye to the Mediterranean's largest island. **AL**

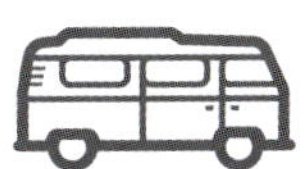

ROAD MAP

Start // Messina
Finish // Palermo
Distance // 757km (470 miles)
Recommended duration // 10-to-15 days
When to go // Any time, though spring and autumn are perfect
Culinary specialities // Marsala wine, *sfincione* (a type of pizza from the Palermo region), *arancini* (rice balls stuffed, breaded and fried)

THE PERFECT SLEEP SPOT

Description // Parking along the road near Etna
GPS coordinates // 37.693077, 14.980686
Light pollution // None
Access // Easy, by road
Facilities // Picnic tables
Parking // 10 spaces
Little extras // Overnight option with a superb view of the Etna crater, 6km (4 miles) away. Many vanlifers have witnessed eruptions from this spot.

Opposite, from top: Spiaggia del Dottore in Sardinia, Italy; Porto de La Cruz in Tenerife, Canary Islands, Spain.

MORE LIKE THIS
ISLAND HOPPING

MALTA

Beaches, cliffs, terraced fields and left-hand drive – that's Malta. Capital Valletta, founded in the 16th century, boasts a rich heritage. Twenty minutes away, the Hal Saflieni hypogeum is a unique prehistoric underground necropolis. Continue south to the fishing village of Marsaxlokk. A colourful stopover not to be missed, it's also just a stone's throw from St Peter's Pool, a blissful natural swimming hole. On the south coast are the Blue Grotto and the Dingli Cliffs, where you can park your camper facing the sea. Drive inland to Mdina, the ancient capital, especially enchanting at dusk – leave the camper behind and explore the narrow streets on foot. For something completely different, visit Popeye Village, a film set turned theme park. Take the ferry to the neighbouring island of Gozo, home to megalithic temples and beautiful landscapes. Everywhere, a multitude of sleeping spots offer great views.
Start/Finish // Valletta
Distance // 147km (91 miles)
More information // visitmalta.com

TENERIFE (SPAIN)

Travelling by camper to the largest island in the Canary archipelago allows you to get off the beaten track. On the west coast, explore the cliffs of Los Gigantes, which rise up to 600m (1969ft). Hiking trails and numerous boat excursions are available. At the northwestern tip of Tenerife, spend the night by Punta de Teno's red-and-white lighthouse. Heading east, there's a succession of beaches and natural pools including gorgeous Charco de la Laja. Push east to Anaga Rural Park, passing through La Orotava and San Cristóbal de La Laguna, two of the island's most picturesque towns. Finally, head south along the TF1 coastal road: the village of El Médano is renowned for its kitesurfing spot overlooking the Montaña Roja volcano. If your van is a 4x4, explore the volcanic landscapes of Teide National Park, in the centre of the island.
Start // Los Gigantes
Finish // Teide National Park
Distance // 258km (160 miles)
More information // hellocanaryislands.com

NORTHERN SARDINIA (ITALY)

Bays, white sandy beaches and turquoise waters are all part of this road trip along Sardinia's northern coastline. Before setting off, be sure to visit Olbia's medieval basilica of San Simplicio and the Nuraghe Riu Mulinu, an archaeological site. Then head north on the SS125. Stroll among the rocks at Capo Testa, a lunar landscape enveloped by crystal-clear waters. With your windows open, drive west on the SP90, which zigzags between the jewels of the coastline. Have a swim in the Costa Paradiso cove, feast on fresh lobster in Castelsardo and eat an ice cream in Stintino. Continue 63km (39 miles) south and you'll find the magnificent Porto Conte Regional Nature Park, with hiking trails and a popular beach. Follow the SP55 to Alghero. Park outside the city walls and walk the cobbled streets of the old quarter, renowned for its Catalan Gothic heritage.
Start // Olbia
Finish // Alghero
Distance // 283km (176 miles)
More information // sardegnaturismo.it

FROM LISBON TO THE DOURO VALLEY

Take a trip to the sunny Costa de Prata and central Portugal, driving through a rich architectural and cultural heritage and a wide variety of landscapes.

With the window wide open and *fado* music on the radio, I approach Lisbon, the first stage of a route that will take me via the Costa de Prata to Porto and the Douro Valley.

Portugal's capital rolls out the red carpet to welcome visitors with its incredible steel bridge over the Tagus River, a lookalike of San Francisco's Golden Gate Bridge (it was built in 1966 by the same company), under the protective gaze of the immense Cristo Rei – a replica of Rio de Janeiro's Christ the Redeemer statue. I stop for an extended stay in the port's huge car park, Rua da Cintura do Porto de Lisboa. It's cheap, but rather noisy due to the nearby railroad and clubs – bring earplugs. The city centre and beach are a 30-minute walk away.

It's best to be in shape and wearing comfortable shoes to explore Lisbon, spread, as it is, over several hills. It's a steep climb up to 11th-century São Jorge Castle, but worth it for the shady terraces, known as *miradouros*, overlooking the city and Tagus. Lisbon is a dynamic, creative mix of Baroque facades covered in *azulejos*, Moorish gardens and lively neighbourhoods; a multicoloured maze where you'll never get lost for long.

After devouring a delicious *pastel de nata*, a traditional custard tart, at the Pastéis de Belém shop, I take line 28 of the legendary yellow tram system, passing some of the city's most beautiful sights: the Basílica da Estrela, the lively streets of Baixa and Alfama. Top tip: the streets are narrow so keep your elbows tucked in. Next stop is the LX Factory where disused warehouses

have been renovated to house designer boutiques, bookshops and trendy restaurants, against a backdrop of vivid street art.

It's time to hit the road again. I follow the coast along the N247 and make my first stop at Cabo da Roca, a steep, wild cliff that is the most westerly point in continental Europe. Just inland, it's easy to spend the rest of the day visiting the romantic parks and exuberant palaces and castles of Sintra and the surrounding area. The road winds through wooded hills in a long, one-way loop, and I fall in love with the fantastical Palácio Nacional da Pena – all domes, crenellated towers and bright colours – and the extravagant, Gothic manor house Quinta da Regaleira, with its well and spiral staircase leading to mysterious underground galleries.

At the end of the day, a seaside spot in Praia da Mexilhoeira (50km/31 miles north via the N247) is the perfect place to spend the night. As soon as I wake up, the refreshing spray of the ocean beckons and I run to the water's edge. I love this life without routine, letting myself be amazed by Mother Nature, having my nose tingle in the morning freshness, filling my lungs with salty air. I feel lucky and free when I travel by camper van.

Continuing north on the N247 soon brings you to the Costa de Prata. This stretch of coast is home to timeless places such as the charming medieval village of Óbidos, which is in a remarkable state of preservation. A stroll among the whitewashed houses covered in red tiles, sitting behind the ramparts, is highly recommended. I then make a detour to Nazaré, a picturesque town known to surfers the world over for its incredible Praia do Norte. This beach is where, from October to March, you'll find the world's biggest waves: the record for the highest wave ever surfed took place here in 2017 – 24.38m (80ft). I'm amused by the number of people who offer me a room to rent even though I'm driving around in a converted van – '*Não, obrigado*' – and head to São Miguel Lighthouse, atop a cliff separating the touristy beach of Nazaré from the wild and windy Praia do Norte. The view is exceptional.

Pushing north, next on the itinerary is Batalha Monastery, a masterpiece of flamboyant Gothic art, with lace-like stonework and a fabulous royal cloister. Then it's on to the old university town of Coimbra, Portugal's medieval capital, majestically perched above the Mondego River and notable for its steep streets and cathedral.

Next morning, as I'm about to leave the spot where I'd spent the night, I notice that my dirty water tank is spilling and rubbing on the ground. I jump into action, throwing down a towel and sliding under the vehicle. Nothing serious, it's just the tank's retaining bar that's come loose. In my toolbox, I retrieve a size 12 wrench to tighten the bolts. With the job done, I stand up again, my hands black, when a Portuguese man kindly approaches me to offer his help. I politely decline, my proud smile speaking volumes as I relish this small DIY victory. I can hardly get through the camper's door, my head is so big.

AZULEJOS

The term '*azulejo*' comes from Arabic and means 'small polished stone'. These glazed, hand-painted earthenware tiles were first imported from Spain in the early 16th century by King Manuel to cover the walls of his palace in Sintra. Over time, the tiles have become one of the Portugal's beloved icons and can be seen covering the facades of many public buildings, churches and homes.

Below: Cabo da Roca. Above: Palacio Nacional da Pena in Sintra. Opposite: On the bridge over the Tagus in Lisbon. Page 65, from top: Lisbon tramway; Douro landscape.

'I fall in love with the fantastical Palácio Nacional da Pena – all domes, crenellated towers and bright colours.'

ROAD MAP

Start // Lisbon
Finish // Douro Valley
Distance // 618km (384 miles)
Recommended duration // 10-to-15 days
When to go // At the beginning or end of summer – when temperatures rise, the lack of shade makes itself felt.
Culinary specialities // *Pastéis de nata* (custard tarts), *francesinha* (a kind of meat sandwich topped with melted cheese), *bolinhos de bacalhau* (cod croquettes)

THE PERFECT SLEEP SPOT

Description // Large car park in the dunes.
GPS coordinates // 39.153301, -9.36895
Light pollution // None
Access // Easy, on a dirt track
Facilities // Public toilets
Parking // 30 pitches
Little extras // Accessible to all vehicles. Quiet and deserted in the evening. Direct access to the beach (supervised by lifeguards) for swimming and surfing.

The rest of the day involves the lush Buçaco National Forest – home to many plant species, from cedars to tree ferns – and the town of Águeda, where the AgitÁgueda Festival is taking place. Street art covers the walls, multicoloured umbrellas hang in the streets and a huge podium is being installed. Even my van is playing along and posing in front of the scenery.

Culture fix enjoyed, the sun beckons me to Aveiro Beach, 30km (19 miles) away, for an afternoon of idleness and swimming. I rinse off my salty skin in the public showers, then set up for the night under a bridge near Aveiro's city centre with its canals, small bridges and painted boats, called *moliceiros*.

Hours later, a ray of sun sneaks in through the camper's skylight, which has been open all night. I smile as I stretch and think about the day's programme – visit the church of Santa Maria de Válega, covered in more *azulejos*, then finish off the trip in Porto and the Douro Wine Valley. More adventures to come. **AL**

Opposite: La Morra, in the Piedmont region, Italy.

MORE LIKE THIS
WINE ROUTES

THE MOSELLE VALLEY (GERMANY)

Fairy-tale castles, medieval villages, vine-covered hillsides – the banks of the Moselle River offer a beguiling journey into a land of romance. From Trier, home to Roman monuments and Germany's oldest cathedral, the meandering river takes you to Bernkastel-Kues, home of Moselle Riesling, and Traben-Trarbach, with its Art Nouveau villas. Continuing north, you reach the Prinzenkopf observation tower and the Bremm lookout. From these viewpoints, there's a superb panorama of the blue ribbon of water winding through the vineyards. Linger in Beilstein, with its attractive cobbled streets lined with half-timbered houses. Unless, of course, you'd prefer to explore Cochem's squares and its hilltop castle. And all of this is merely a marvellous prelude to the historical treasures of Koblenz, at the confluence of the Rhine and Moselle rivers.

Start // Trier
Finish // Koblenz
Distance // 203km (126 miles)
More information // visitmosel.de

THE PIEDMONT WINE ROUTE (ITALY)

Between Genoa and Turin you find the sunny, vineyard-lined roads of Piedmont. Head for Acqui Terme, in the Monferrato region, famous for its red wine (Dolcetto d'Acqui) and the sulphur hot spring that gushes out in the heart of the town. View the city from the gardens of the 11th-century Castello dei Paleologi. Through grape-covered hills, drive to Canelli, celebrated for its production of Moscato d'Asti, a renowned sparkling white wine. Continue your journey to the Castello di Grinzane Cavour, home to a museum dedicated to Piedmont's wine culture and a wine cellar for tasting. Visit the 14th-century fortress at Serralunga d'Alba before stopping off at the village of Barolo, birthplace of the 'king of wines, wine of kings'. End your itinerary in the hilltop village of La Morra for views over this land beautifully shaped by vines.

Start // Acqui Terme
Finish // La Morra
Distance // 85km (53 miles)
More information // piemonte.italiaguida.it

TOKAJ WINE REGION (HUNGARY)

Sitting in the foothills of the Zemplén Mountains, the vineyards that produce the prestigious Tokaj wine are spread over 28 municipalities. Here, grape-growing hillsides mingle with a wilder landscape of rivers and forests, the ideal setting for a relaxing road trip. Start with the Gombos-hegy and Kőporosi wineries, located in the miniature hillside village of Hercegkút. Visit Sárospatak to explore its castle, home to one of the region's finest Tokajs. En route to the southwest, stop at other castles associated with wineries, such as Oremus in Tolcsva, whose cellars were hand-hewn out of volcanic rock and date back to the 13th century. Finish your journey in Tokaj, the village that gave its name to the appellation. At the Wine Museum you can find out all about this liqueur-like beverage, produced by a fungus that justifies its name – 'noble rot.

Start // Hercegkút
Finish // Tokaj
Distance // 62km (39 miles)
More information // visittokaj.com

ACROSS SLOVENIA AND CROATIA

Follow a stretch of road between two countries and their superb capitals, before losing yourself in the natural setting of the Plitvice Lakes.

The Slovenian capital wakes up under snow. Having arrived late in the evening the day before, Camille, José and I are delighted to explore it under its thick white coat. All three of us love these Southeast European cities, elegant and full of life at the same time. In fact, we're looking forward to visiting Zagreb too, in a few days' time, as soon as we've crossed the Croatian border. A long drive then takes us south to the Plitvice Lakes, a grand spot and a must for nature lovers.

My companions and I begin our tour of beautiful Ljubljana. The city centre is not large, which contributes to its charm. We appreciate the refined, uncluttered architecture of the middle-class houses, as well as the colourful, flashier religious buildings. However, it's on the bridge-lined banks of the Ljubljanica River that our hearts are won over. The peaceful atmosphere is so intoxicating that we spend the evening wandering its shores. Before returning to the van, which we've left on the outskirts of the town, we walk to the castle through a maze of steep streets. It's worth the effort. Standing at the highest point of the fortress, guardian of the city for 900 years, we enjoy a breathtaking view over a sea of crimson roofs, and capture with our eyes an image of the capital we will treasure.

On our way to Zagreb we enter the heart of Lower Carniola, a region of vineyards and forests, where isolated villages topped by elegant bell towers dot the hillsides. After 70km (43 miles), we stop to briefly explore the historic centre of Novo Mesto. Tucked in a bend of the Krka River, the old town with its multihued buildings is a pleasant sight to behold. We stroll Glavni Square, the town's hub, where shops cluster around a pretty fountain. A few steps away, the mimosa-yellow church of St Leonard shines brightly. We wander off to do a bit of shopping and discover a vast industrial zone. In this district, as in those of many manufacturing towns, the magic has gone.

But that doesn't stop our enjoyment of this road trip. We cross the Lower Save Valley and linger in the village of Kostanjevica na Krki, the smallest in the country, built on an island. In this rural

landscape on the edge of Slovenia, we take a long walk along the Krka, appreciating this unrivalled haven of peace. However, the most beautiful memories are not always the most romantic, and our wanderings through Zagreb after crossing Croatian customs confirm this. A torrential downpour that lasts several days gives us little respite to roam the streets: just enough to get to St Mark's Church, an iconic landmark of the upper town, whose red, cyan and white roof bears the coats of arms of the capital on one side, and of Croatia, Dalmatia and Slavonia on the other. We take refuge in a pub, forced to order a few pints to kill time. What could have been a dreary winter's evening is transformed into a wonderful moment of sharing.

Only José and I are continuing our adventure further south, through the Croatian countryside – not all of us have the privilege of working as digital nomads. Around 140km (87 mile) of road lined with copses, remote hamlets and large, isolated farmhouses separate us from the turquoise lakes of Plitvice. Along the way, we stop off not far from the Bosnian border at Crni Potok, a ghost-like hamlet of 150 souls. We drift off to sleep in the back of the van, wrapped in an almost oppressive silence. At dawn, just as we're getting ready to get back behind the wheel, a man appears. He's blind and seems unsettled by our presence so begins to call out to his companion, who sticks her head out of a nearby window. The woman sees our smiling, worried faces and invites us without hesitation to a veritable feast. It's barely 8 o'clock, and sitting around a full bottle of rakia in this little kitchen, José and I are slightly dazed by the situation. The couple are adorable and constantly serve us large glasses of spirit, accompanied by a bowl of coffee and homemade doughnuts. Our unusual breakfast is not lacking in local character, and even makes us loquacious – the four of us manage to communicate with the help of gestures and theatrical intonations, and so we laugh for most of the morning.

We decide to wait until the next day to set off for the Plitvice Lakes National Park. With the camper's tyres hugging the road, the jovial atmosphere gives way to meditation, fuelled by the landscapes passing by. Our inner journeys sometimes come to a halt, for a quick chat or exchanges of ideas, before we return to our own thoughts. On the road, time stretches, reflections take shape.

We finally reach the edge of the national park, situated in the Dinaric Alps, and quickly put on our hiking boots after leaving the camper in one of the car parks. This large natural wonder boasts 16 lakes linked by countless waterfalls, as well as limestone caves and dense forests home to grey wolves, brown bears and lynx, among other mammals. We won't be seeing any of them – they're too elsuive – but knowing they're nearby is a real thrill. A million tourists come here every year, so of course the site is protected and we have to stay on a large path built of logs so as not to encroach on the wilderness.

VISITING ZAGREB

The Croatian capital is the perfect destination for an urban getaway, before heading off to Plitvice or the Adriatic coast. Its upper town, with colourful houses, cobblestone streets and many museums, will delight art and culture lovers. A very different atmosphere prevails in the lower town, particularly around the bustling Dolac market, where bright red parasols abound. You're sure to be surprised by Zagreb, a city full of contrasts.

Below: Plitvice National Park. Above: Zagreb. Opposite: Forest near Ljubljana. Page 71, from top: Kongresni Square, Ljubljana; Lake Plitvice.

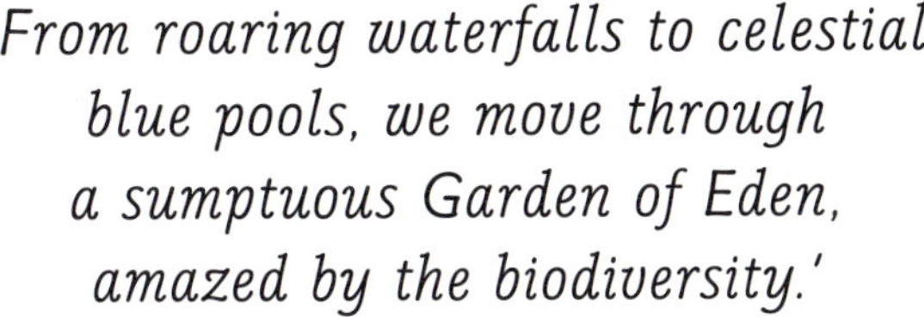

'From roaring waterfalls to celestial blue pools, we move through a sumptuous Garden of Eden, amazed by the biodiversity.'

It's February and quiet and we're lucky enough to be the only ones, or almost the only ones, walking the trails. It doesn't take long to realise why this national park, in the middle of Croatia, is one of the country's most beautiful destinations. From roaring waterfalls to celestial blue pools, we move through a sumptuous Garden of Eden, amazed by the biodiversity. Nature is singing and the sun is shining, and spring is just around the corner. **AD**

ROAD MAP

Start // Ljubljana (Slovenia)
Finish // Plitvice Lakes National Park (Croatia)
Distance // 307km (191 miles)
Recommended duration // 5-to-7 days
When to go // Avoid summer to enjoy the most popular spots when they're less busy.
Culinary specialities // *Štrukli sa sirom* (fresh cheese puff pastries from the Zagorje region, near Zagreb)

THE PERFECT PHOTO SPOT

Description // In the heart of Plitvice Lakes National Park
GPS coordinates // 44.86452516267551, 15.56196027902734
Access // On foot, after parking in one of the dedicated car parks
Activities // Hiking, photography
Visitor numbers // It's more pleasant to visit outside the high season.
Little extras // Continue your adventure at the impressive Una waterfalls, just 40km (25 miles) across the Bosnian border

Opposite, clockwise from top: Preikestolen, Norway; Vintgar Gorge, Slovenia; Forni di Sopra, Italy.

MORE LIKE THIS
HIKING COUNTRYSIDE

SOUTHWEST NORWAY

Departing from Stavanger, a major coastal town in southwestern Norway, head northeast along the Lysefjord. To best explore the 'Fjord of Light', treat yourself to a short boat trip, then lace up for the iconic Preikestolen hike – you'll discover a jawdropping view from the heights of this 604m (1982ft) cliff. Return to your vehicle and retrace your steps to the island of Karmøy, whose marshes and white sandy beaches are a joy to discover on foot, then stop off in the pretty port of Haugesund. Continue north to the Bømlo archipelago and drive to Bremnes to admire the fishing huts that stand on the wild coastline. Last but not least, after a three-hour drive, you reach Trolltunga, a must-see hike, where a tongue of rock jutting out over an immense abyss will leave you speechless. A natural spectacle of breathtaking beauty.

Start // Stavanger
Finish // Trolltunga
Distance // 535km (332 miles)
More information // visitnorway.com

TOUR THE FRIULIAN DOLOMITES (ITALY)

Begin your Dolomites drive by setting course for Belluno, a charming Veneto town straddling the Piave River. Let yourself be seduced by the Piazza Duomo, replete with a cathedral, a palace and the ruins of a castle, before heading north into the mountains and the focus of this trip. It's on the heights of Forni di Sopra, a small winter sports resort, that you'll experience your first beautiful hikes on numerous marked trails. You may be lucky enough to spot some wild animals (ibex, golden eagles), before sampling the delicious local cuisine. For more alpine scenery, drive 60km (37 miles) to the Tagliamento Valley, where you'll have the chance to go from waterfall to lake, including Lago di Cornino, a turquoise jewel perfect for swimming. Further south, the Valcellina and its magnificent gorges offer a final breath of fresh air before returning to Belluno.

Start/Finish // Belluno
Distance // 249km (155 miles)
More information // visititaly.com

TRIGLAV NATIONAL PARK (SLOVENIA)

Alpine valleys, blue-green rivers and powerful waterfalls are in store if you take the road to Triglav National Park in northwest Slovenia. In the eastern Julian Alps, the resort of Kranjska Gora is a strategic starting point for exploring the region – hikers will love the larch forest at the foot of Triglav, Slovenia's highest mountain (2864m/9396ft). Next drive east, still within the park, to visit the Vintgar Gorge on foot: a long, surreal trail on wooden footbridges overlooks the translucent Radovna River. Back in the camper, cross the Pokljuka karst plateau and its coniferous forest to the south of the park for the Tolmin Gorge. The latter offers an exceptional spectacle – pure water rushes through a narrow canyon, with vertical cliffs rising above. Finally, stop near the Kozjak Waterfall and follow the signposted path to appreciate the beauty of the area, before returning to Kranjska Gora.

Start/Finish // Kranjska Gora
Distance // 212km (132 miles)
More information // slovenia.info

ADVENTURES IN ASTURIAS AND GALICIA

Navigate northwest Spain's beaches and mountains, travelling across Asturias and Galicia to Santiago de Compostela.

I turn down the car radio and exchange a smile with Adrien, who's driving, before resting my head against the window. It's good to be a passenger and just relax. We're off to discover the unusual landscapes of northwest Spain, with Santiago de Compostela as our ultimate goal.

From Bilbao, we head west to the Picos de Europa National Park, and, at Caín de Valdeón, we hike along the Ruta del Cares. This trail follows a deep canyon to Poncebos. It's best to get to Caín early in the morning, so you can park easily and walk without feeling rushed for time, because while the route is not particularly difficult, it is long (24km/15 miles round trip), and sometimes vertiginous. In the evening, exhausted, we take up temporary residence off the side of the road.

Next day starts with the glacial lakes of Covadonga. Getting there means passing the beautiful Cangas de Onís bridge, which dates back to the 13th century, and then, around a bend in the road, majestic Covadonga Basilica appears, perched on a rock in an impressive, verdant mountain setting. You don't have to be

a believer to be moved by the beauty of this site, and by mutual agreement, we choose to stop and visit the splendid church.

A dozen kilometres separate us from the Covadonga Lakes themselves, via the CO4, certainly one of the most beautiful roads in Spain (in high season, it attracts so many people that access for private vehicles is restricted, with buses providing daytime access to the lakes). From every angle, the meadows and mountains are stunningly beautiful. We're surrounded by free-ranging cows with clanging bells as we skirt part of Lake Enol before reaching the car park. The area is very busy, but given its size, there's plenty of room for everyone. Various hiking trails begin at the lakes: we take one that weaves its way through an old mine and then opens out onto the plain of Lake Ercina, where we enjoy a peaceful picnic.

Back at the camper, we head north, down from Covadonga, and as evening falls, we find a parking area near the Mirador del Fitu, a viewpoint overlooking a picturesque landscape between mountains and ocean. The sky has cleared completely, promising ideal conditions for star gazing. Adrien takes out his guitar and plays a few notes to accompany the sunset. These are the moments that make us love vanlife so much.

First thing in the morning, Adrien takes the wheel, while I scout out the route that will take us to Playa del Silencio, the 'beach of silence', near Cudillero, a wonderful pebble beach surrounded by amphitheatre-like cliffs. When we park the van on the side of the one-way road, it's raining and the place is deserted. Waiting for the weather to clear, we install a set of wheel chocks to

SURFING AT DONIÑOS BEACH

Doniños Beach in Ferrol, a port city in the A Coruña province, is renowned as one of Galicia's best surf spots, with large, consistent waves all year round. The beach stretches over 2km (1.5miles) of wild landscape, between ocean and mountain, and offers a multitude of waves for surfing rights and lefts. The sunsets are pretty idyllic too.

Below: Picos de Europa National Park. Above: Santiago de Compostela Cathedral. Opposite: Lake Ercina. Page 77, from top: Cangas de Onís bridge; Playa del Silencio.

compensate for the inclination of the terrain, and position the vehicle perfectly horizontally. Adrien starts cooking, while I sit on the bench with a hot mug in my hands, gazing out of the window at the ocean. As soon as the rain stops, we jump outside, guided to the beach by the smell of the sea. The sound of rolling pebbles, carried away with each wave, resonates and bewitches us. Sitting on the shore, we savour the moment, our senses alert.

Back in the camper van, it's time to go west. Our next stop is the fabulous Praia das Catedrais ('cathedrals beach') in Galicia – its name derives from its 30m-high (98ft) natural arches, looking like Gothic flying buttresses fashioned by the elements. The beach is only accessible at low tide and, unfortunately for us, the weather is rough and the choppy seas have not receded sufficiently – the cathedrals won't be revealing their treasures today.

We return to the A8 and drive through more rain to reach a riverside parking area for the night at Fiopans. I fall asleep immediately despite the ongoing storm.

Santiago de Compostela is only 20km (12 miles) away. To be on the safe side, we opt for paid, guarded parking (free spaces in the city are rare, and there are many reports of theft). We're naturally drawn to the impressive cathedral on Praza do Obradoiro, where many pilgrims converge, endpoint of their Camino walk. The emotion is palpable: some howl with joy, others cry. It's the culmination of long hikes, patience and hope. We visit the very interesting museum dedicated to the pilgrimage, then wander from square to square, among the golden-tinted monuments, enveloped in a singular atmosphere here, in one of Spain's many magical places. **AL**

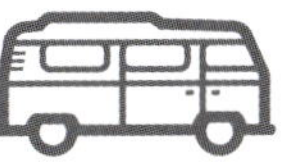

ROAD MAP

Start // Bilbao
Finish // Santiago de Compostela
Distance // 770km (478 miles)
Recommended duration // 12-to-15 days
When to go // Year round
Culinary specialities // Tapas, *carbayones* (puff pastry filled with almonds, egg yolk and sugar), *bollo preñao* (bread roll stuffed with chorizo and cooked with cider)

THE PERFECT SLEEP SPOT

Description // Seaside parking with spectacular views of meadows, beaches and surrounding cliffs.
GPS coordinates // 43.623256, -5.878933
Light pollution // None
Access // Easy, but the path can be muddy in wet weather.
Facilities // None
Parking // 15 places in the heart of nature
Little extras // Departure point for walks and swimming opportunities

Opposite: Bicaz Canyon, Romania.

MORE LIKE THIS
SPECTACULAR GORGES

NORTHERN PINDOS NATIONAK PARK (GREECE)

Want to visit Europe's deepest canyon? Head for the sublime Vikos Gorge in western Greece and you can. This gigantic, 900m-deep (2953ft) fault, carved out by the Voidomatis River, stretches for 12km (7.5 miles) between Vitsa and Papingo, in Northern Pindos National Park. Leave the camper in Monodendri and hike through rock sculptures to the gorge. Then discover the traditional grey stone hamlets of Zagoria, linked by ancient stone paths and punctuated by staircases and beautiful arched bridges. Visit Aristi and Papingo, and admire the three arches of Kipi's 200-year-old Plakida Bridge. Thrill-seekers can try their hand at rafting in the gorge too – the water is renowned for its purity. Extend your road trip to Lake Ioannina, calling at its handsome village and small island with Byzantine monasteries. To sleep, choose a lakeside spot.

Start // Vikos Gorge
Finish // Lake Ioannina
Distance // 130km (80 miles)
More information // pindosnationalpark.gr

PIENINY NATIONAL PARK (POLAND)

In southern Poland, Pieniny National Park covers three strikingly beautiful mountain ranges. After a trip to the Wodospad Zaskalnik Waterfall, park in Szczawnica and relax at the Plac Dietla spa. Float down the Dunajec Gorge on a raft, operated by boatmen dressed in traditional costume. See the peaks of the Three Crowns Massif, part of the famous Pieniny Mountain Range. Drive to Sromowce Nizne, and climb up to the spiralling Okraglica observation platform, which offers great views over the Dunajec Valley and the Tatra Mountains. Contemplate the castles of Lake Czorsztyn, make a detour to Grandeus Hill for its panoramas of the Tatras, Pieniny and Gorce mountains, and discover pretty spots in the Białka Gorge Nature Reserve whose rocks are home to protected vegetation.

Start // Wodospad Zaskalnik Waterfall
Finish // Białka Gorge Nature Reserve
Distance // 55km (34 miles)
More information // piepn.gov.pl

BICAZ GORGE (ROMANIA)

Test your driving skills on the 8km (5 miles) of twisting tarmac on Romania's 12C national road, which follows the course of the Bicaz River through the Bicaz Gorge. Dramatic rock faces rise 300-400m (984–1312ft) high – a climbing and *via ferrata* (protected climbing area with fixtures and cables) paradise. At times, the narrowness of the valley can provoke a slight feeling of fear, but fascination usually wins out. Topped by a cross, the highest point in the gorge (1120m/3675ft) is easy to spot from the road. At the head of the gorge, you'll discover the pretty Red Lake, where you can rent a boat and go hiking. The 12C continues to Gheorgheni via the superb Bucin Pass. The whole region has plenty to offer: hike to the Piatra Singuratică cabin from Balan; discover hidden caves; contemplate waterfalls canoe the local lakes. The choice is yours.

Start // Bicaz dam
Finish // Piatra Singuratică
Distance // 116km (72 miles)
More information // cheilebicazului-hasmas.ro

HEADING SOUTH FROM FRANCE TO SPAIN

A change of scenery is guaranteed in the Basque Country, Navarre and Aragón on the Franco-Spanish border.

It's late when we leave Biarritz and set off on the A63. Adrien's camper doesn't attract the attention of customs officers and we enter Spanish territory without being checked. Our programme for this van vacation? A tour of various, little-frequented destinations along northern Spain's Basque coast, diverting to the southern tip of Navarre and up into western Aragon, then back to France via the Pyrenees.

We pass San Sebastián and switch off the engine 30km (19 miles) further on at the port of Zumaia, where we find an official (and free) off-season place to stop. Zumaia lies at the heart of the Basque Coast Global Geopark where spectacular striated rock outcrops reveal millions of years of geological history. We've planned to be here for low tide to walk the Flysch Route, a 15km (9 mile) cliffside path linking Zumaia and Deba. Between the green of the pastures and the clear waters of the ocean, the rock layers create a surreal vision.

Back in the van, continuing westwards, we make a detour to the intriguing abandoned castle of Butrón before reaching Bilbao. As luck would have it, we find a free parking space in the Deusto neighbourhood, about twenty minutes from the Guggenheim Museum, with its extravagant curves designed by Frank Gehry. Admiring this architectural feat, I watch the titanium cladding change colour as the sky changes, sometimes silver then suddenly gold. The city is brimming with contemporary art works: Louise Bourgeois' giant *Spider*; Jeff Koons' huge, flower-covered *Puppy*; La Salve Bridge and the Zubizuri footbridge; plus arts centres and skyscrapers.

As the sun sets, it's time to find a place to spend the night. I take control of the van and leave the coast to head inland. My co-driver reviews the possibilities listed on his dedicated app. One of the only places in the province of Álava where wild camping is permitted is a pretty clearing south of Salvatierra, off the A2128, a 90-minute drive away. Perfect. One of the great joys of sleeping in a camper is opening the door wide each morning to relish the pleasure of seeing what new

SAN JUAN DE GAZTELUGATXE

Located 35km (22 miles) northeast of Bilbao, San Juan de Gaztelugatxe is an iconic Basque islet, linked to the shore by a pedestrian bridge. A 241-step path leads to the island's highest point, occupied by a chapel. The site was one of the filming locations for *Game of Thrones*.

landscape is waiting outside - in this case, it's forests and fields as far as the eye can see.

Our morning routine begins with some personal grooming. Adrien designed his camper primarily for surfing sessions on sunny days. Meaning he chose not to install any heating or water heaters. To wash, therefore, we need to boil water in a large saucepan on the gas stove, pour some of it into our teacups to accompany our breakfast, then add tap water to what's left in the pan. This provides water with the desired temperature for rinsing off after soaping up with a washcloth.

Ablutions complete, our next destination is just a few minutes' drive away, in Navarre – the Urederra spring, or 'precious water', located in the middle of a protected area. We stop in the huge car park in the small village of Baquedano, at the foot of the Sierra de Urbasa, and begin our walk. In the centre of a forest of beech and oak trees we find a waterfall whose crystalline water fills incredible sky-blue-coloured natural pools, contrasting wonderfully with the orange leaves on the trees. We then move on to Olite, where we visit the Palacio Real, the residence of the kings of Navarre until the 16th century. The immense Gothic building, with its many towers and terraces, has a central location in the town.

Our house on wheels finally takes us to the Bardenas Reales Nature Reserve, 46km (29 miles) to the south via the N121. Its surprising lunar landscapes recall the deserts of the American West. The information centre provides us with a map of car and bike paths, and the hostess warns us that, in wet weather, many areas are flooded and become impassable or even dangerous. She also points out that the park's management accepts no responsibility and provides no assistance in the event of accidents – it's clearly a place where having your vehicle properly insured is a very good idea. Finally, to preserve the ecosystem, regulations strictly prohibit all forms of camping within the park. With these considerations in mind, we spend two wonderful days exploring the wild, arid landscape. The first night is in a camper van park next to the fascinating Cuevas de Arguedas cave dwellings; the second is spent, less poetically, at the campsite, doing laundry, filling the water tank and taking hot showers.

Back on the road and we're northbound, driving towards Foz de Lumbier, an enchanting 1300m-long (4265ft) canyon. In the car park, Adrien checks the condition of our bikes, while I prepare some sandwiches, before we go for a ride along the gorge, under the menacing gaze of a dozen vultures and

Opposite, from left: Mallos de Riglos; the Castildetierra, Bárdenas Reales; striated rock outcrops at Zumaia. Above: Bárdenas Reales. Page 83: Bárdenas Reales landscape.

'Spectacular striated rock outcrops reveal millions of years of geological history.'

watching out for tunnels in total darkness – bring a headlamp to avoid accidents. Next on the itinerary is the Yesa Reservoir, 20km (12 miles) to the east in Aragón. The dry, whitish limestone soil gives the shores of the reservoir a moon-like appearance. By chance, we discover an open-air hot spring where you can bathe, then the ghost village of Esco, deserted when the dam was built. As daylight fades, we drive along the N240 through lush green plains, with the snow-capped peaks of the Pyrenees as a backdrop.

At Puente la Reina de Jaca, we turn off onto the A132, which runs alongside the Gallego River. Round a bend in the road, the impressive rock faces of the Mallos de Riglos make their jawdropping appearance, leaving us speechless. We opt for wild camping near these colossal natural wonders. I know I won't sleep a wink all night, kept awake partly by the fear that we might be moved on – but mostly by my impatience to see the sun rise over these amazing rocks. **AL**

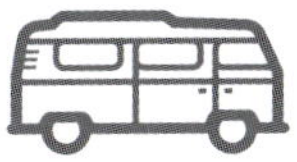

ROAD MAP

Start // Biarritz
Finish // Mallos de Riglos
Distance // 854km (531 miles)
Recommended duration // 10-to-15 days
When to go // Year round
Culinary specialities // *Ajoarriero* (a dish consisting of vegetables, egg and fish, often cod), *canutillo* (a pastry cone filled with custard)

THE PERFECT SLEEP SPOT

Description // Large, flat parking lot near Bardenas Reales Nature Reserve
GPS coordinates // 42.172404, -1.590131
Light pollution // Low
Access // Dirt road
Facilities // None
Parking // 20 places
Little extras // Good quality 4G internet, convenience store nearby with waste disposal service and water. Don't miss the pretty abandoned cave houses just across the road.

Opposite, from top: Aguas Tuertas valley, Spain; Ordesa and Mont Perdu national parks, Spain.

MORE LIKE THIS
SPANISH PYRENEES

BETWEEN ALT PIRINEU AND AIGÜESTORTES

The village of Os de Civís is a good starting point for an assault on the Catalan Pyrenees. Cross the Alt Pirineu, a rugged mix of varied landscapes with Mediterranean and alpine forests. Follow the C13, the manmade boundary between this and the Aigüestortes National Park, and wind your way up the LV5004 to Espot. There are several trails here, including one leading to the Estany viewpoint, which offers a fabulous view of Lake St Maurice. Return to your vehicle and drive through La Guingueta d'Àneu, a village lined with picnic areas, before heading northwest along the C28 for more hikes: the Gerber Valley and its azure lakes; the Colomèrs lake cirque; or, in the Val d'Aran, the gigantic Saut deth Pish Waterfall, 50m (164ft) high. Finally, head south to the medieval village of El Pont de Suert, gateway to the Vall de Boí and its remarkable Romanesque churches.
Start // Os de Civís
Finish // El Pont de Suert
Distance // 222km (138 miles)
More information // spain.info

ARAGONESE PYRENEES

From Lanuza, a village near the Col du Pourtalet, head south on the A136 and join the twisting N260 which you will take eastwards. For a refreshing break, the Forcos Ravine (3km/2 miles north of Fiscal) has a winning combination of waterfalls, vegetation and rocks. Next stop, Aínsa – a splendid medieval town atop a hill, and a local adventure-sports hub (canyoning, *via ferrata* and more). Ordesa National Park and Mt Perdido are close by so why not detour there? The Añisclo, Escuaín and Pineta valleys that encircle Mt Perdido offer a wealth of hiking opportunities, sprinkled with beautiful gorges and waterfalls. Go back to the N260 and continue towards Benasque, close to the two highest Pyrenean mountains, Aneto and Posets. The area is a good base for hiking to the peaks, exploring the high valleys and rafting.
Start // Lanuza
Finish // Benasque
Distance // 230km (143 miles)
More information // turismodearagon.com

AROUND THE WESTERN VALLEYS NATURAL PARK

Head for the beautiful hamlet of Siresa, north of Hecho, to admire St Peter's Monastery, a fine Romanesque building from which Christianity spread to the rest of Aragón in the Middle Ages. This village is a gateway to the Western Valleys Natural Park, where you'll discover majestic cirques, sharp peaks and bluish lakes. For the ultimate adventure, follow the unpaved trail into the Aguas Tuertas Valley (small vehicles only). Water, pastures and horses are the order of the day here. Make a U-turn to visit Biniés, and admire its charming castle, with imposing towers. Around 40km (25 miles) to the east, Rapitán Fort overlooks a lovely mosaic of greenery. Then take the N330 to the peaceful village of Borau, and make a side trip to the impressive Sibiscal Waterfall. Finally, return to the main road to explore the Las Güixas Cave, a fascinating cavern that will appeal to geology buffs.
Start // Siresa
Finish // Las Güixas Cave
Distance // 158km (98 miles)
More information // turismojacetania.com

THE CROATIAN COAST

Cruise the Adriatic coastline discovering relics from another era.

It's been daylight for a while when the smell of coffee fills the camper. Several weeks have passed since my friend José and I left France, and we've established a morning ritual of taking our time over a hot drink. Between sips, we discuss the agenda we've concocted: a van ride down the Adriatic, from Zadar to Dubrovnik. We haven't even gripped the steering wheel yet, but we're already dreaming of the heavenly beaches, historic cities and wonderful views we'll encounter.

To the north of Dalmatia, our first contact with the Croatian coast is Zadar, a characterful city with a fabulous architectural heritage. We dive straight in, visiting the remains of the Roman forum, built between the 1st and 3rd centuries. Temples and ruined columns stretch across a vast esplanade, surrounded by two notable religious buildings: the Cathedral of St Anastasia, a masterpiece of Romanesque art; and the Church of St Donatus, a Byzantine rotunda flanked by a magnificent clock tower. Strolling around this fortified town, sprinkled with enticing beaches, is a joy, especially as we don't meet many other holidaymakers.

Moving on from this excellent first stop, we continue our road trip south, never taking our eyes off the coast. We're speeding along when we spot a hitchhiker on the side of the road. This strikes a chord with us – José and I both owe a huge debt to the 'thumbing' community – so we invite the adventurer to climb aboard our T4. Seemingly somewhat inebriated, he repeats tirelessly, between laughs, 'Super, super, super', clearly happy that providence has placed us in his path. We drop the jolly fellow off just before Trogir, and enter this cute little town.

After parking, it's time for a walk across the bridge to the old town, built on a small island. This jewel of Dalmatia richly deserves its UNESCO World Heritage listing – the palace and castle are linked by a maze of picturesque cobbled streets, and St Lawrence's Cathedral is one of the most beautiful in the country, with a richly sculpted Romanesque portal and charming bell tower offering a 360° view. We leave the medieval heart of Trogir behind and head for its market, just a few hundred metres away. A world of bright colours and mouth-watering aromas awaits. In the midst of the hustle and bustle, we stock up on provisions for the rest of our journey – and buy two huge spinach *burek* pastries to eat on the go.

Less than 30km (19 miles) separate Trogir from the seaside city of Split, but we wouldn't mind it being more – driving along the

steep coastline, against a backdrop of green islands scattered across the water, is far from unpleasant.

As soon as we arrive on the vast Split peninsula, we head for Diocletian's Palace. This astonishing complex of over 200 Roman-era buildings forms a labyrinth of alleyways where bars and restaurants have sprung up. Many of the ancient buildings are still remarkable, and budding historians will find much to enjoy here. But there's more to the city than this, and we enjoy experiencing Split's contrasting sides. The Riva waterfront promenade, lined with palm trees and crowded terraces, has an air of the Côte d'Azur about it. Conversely, at the end of the spit of land, away from the busy streets, there are several beaches where you can find a corner of nature.

We choose to leave Split and head for the small village of Drašnice for a quiet night's sleep – in a van, it's always best to find a secluded spot to rest. Settled near the town's fishing port, under a shining moon, we enjoy ideal conditions.

The morning sun wakes us from our dreams, and we're soon heading south again. Part of this route crosses an 8km (5 mile) strip of land belonging to Bosnia-Hercegovina before re-entering Croatia and continuing towards Dubrovnik, so we present ourselves at the border post. We receive a pretty intimidating welcome. The customs officer, probably in need of something to do, decides to search the entire camper. We're used to this kind

DEALING WITH SUMMER HEAT IN A CAMPER

To avoid heatstroke, it's essential to seek shade when parking – meaning, in the evening, it's important to anticipate where the sun will be next morning. Proximity to water often means cooler temperatures – and the possibility of swimming. Circulating the air in the van, hydrating regularly and resting during the hottest hours are other ways to cope with high temperatures.

'Below the roadway, splendid azure beaches stretch out amongst bushes and cypresses.'

Below from left: Diocletian's palace in Split; Makarska riviera. Above: Lovrijenac fortress in Dubrovnik. Opposite: Port of Zadar. Page 89: Coastal road in Dalmatia.

of situation, so know it's best to remain courteous and smile as he scrupulously checks the contents of our dirty laundry bags and rubbish bins. Inspection over we're off and a second, friendlier, checkpoint takes us back into Croatia.

We're now driving along slightly winding Route 8. Below the roadway, splendid azure beaches stretch out amongst bushes and cypresses, providing opportunities to cool off for a while as temperatures continue to rise. Dubrovnik eventually appears in front of us, overlooked by an immense cliff. We start our visit in the old port, and are captivated by the centuries-old stones of the jetty and the sight of moored boats. Walking on, the narrow, stepped medieval streets are equally enchanting. In the heart of Stari Grad (the walled old town), we come upon Luža Sq, home to the amazing Baroque church of St Blaise, designed in a refined Venetian style, and its neighbouring clock tower, sleek and crowned by a small metal dome.

We're not the only ones appreciating Dubrovnik though – the city is extremely busy and we wander for a while, tramping the stones of the main thoroughfare, the Stradun, with hundreds of other visitors. Everyone, like us, would probably like to be alone to enjoy such a magical place. **AD**

ROAD MAP

Start // Zadar
Finish // Dubrovnik
Distance // 366km (227 miles)
Recommended duration // 7-to-10 days
When to go // Spring and autumn for perfect temperatures
Culinary specialities // *Sarma* (cabbage leaves stuffed with minced meat and rice, cooked in broth)

THE PERFECT PHOTO SPOT

Description // The bell tower of St Lawrence's Cathedral, Trogir
GPS coordinates // 43.51709588083931, 16.251409180398557
Access // On foot
Visitor numbers // Popular with amateur photographers, best to come early in the day
Little extras // Visit the elegantly decorated interior of the building.

Opposite: Road to Sa Calobra, Mallorca.

MORE LIKE THIS UNDER THE SUN

TOWARDS ISTANBUL (TÜRKIYE)

Take a trip to the edge of geographical Europe. Park on the streets of Edirne, Türkiye, close to the Greek and Bulgarian borders. Look up to admire the immense minarets of the Selimiye Mosque, a magnificent edifice dating back to the 16th century. Then head south to the Gallipoli Peninsula and the memorials to the WWI campaigns that took place here. Follow the northern shore of the Sea of Marmara, stopping at Tekirdağ for a Turkish coffee on the waterfront. Look out for beachside parking nearby to enjoy an evening in the camper overlooking the coastline. After a relaxing night, take the road to Istanbul, one of the world's most beautiful cities. Fall under the spell of the Blue Mosque and Hagia Sophia, and lose yourself in the Grand Bazaar. On the other side of the Bosphorus, it's Asia.

Start // Edirne
Finish // Istanbul
Distance // 493km (306 miles)
More information // goturkiye.com

FROM ATHENS TO THESSALONIKI (GREECE)

To visit Athens at your leisure, park on the outskirts and take the metro. Allocate plenty of time for visiting the Greek capital's many marvellous historical sights and succumbing to the delights of its Mediterranean cuisine. Then leave the hustle and bustle for the town of Vólos, from where you can explore the verdant Pelion Peninsula and its peaceful beaches, before heading for Litochoro, a base for Mt Olympus. From the town, a variety of trails will take you closer to the domain of the gods. Leave the E75 – the backbone of this road trip – to spend a few hours in the Axios Delta National Park, home to birds and wild horses, and finish things off in Thessaloniki, a dynamic city where the vestiges of history coexist with modernity.

Start // Athens
Finish // Thessaloniki
Distance // 638km (396 miles)
More information // discovergreece.com

MALLORCA (SPAIN)

Need a strong dose of sun? Head for Mallorca, in the Balearic Islands. It's in Palma, the capital of the Spanish island, that you'll turn on the camper's ignition, ready to explore the scenic roads that this destination has to offer. Bring your swimwear for lounging on the various beaches, such as Cala Pi, a bay set between cliffs. For more sun, sea and sand, don't miss the huge, wild expanse of Platja des Trenc, near Colònia de Sant Jordi. Further east are other heavenly bays, including Cala Mesquida, a beauty of turquoise waters. Next up is a trip to the Cap de Formentor Peninsula, a rugged terrain ideal for walking. The show doesn't end there. To the north, let yourself be carried away by the dizzying curves leading to Sa Calobra, a secluded little port, before returning to stroll between the colourful facades of Palma.

Start/Finish // Palma
Distance // 335km (208 miles)
More information // spain.info

ALONG THE ALGARVE

Bem-vindo to golden sandy beaches fringed by towering rocks and tiny villages with white houses.

The Algarve is Portugal's southernmost region. Its coastline of ochre cliffs pierced by caves, the deep blue of the Atlantic Ocean and its many bays make it a dream destination that attracts a huge number of visitors. Thinking I'd escape the crowds and the heat, I choose June for this east-west road trip – but the sun and the tourists are already well and truly out. Fortunately, tranquil Pego do Inferno Lake, and the small waterfall that flows into it, are waiting for me at the start of this trip. After a dip in the blue-green waters, I head back through the orange and lemon groves to pick up my camper from the car park.

Next stop is Tavira, nicknamed 'the city of a thousand and one churches'. That number might seem an exaggeration – and it is: there are actually 37 of them. The area's soft soil has protected it from concrete development making it a pleasure to wander through its maze of cobbled streets, lined with white houses with air-permeable *reixa* (latticework) doors and *tesouro* (four-sided) roofs. I cross the Roman bridge and climb up to the castle garden – the former Moorish fortress – before getting back in the van and heading for the salt marshes of the Ria Formosa Natural Park. This area of mudflats and lagoons is home to a multitude of birds – including spotted pink

flamingos, cormorants, herons and storks – and lends itself to a slow-paced saunter.

Tearing myself away from this peaceful spot, I head for Faro, capital of the Algarve. Its old town combines cobbled streets and charming squares, all surrounded by medieval ramparts and anchored by the cathedral. But I'm in a hurry to get to the region's famous beaches, so I don't linger and instead continue on to Praia da Rocha Baixinha, a long stretch of sand to Faro's west. This time, travelling out of season pays off as I immediately find a space to park. It's worth noting that since 2021, parking in the Algarve has become an obstacle course for camper van drivers because in an attempt to stem the flow of tourists, local authorities have banned all converted vehicles from parking outside authorised locations. A new law that came into force shortly afterwards relaxed these regulations, allowing parking for up to 48 hours in car parks in a single municipality. However, a ban (with heavy fines) remains the rule in Natura 2000-listed and other protected coastal zones, plus certain localities. With my mind at ease, I make my way down the stairs to the beach with its backdrop of red and white cliffs. Even with just your feet in the water here, it's easy to grasp the power of the ocean. Surfers take it up a level and have a blast until the last light of day. Chased away by the mosquitoes, I return to my house on wheels where I plan to spend the night – but am in for a shock. I forgot to park in the shade and the heat inside is stifling. Quickly, I open the doors and windows as wide as possible, put up the mosquito nets (which I take care to moisten) and turn on my little fans. I see that a hot day is forecast for tomorrow, so decide to adapt my plans and head inland.

Located 32km (20 miles) to the north, my destination is Alte, considered to be one of the Algarve's most traditional villages. Its whitewashed houses, with their open fireplaces, are nestled in the green, fertile hills of the Serra do Caldeirão. Just a stone's throw away, the Fonte Grande, fed by the springs of the Alte River, is a peaceful, shaded pond, ideal for picnics and bathing. I take the N124 westwards again and stop off at Silves, the ancient Moorish capital. An imposing castle with red sandstone walls still bears witness to this era. The white town, with its steep streets, daily market and lively cafe terraces, exudes a relaxed atmosphere. Less than five minutes' drive away, I reach Quinta do Sol Poente farm, where I've reserved a pitch for the night. Nuno and his family give me a warm welcome. The property is huge, in the middle of a wilderness dotted with orchards. There are hanging hammocks, an adorable dog and cat, and a vast water tank that doubles as a swimming pool – a place of peace.

I leave this special spot early to head back to the ocean. It takes several days to explore the many bays between Porches and Lagos. Golden sandy beaches, rocks sculpted by erosion, jagged cliffs – the entire coastline is fabulous. I visit two

THE ALGARVE'S WEST COAST

Largely protected by the Parque Natural do Sudoeste Alentejano e Coste Vicentina, the Algarve's west coast is home to some of the region's best surfing. In the north, picturesque Odeceixe is a village of small blue houses, dominated by a windmill. Let yourself be seduced by its beautiful beach, sheltered between the cliffs where the Seixe River meets the ocean!

Below: Ponta da Piedade, near Lagos. Above: Alte. Opposite: Faro street. Page 95, from top: Bordeira street; Praia de Benagil.

'It takes several days to explore the many coves between Porches and Lagos. Golden sandy beaches, rocks sculpted by erosion, jagged cliffs – the entire coastline is fabulous.'

natural arches at Praia da Marinha, Praia de Benagil's cave with a natural skylight in the ceiling, accessible by swimming, and Praia dos Estudantes, a beach overlooked by a bridge between two cliffs.

Heading south, 35km (22 miles) after Lagos, is the Sagres headland, marked by an impressive 15th-century fortress. I admire the mosaic stone compass and the well that lets you hear the roar of the ocean and feel the wind rising from below. Another promontory, Cabo de São Vicente, lies 6km (4 miles) further on and is dominated by a lighthouse with a bright red lantern. The camper van rocks in the wind. I've reached the southwestern tip of Europe; it feels like the end of the world. **AL**

ROAD MAP

Start // Pego do Inferno
Finish // Cabo de São Vicente
Distance // 250km (155 miles)
Recommended duration // 10-to-15 days
When to go // All year – except summer, when it's crowded, expensive and hot
Culinary specialities // *Cataplana* (fish and meat stew), *xarém com conquilhas* (corn porridge-based dish with clams, bacon or chorizo)

THE PERFECT SURF SPOT

Description // Amado, a long beach famous for surfing, 30km (19 miles) north of Cabo de São Vicente
GPS coordinates // 37.1652, -8.90371
Light pollution // None
Access // Large car park at the end of a dirt track. There's also a shuttle service from Carrapeteira.
Facilities // Fast food, showers and public toilets
Parking // The beach is big enough to offer plenty of space even during the summer season.
Little extras // Huge wild beach with surf lessons and equipment rental

Opposite: Zagare Bay, Italy.

MORE LIKE THIS
BEACH DESTINATIONS

COSTA BRAVA (SPAIN)

The Costa Brava means holidays in the sun: beaches; coves hidden in the vegetation; invigorating swims; crystal-clear waters; walks along coastal paths; charming fishing villages. The menu is long and appealing, and travelling by camper allows you to pick and choose as you please. Looking for a long sandy beach? Stop at Platja de Santa Margarida, Platja de Sant Pere Pescador or Platja de Pals. Are you more of an intimate cove type? Cala el Golfet, Cala Estreta and Cala s'Alguer tick that box. There are also pretty little ports such as Palamós, not forgetting the Cadiretes Massif, further south. Take the contorting road between Sant Feliu de Guíxols and Tossa de Mar, overlooking the Mediterranean Sea, to soak up all its beauty. If possible, visit out of season, to avoid the heat and to make finding parking easier.

Start // Platja de Santa Margarida
Finish // Cadiretes Massif
Distance // 90km (56 miles)
More information // costabrava.org

GOTLAND ISLAND (SWEDEN)

Take your camper on the ferry to Visby, capital of Gotland. Once you've managed to drag yourself away from this captivating medieval town, head north. Park at Lickershamn and walk down the steep path under the pines to a cliff-backed beach. After a refreshing swim, enter 'Grostäde' in your GPS, and in no time you'll be driving through woods on a stony track. At your destination are six tiny fishing huts and a few boats by the water's edge. Nearby, the Blå Lagunen is a limestone quarry whose turquoise waters have made it a popular swimming lake. From Fårösund, take the ferry and explore the small island of Fårö, just a stone's throw away, with its attractive Rauk Langhammars (rock formations), Norsta Aurar sandy beach and Helgumannens fishing village. Then return to Visby.

Start/Finish // Visby
Distance // 208km (129 miles)
More information // visitsweden.com

THE GARGANO PROMONTORY (ITALY)

Between the highlands sheltering the Foresta Umbra, the last vestige of Puglia's ancient forests, and the cliffs plunging into the sea, the panoramic road along the Gargano Promontory is one of Italy's most beautiful. Set off from Manfredonia, where you'll learn about the heritage left by the Swabians, and head north. Discover Punta Rossa Beach, Zagare Bay and La Pergola cove. Stop off at Vieste, a fishing town on a rocky outcrop, after which wonderful beaches follow one after another: Punta Lunga, Scialmarino and Sfinalicchio, with their bars and restaurants. Take care as the road to Peschici is winding. Thanks to its whitewashed houses and maze of alleyways, this village is reminiscent of North African towns. Swim at the sandy beaches on both sides of Rodi Garganico's cliff, before finishing on a high, cruising through the greenery of Gargano National Park.

Start/Finish // Manfredonia
Distance // 187km (116 miles)
More information // italia.it

A TOUR OF THE DOLOMITES

In the heart of the Italian Alps, spectacular nature invites you to hike and contemplate.

I arrive in Bolzano, the gateway to the Dolomites, eager to discover this region of the Italian Alps that has been filling my daydreams for years. With images of spiky rocky ridges and blue lakes in my mind, I park the camper without difficulty not far from Klebenstein Castle, a little way from the town centre, which I reach on foot. In Piazza Walther, the lively central square, it's interesting to note the Germanic influences in this Italian region – German is the common language of a majority of the population in the South Tyrol, although this is less true in Bolzano, due to Mussolini's policy of forced Italianisation. I walk the colourful streets of the old town and marvel at the Duomo, a cathedral with a chiselled Gothic bell tower and a roof decorated with polychrome glazed tiles. My first pretzel here is enjoyed under the gentle rays of the still-warm October sun.

By evening, in the back of the van, the mercury on my thermometer has plummeted though, and I huddle under thick blankets to resist the cold. In the early hours of the morning, I wake up to the sound of rain hitting the roof above me. Next day's planned hike is dropped, and instead I take the road to Bressanone, a town with a medieval core, located 50km (31 miles) north on the SS12 in a breathtaking alpine setting. I find a car park in the inner suburbs – it's always good to avoid driving a camper in narrow, ancient streets. In the early afternoon, the sky clears and I take the opportunity to explore the town's pedestrianised streets, adorned with pretty arcades, and take a few shots of the Baroque cathedral. The cloister is impressive, its vaulted ceilings covered with frescoes worthy of the greatest masters.

My next long-awaited destination is Lago di Braies. This breathtaking lake is a landmark of the Dolomites, and in these touristy regions, the magic of the place belongs to those who get up early. After sleeping in the nearby village of Ferrara, I arrive at 6am and stop in a still-empty car park. Walking towards the water I discover a picturesque hut on stilts where small wooden boats are moored. The surrounding snow-capped mountains, planted with an army of conifer trees, are gracefully reflected in the mirror-like surface of the lake. I take the path around the shoreline, alone in the world, telling myself it's crazy that this place is real. When I return to the starting point, the visitors are now numerous. It's time to get back on the road.

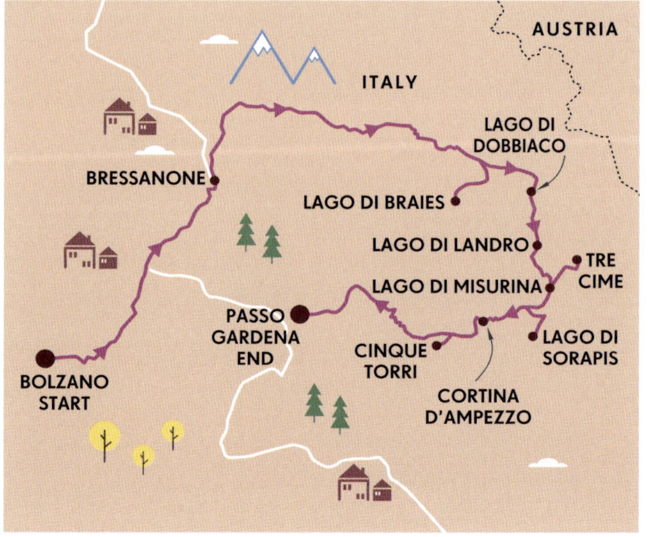

THE CINQUE TORRI

The Giro delle Cinque Torri is an easy trail that cuts impressively through a fault in the heart of the 'five towers' rocky landscape. Part of the route, the Trench Path, is a moving memorial to the fighting that took place here during WWI. Owners of large vehicles should park along the SR48 (free) rather than at the foot of the Cinque Torri, in order to avoid a very narrow road.

'Walking towards the water I discover a picturesque hut on stilts where small wooden boats are moored. The surrounding moutains . . . are gracefully reflected in the mirror-like surface of the lake.'

I continue my adventure on the banks of Lago di Dobbiaco, another little blue lake in the Val Pusteria, another of the Dolomites' iconic sites. Wild, unspoilt nature awaits me. As soon as I've parked, I slip on some knee-high boots – this marshy area is home to an abundance of wildlife, including vipers – and set off for a walk around the lake, a soothing stroll in a seemingly untamed environment.

Lunch calls for a change of scenery and a good option seems to be Lago di Landro and its immense, immaculate beach, 8km (5 miles) south on the SS51. From the turquoise tones of the water, you'd expect white sand, but it's actually a greyish clay that gives this lake its colour palette. Settled in my van, facing the mountains, a cup of tea in hand, I let my gaze and thoughts drift off over the crystal-clear water.

In the early hours of the morning, I set off to hike the Tre Cime, three peaks reaching around 3000m (9843ft), 20km (12 miles) from Cortina d'Ampezzo. I leave the camper at the edge of Lago di Misurina to hitchhike to the start of the walk, thus avoiding the somewhat costly toll. Success. I arrive at the foot of the Tre Cime just as day is breaking. After thanking my drivers, two Germans, I set my sights in the direction of the Rifugio Auronzo, with only the wind, the rock and the last stars to accompany me. Slender rays of sunlight appear, making the moment almost solemn. Step by step, I reach the Auronzo, then the Lavaredo and finally the Locatelli huts. As the Tre Cime tour is relatively easy, I finish this magnificent loop mid-morning, leaving me time to explore other nearby trails. Then, at the end of the day, I have to walk another 8km (5 miles) back to Lago di Misurina to get to the van – that evening, I fall asleep instantly.

Another early wake-up call, but it's well worth it as today I'm heading for Lago di Sorapis, probably one of the most beautiful lakes in the Dolomites. From the Passo Tre Croci car park, I follow the GR215 markers towards the Vandelli refuge. The forest around me is decked out in its seasonal finery – autumn is well underway and blazing colours brighten the route. However, I keep my eyes on the trail, which has some tricky sections and

Opposite: Tre Cime. Above: Lago di Braies. Below: Lago Landro. Page 101, from top: Passo Gardena road; At the edge of a wood.

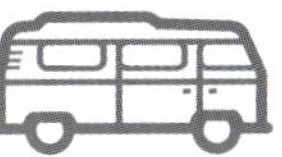

ROAD MAP

Start // Bolzano
Finish // Passo Gardena
Distance // 245km (152 miles)
Recommended duration // 7-to-10 days
When to go // Autumn, to enjoy the seasonal colours and escape the crowds
Culinary specialities // *Apfelstrudel* (a traditional apple, raisin and cinnamon cake)

THE PERFECT PICNIC SPOT

Description // Parking on the banks of Lago di Landro, with a wonderful view of the landscape
GPS coordinates // 46.633541968657866, 12.231358213463745
Access // Free parking along the SS51 road
Facilities // None
Visitor numbers // Depends on season
Little extras // A pleasant after-dinner stroll along the shoreline

metal ladders, allowing you to scramble up the cliffside with minimal risk. Relieved to reach the lake, I gaze deep into its turquoise water. This fascinating place certainly rewards the 5.45am start.

Back at the van, I spend the night in Ortisei, the starting point for more legendary hikes, but I feel the need to rest above all. I take a short walk to the Cinque Torri, a superb group of five stone towers, then let myself be mesmerised, at the wheel of the T4, by the road leading to the Passo Gardena. At 2121m (6959ft) above sea level, this pass on the SS243 offers wide views over the alpine pastures of the Gardena and Bardia valleys. In the distance, under a dark sky, a sharp rock face brazenly attempts to pierce the clouds. Here, more than anywhere else, I feel tiny in the face of nature's power. **AD**

Opposite, from top: Stelvio Pass road, Italy; Silvretta Alpine road, Austria.

MORE LIKE THIS A TRIP TO THE ALPS

SWISS TICINO

Whether you're a fan of skiing, hiking or mountain biking, the resort of Andermatt is the perfect place to start your mountain road trip. After a breath of fresh air and a bit of local cheese, follow the twisting road into Ticino, then straight on to Bellinzona, the canton's splendid capital, huddled in the heart of a rocky massif. Allow yourself a detour to the shores of Lake Lugano to stroll through the elegant streets of the eponymous town. All you'll want to do next is discover Locarno, another exceptional place, on the shores of Lake Maggiore. Take the camper west out of town and venture into the Melezza River Gorge, which features an impressive Roman bridge, pretty churches similar to those in the Italian Alps and magnificent, deep-blue Lake Palagnedra.

Start // Andermatt
Finish // Lago di Palagnedra
Distance // 172km (107 miles)
More information // ticino.ch

THE STELVIO PASS (ITALY)

Experience a sensational drive along the legendary Stelvio Pass, one of the most beautiful routes in the world. The road is only open from the end of May to the end of October and features dozens of hairpin bends, forcing you to keep a firm grip on the steering wheel. Near Lake Como, Valtellina is the starting point for this legendary tour, which takes you all the way to Bolzano, gateway to the Dolomites. While the whole itinerary is captivating, the section from Bormio to Trafoi is the most spectacular. In the middle of Stelvio National Park, with its remarkable flora and fauna, your heart will jump at the succession of breathtaking Alpine landscapes. This narrow ribbon of road hugs the Swiss border and reaches an altitude of 2758m (9049ft) – the second-highest pass in the Alps. At the top, take a photo while your engine recovers.

Start // Valtellina
Finish // Bolzano
Distance // 197km (122 miles)
More information // italia.it

MOUNTAINS OF WESTERN AUSTRIA

Enjoy the flat shores of Lake Constance in Bregenz before embarking on the Silvretta High Alpine Road in your camper. Around the Bielerhöhe Pass and its pretty reservoir, pause to admire Piz Buin (3312m/10,866ft), surrounded by magnificent craggy terrain. Then return to civilisation in the lively mountain resort of Sankt Anton am Arlberg, where you can sample the local gastronomy after a long walk or bike ride. Head southeast again, following the beautiful Inn Valley to Fiss, a small Tyrolean town offering plenty of outdoor activities, before reaching the refined streets of Innsbruck, the elegant regional capital. Note that this scenic drive is only open during the summer months, as weather conditions are too difficult the rest of the year.

Start // Bregenz
Finish // Innsbruck
Distance // 306km (190 miles)
More information // austria.info

FROM ATHENS TO THE SOUTHERN PELOPONNESE

Epicureans will be delighted by this itinerary, which combines old ruins, gourmet delights and a hidden paradise.

Having just about managed to park in the narrow, hectic streets of Athens, I intend to explore the city without getting back behind the wheel. If I were to judge by this first impression, I could almost regret having come here with my camper van. But fortunately I know that the rest of Greece is an Eden for vanlifers – you can park in a thousand idyllic places, many roads offer wonderful views, the sun shines most of the time and the cost of living is relatively low. As soon as I leave the capital, I know I'll be able to enjoy a rural road trip via the Corinth Canal to Kalamata in the south of the Peloponnese, taking in mountains and olive groves on the way.

While Athens is not ideal for travellers with vehicles, it is a dream destination for history buffs, who hone in on the Acropolis. As this world-famous 'upper town' attracts tourists from all over the planet, I get up early to avoid the crowds. The ancient heart of the Greek metropolis contains several celebrated temples, including the famous Parthenon, a structure supported by 46 marble columns and dedicated to the goddess Athena. Just as stunning as the architecture of the Acropolis, are the views it presents – from its hilltop location you can survey the whole city. This panorama makes me want to lose myself in the city's streets, away from the busy areas of Monastiráki and Pláka. I stroll aimlessly and my wanderings lead to the central market, whose halls are filled with tempting stalls selling spices, dried fruits, cakes, olives and cheese. I don't even try to resist and soon find myself with my arms full of delicacies.

Before leaving the Attica region surrounding Athens, I visit Piraeus, Greece's principal port, taking the metro and getting off at the Piraeus stop, the terminus of line 1. Leaving the docks behind, I walk along the coast to Zea Marina and am transported to another world. Here, luxury yachts compete in grandeur, while I, surrounded by all this opulence, bite into my modest feta cheese sandwich. I continue my exploration of Piraeus and fall under the spell of the place. This town, built

KALAMATA OLIVES

The cultivation of Kalamata olives, exported worldwide, provides a livelihood for many families. Trees are so precious that they are passed down from generation to generation, and the fruit is harvested by hand or with a rudimentary machine, before the oil is extracted cold in small local presses. Olives are also preserved whole, in brine, after soaking in water for 15 days.

'I stroll aimlessly and my wanderings lead to the central market, whose halls are filled with tempting stalls selling spices, dried fruits, cakes, olives and cheese.'

2500 years ago by Themistocles, has a unique feel thanks to its mix of industrial warehouses, historic relics, art galleries, fine restaurants and a seaside resort popular with wealthy holidaymakers.

But I can't wait to get on the road and head inland. So I set course for Corinth, well-known for its canal and archaeological remains. Many travellers take excursions from the capital, 80km (50 miles) away, to visit ancient Corinth and its citadel, Acrocorinth, the nearby theatre of Epidaurus and the ruins of Mycenae. But I'm more interested in the famous canal, a 6km (4 mile) trench linking the Aegean Sea to the Ionian Sea – one of the biggest construction projects in history. I park at the canal's western end, and set off to explore the area on foot. The sides of the canal rise 52m (170ft) from the water below, revealing a multitude of rock strata in sandy and ochre tones. I feast my eyes on this feat of engineering, then head back to the camper before daylight fades. My evening's agenda will be as simple as possible: admire the sunset while tasting the region's famous grapes – nature's sweets.

Continuing southwards across the Peloponnese, I notice that local driving can be surprising when you're not used to it. In Greece, for example, the secret to a smooth ride is to keep as far to the right as possible. As the kilometres go by, I take in as much of the mountainous, wooded terrain as I can, as well as the hills planted with olive trees, which seem to stretch on forever. After a few hours' on the road, I arrive in Kalamata, a major olive-growing area (most of them fleshy and dark purple), which I know from having spent several months there. I love this city. It's built on a human scale and little affected by mass tourism meaning it's a great place to live. The tiny Agioi Apostoloi Church, with its russet stones crowned with tiles, and the ruins of Villehardouin's Castle are among my favourite places. What's more, Messinia's capital boasts several kilometres of beach, plus a pretty marina with affordable cafes.

Opposite: Corinth Canal. Above: Ruins of ancient Corinth. Below: Olive grove near Kalamata. Page 107, from top: Athens acropolis; Kalamata surroundings.

ROAD MAP

Start // Athens
Finish // Megali Mantineia
Distance // 271 km
Recommended duration // 5-to-7 days
When to go // Spring, autumn and winter to avoid the heat (plus, there are fewer crowds at tourist sites)
Culinary speciality // *Horiatiki salata* (salad with tomatoes, cucumbers, olives, onions, feta and oregano)

THE PERFECT SLEEP SPOT

Description // Yurt overlooking the Gulf of Messinia
GPS coordinates // 36.95547208206742, 22.168649081012447
Access // Medium, via a small, steep asphalt road
Facilities // Yurt with electricity, toilet and wi-fi
Reservations // Book in advance on Airbnb.
Little extras // Admire the sunset over one of the most beautiful views in the entire region.

All that said, the main reason I'm in the Kalamata region is to visit my Greek 'granny', Diane, a lively pensioner who I met here years ago on a hitchhiking trip across Europe. To celebrate our reunion, we head for the nearest tavern, where we order *saganaki* (fried sheep's cheese), Greek salad, courgette fritters and *tzatziki* (yoghurt with cucumber, herbs and lemon). We then return to Megali Mantineia, the village where Diane has set up her yurt. She's been living here for over fifteen years, in the middle of the olive groves, combining ecology and the good life on a daily basis. From the garden table where we share our meals, the view of the Gulf of Messinia is enchanting. Every evening, this little paradise on Earth throws up a new spectacle, a mix of indescribable colours setting the sky ablaze. A breathtaking inferno that seems impossible to tire of. **AD**

Opposite: Temple of Athena Pronaia in Delphi, Greece.

MORE LIKE THIS
BACK TO THE PAST

ANCIENT GREEK CITIES

The slopes of Mt Parnassus are the starting point for this tour of Greece, with its focus on antiquity. Begin your time travelling at Delphi, visiting the sanctuary of Apollo where the oracle delivered her prophecies. Then head for Athens, stopping for 48 hours to admire the Acropolis and the Temple of Hephaestus. Parking won't be easy, so opt for a private, guarded car park, and make tracks in the evenings to sleep near the coast. Alternatively, drive straight to the Peloponnese and visit the citadel of Mycenae and its Lion Gate, then the charming city of Nafplio, with its pretty port and interesting archaeological museum. Not far away are the acropolis of Tiryns and the theatre of Epidaurus, sitting in wooded hills. Drive through olive groves towards Olympia, iconic location of the first Olympic Games.

Start // Delphi
Finish // Olympia
Distance // 515km (320 miles)
More information // discovergreece.com

ANCIENT SICILY (ITALY)

By camper, you'll arrive in Sicily's northeast, rolling off the ferry at Messina – perfect for a visit to the isolated ruins of the ancient Greek city of Tyndaris, on the edge of a cliff, surrounded by olive groves and cypress trees. Cut through the SS185 mountain road and make a detour to Taormina and its Greek theatre. Pass Catania. If you have time, visit Syracuse – its archaeological park (Neapolis) includes another Greek theatre, a Roman amphitheatre and an ancient quarry. Retrace your steps back to Catania and cross the centre of Sicily, following a winding road to the ruins of the Roman villa of Casale where you'll find well-preserved mosaics and paintings. Drive to Agrigento to see its Valley of the Temples, then follow the coastline to the archaeological site of Selinunte. You'll find choice options for a picnic break here, plus a heavenly view of the sea.

Start // Tyndaris
Finish // Selinunte
Distance // 528km (328 miles)
More information // visitsicily.info

CRETAN RUINS (GREECE)

Served by several ferry lines, Heraklion marks the start of your road trip around Crete, following in the footsteps of the Minoans. Admire the splendid art of this pre-Hellenic Cretan civilisation at Heraklion Archaeological Museum, then walk along the harbour, dominated by a splendid Venetian fortress. Take a trip 34km (21 miles) east to see the ruins of Malia Palace. On this coastal road, there are several spots where you can sleep with a view of the sea. Next, be wowed by the majestic remains of the palace of legendary King Minos at Knossos, 5km (3 miles) south of Heraklion, then by those of the palatial city of Phaistos, to the south. On the way back, a beautiful stopover awaits at the ruins of the Minoan necropolis of Armeni, just before the pretty coastal town of Rethimno. Finally, return to the wine-growing region around Heraklion to toast your Cretan journey.

Start/Finish // Heraklion
Distance // 284km (176 miles)
More information // incrediblecrete.gr

WESTERN EUROPE

A TWO-COUNTRY TRIP

Enjoy French vineyards then cross almost the whole of Germany, from city to forest to Berlin.

Autumn has always been my favourite season. There's nothing more beautiful than seeing landscapes draped in their russet mantle, while wildlife has one last burst of energy before winter. A camper van makes it easy to take in this majestic spectacle, allowing you to criss-cross remote countryside and wilderness, to stop at the edge of the woods whenever the mood – and colours – take you. It's in one balmy, autumnal October that I decide to embark on a road trip from Alsace in France to Germany's capital Berlin, with nature breaks and stopovers in charming villages on the way.

Colmar, close to the German border, is a perfect starting point for this tour. With no difficulty, I find a parking space, then head off into the town's enormous pedestrian zone, with its splendid traditional mansions. In the picturesque Little Venice neighbourhood, the Lauch River is lined with colourful half-timbered houses on whose many chimneys storks build rough nests, which they occupy in spring and summer. At the tourist office, I'm told that it's possible to see these great waders all year round, in the nearby Grand Ried Nature Reserve. I return to my camper and drive for a handful of kilometres past golden hillsides, where the sun shines on a sea of vineyards. When I reach the reserve, I realise the tourist office people knew what they were talking about. A long walk through a forest leads to a reedbed, where I use binoculars to observe a whole group of storks, busy fishing in shallow water. Several fallow deer with red coats spotted with white also make an appearance. To top it all off, there's no shortage of places to set up my van for the night, so I can extend my nature detour into the next day.

Now it's time to cross the Rhine into Germany to join the A6 after Karlsruhe, following a route that's dotted with vineyards and vast forests. One of the first stops on my way to Berlin is Rothenburg ob der Tauber. This medieval city between Stuttgart and Nuremberg has retained plenty of historical charm and is a deservedly popular stop on Germany's Romantic Road. After parking under the city walls, I stroll along the cobblestones, gazing up at the pretty red-tiled roofs of the buildings. The old taverns haven't aged a day. Equally picturesque are the

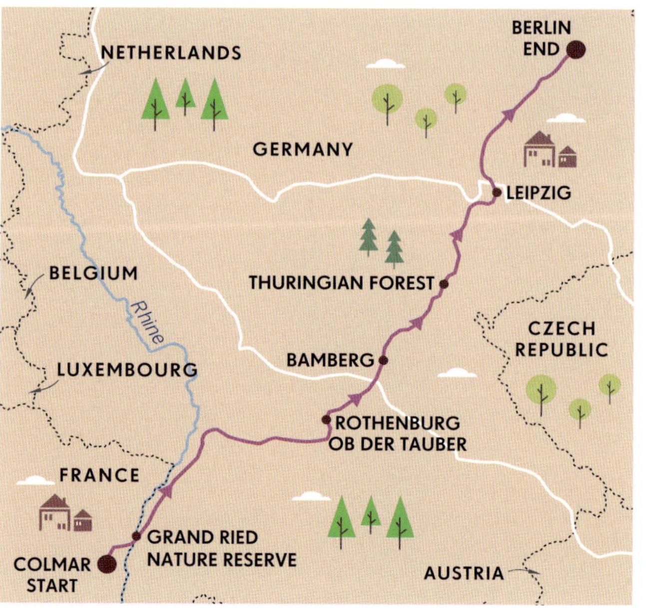

'A long walk through a forest leads me to a reedbed, where I use binoculars to observe a whole group of storks, busy fishing in shallow water.'

ramparts and the Doppelbrücke, a double-decker bridge spanning the Tauber River.

Heading northeast, the 470 cuts through wooded countryside dotted with small villages. Bamberg, the city of seven hills criss-crossed by canals, is my next stop. In the heart of this medieval Bavarian gem, I enjoy the well-preserved architecture of the old town's streets. St Peter's and St George's Cathedral, built of grey stone and bristling with four spires, impresses me with the treasures it contains, including the 13th-century Bamberg Horseman statue and the marble tombs of Holy Roman Emperor Henry II and his wife.

After 150km (93 miles) following the course of the Main and then the Rodach rivers, I allow myself a moment's respite, to breathe a little fresh air in the Thuringian Forest. Here, the terrain is rougher than on the rest of the route and, despite the rain, I decide to go walking through the forest. It turns out to be an excellent idea. The salamanders are out and about, and I'm lucky enough to be able to admire their black and yellow tones, while an owl hoots in the distance. The moment seems timeless.

I now have Leipzig in my sights and choose to get there on the A9 motorway to clock up a hundred kilometres without detours. On German *autobahns*, contrary to popular belief, few drivers seem to exceed 130kph (80mph), and as far as I'm concerned, there's no risk of speeding – my T4 is moving slowly but surely. It takes me over an hour to reach this pretty Saxon town where I head straight for the central square after parking. The Marktplatz, surrounded by restored medieval buildings, is delightful. Wandering around at random, I discover various green spaces, including Rosental Park. Its high tower is said to offer a spectacular view of the town and surrounding forest so, step by step, I climb the huge staircase. I'm not disappointed.

The next day, I reach Berlin, after 190km (118 miles) of straight road, cutting through oak woods and wet meadows. Although driving in the capital is not complicated, I prefer to leave my van in a residential area and visit on foot. I spend several days soaking up the richness of this European cultural hub, where museums and art galleries flourish. A visit to Berlin also means remembering the city's tumultuous past by visiting Checkpoint Charlie, the Holocaust Memorial and the sombre remains of the Berlin Wall. While the city's historical architecture includes many highlights (the Reichstag, Charlottenburg Palace, the Brandenburg Gate), there are also some amazing contemporary buildings, notably on Potsdamer Platz. Not to mention a slew of some of Europe's best clubs and underground bars, which will leave night owls with unforgettable memories. **AD**

VISIT POTSDAM

Located 25 km from Berlin, Potsdam is a peaceful, photogenic city of palaces, parks and Cold War sites (including the 'Bridge of Spies'). Château de Sans-Souci, the residence of former Prussian king Frederick the Great, is a real gem. To extend your Potsdam getaway, you can sleep in a van on the banks of the Havel.

Opposite, clockwise from left: In the forest; Réserve naturelle du Grand Ried; Berlin. Page 115: Bamberg.

ROAD MAP

Start // Colmar
Finish // Berlin
Distance // 879km (546 miles)
Recommended duration // 7-to-10 days
When to go // Autumn, to enjoy the magnificent colours of the forest
Culinary speciality // *Kartoffelpuffer* (a gourmet potato pancake baked in a pan)

THE PERFECT PICNIC SPOT

Description // Car park of a lovely chapel in the middle of the woods in Grand Ried Nature Reserve
GPS coordinates // 48.229290110050165, 7.464785085729902
Access // Easy, via a small road off the D424
Facilities // None
Visitor numbers // Generally less frequented, apart from a few hikers and cyclists
Little extras // Spot deer from afar

Opposite, from top: Amrum Island, Germany; Elegant avocet.

MORE LIKE THIS
BIRDWATCHING

THE WADDEN SEA (NETHERLANDS AND GERMANY)

Meet the wildlife along the Wadden Sea coast, from the Netherlands to Germany. First, head to Lauwersmeer National Park, classified as a Dark Sky Reserve, an area where you can appreciate a sky full of stars free from light pollution. Drive to De Kiekkaaste observation hut and use binoculars to spot birds and seals in the Dollard Estuary. Then it's on past Bremen and Hamburg to the Kronenloch Nature Reserve, a favourite with birdwatchers. You'll see black-tailed godwit, barnacle goose and great crested grebe, among others. For a picnic, stop at Sankt Peter-Ording, where a car park on the beach of the peninsula offers views out to sea. Finally, explore the beautiful North Frisian Islands on one of the many ferries.

Start // Lauwersmeer National Park
Finish // North Frisian Islands
Distance // 616km (383 miles)
More information // holland.com

AROUND GRAN PARADISO (ITALY)

Straddling the Aosta Valley and Piedmont, Gran Paradiso National Park welcomes nature-loving vanlifers. Make your way to the alpine village of Cogne, from where you can follow various trails through the heart of the park to admire golden eagles, buzzards, hawks and even ibexes. Nearby, stop off in Aosta, a city of sumptuous architecture that retains traces of its Roman past. Continue the trip in the medieval village of Bard (note its monumental fortress) and the colourful streets of Ivrea, a town with a remarkable cathedral. Follow a twisting, narrow road, lined with glaciers and flowery meadows, to spend the night in the car park of the Savoia refuge (on the Colle del Nivolet), with expanisve views over the lake of the same name. Finally, step back in time and end your Italian adventure in the elegant city of Turin, on the banks of the River Po.

Start // Cogne
Finish // Turin
Distance // 287km (178 miles)
More information // italia.it

THE ARDENNES (BELGIUM)

Head for the south of Belgium for a green trip to the heart of the Ardennes. As well as wild boar and foxes, you'll have the chance to spy many birds: black storks, shrikes and owls are just some of the feathered inhabitants of this haven of peace. To lose yourself in this mix of deciduous and coniferous trees, visit Laneuville-au-Bois, the trailhead for many hikes. Then follow a country road to the charming town of La Roche-en-Ardenne, whose feudal castle dominates the Ourthe Valley, and follow the river to find some nice places to set up your van. Next day, move on to the village of Dochamps for another walk through the Ardennes forest, then drive through meadows to the Bayehon Waterfall at Longfaye. Finish at Hautes Fagnes-Eifel Nature Park, where cranes, falcons and grebes occupy the marshes.

Start // Laneuville-au-Bois
Finish // Hautes Fagnes-Eifel Nature Park
Distance // 83km (52 miles)
More information // visitardenne.com

AN AUSTRIAN TOUR

Celebrated cities and Alpine panoramas are part of this musical road trip through Austria.

Mozart's *Requiem* crackles through my van's antiquated speakers, getting me in the mood for this journey – it's impossible to visit the musical heart of the continent without soaking up the harmonies that continue to move contemporary music lovers. I'm about to visit four towns of dazzlingly refined architecture. Vienna, my ultimate destination, should be its crowning glory, but Innsbruck, Salzburg and Graz are also full of promise.

In Innsbruck, I'm joining two friends whom I met six months earlier on Spain's Camino de Santiago pilgrimage route. Who would have thought then that we'd find ourselves in the multicoloured streets of Tyrol's capital? I park at the bottom of their building. I've been travelling alone through the Alps for several weeks now, so I'm happy to be surrounded by friends this evening, recalling precious memories.

We walk the length and breadth of the city, lively and soothing at the same time. Maria-Theresien-Strasse, Innsbruck's backbone, has a handful of street musicians entertaining passers-by and is the perfect place to enjoy a pistachio ice cream while taking in the show. All around us, the shop window displays contrast with the snow-capped peaks in the background. This is all great but the mountains are calling.

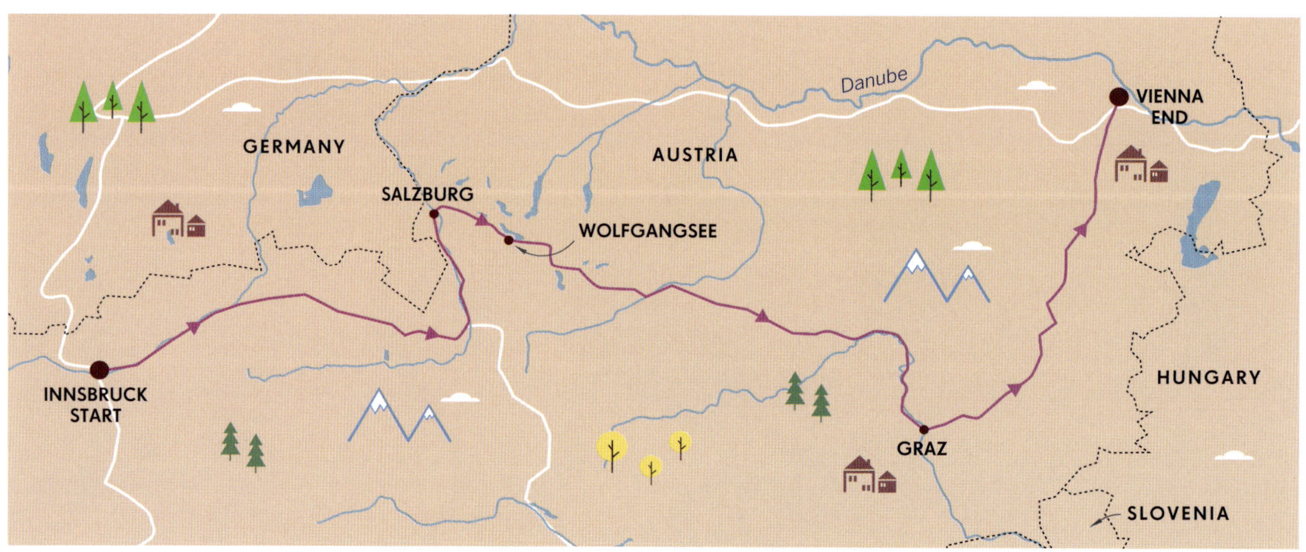

The next day, to get back in touch with the pleasures of walking, we head for the Nordkette, the mountain range overlooking Innsbruck. The wooded Arzler Alm Trail is reputed to be easy, but it's steep enough to give us a hard time. The effort makes us hungry and, as luck would have it, there's an alpine chalet at an altitude of 1067m (3501ft) where we pounce on a plate of *knödel*, traditional potato dumplings, which we devour without leaving a crumb.

After these few days of shared happiness, I have to get back on the road, destination Salzburg, about 200km (124 miles) to the east, on the German border in the foothills of the Alps. From the top of a steep hill in the centre of Salzburg, the Hohensalzburg Fortress has watched over the city for 900 years. It was at the foot of the fortification's thick walls that Mozart was born and it seems only right that I take the time to visit his birthplace, which has been converted into a well-presented museum. I then take a long stroll down Getreidegasse, a shopping street whose Baroque facades feature lovely wrought-iron signs. Here and there I come across groups visiting the town following in the footsteps of *The Sound of Music*, singing and taking photos at the film's locations. As for me, I never tire of walking along the banks of the Salzach River in the centre of the city, which offers a magnificent sweep of Salzburg, its Baroque bell towers and domes, its impressive fortress and the peaks of the Alps in the distance.

Back behind the wheel of the camper, I decide to get back to nature again before my next urban leg. After taking route 158, I set my van down on the banks of the Wolfgangsee, loomed over by the Schafberg mountain (1783m/5850ft). An old-fashioned steam train, the Schafbergbahn, climbs to the summit in summer, using Austria's steepest cogwheel railroad. The impression the hypnotising deep blue of the water makes won't let me leave until the next morning.

I continue eastwards towards Graz, a city whose architecture is a harmonious blend of Renaissance, Baroque and contemporary. A walk on the Schlossberg here gives you a stunning view of the old Altstadt district from the 123m-high (404ft) hill, with the city's iconic clock tower in the foreground, square and imposing. I walk towards the Murinsel, a tiny artificial island built on the Mur River where a modern, shell-shaped structure, floating in the middle of the water between two metal footbridges, houses a cafe and theatre under its thousand windows. A most unusual place, in bold contrast with the surrounding historic buildings!

Following the small roads 54 and 17, I finally reach Vienna, after four hours of driving through countryside. As always when I arrive in big cities, I look for a place to park so I can explore more freely. I find my happiness on the outskirts, right on the banks of the Danube. Several days won't be too many to visit the romantic capital. Architectural and cultural treasures abound – Schönbrunn Palace, St Stephen's Cathedral, the

THE AUSTRIAN TYROL

The Austrian state of Tyrol lies to the northeast of the Alpine region of the same name. Its craggy landscapes attract many travellers in all seasons, who come to enjoy winter sports, hiking, mountain biking and climbing. These outdoor activities can be combined with visits to local cities containing exceptional architecture – such as Innsbruck or Lienz – not to mention delicious mountain cuisine.

Above: Graz's old town square. Below: Mozart's birthplace in Salzburg. Opposite: A break between two hills. Page 121, from top: Salzburg; Innsbruck and the Nordkette mountains; Fountain in Vienna's Belvedere Palace.

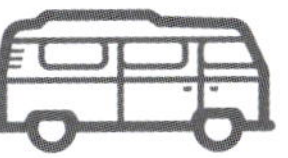

ROAD MAP

Start // Innsbruck
Finish // Vienna
Distance // 674km (419 miles)
Recommended duration // 7-to-10 days
When to go // Year-round for the cities; winter for skiing and other snow sports
Culinary specialities // *Knödel* (bread, potato or semolina dumplings that can be savoury – filled with cheese, bacon or spinach – or sweet)

THE PERFECT PICNIC SPOT

Description // On the Arzler Alm Trail (view of the Alps)
GPS coordinates // 47.29668218308569, 11.4040323356217
Access // On foot, following the signposted hiking trail from Innsbruck or Hungerburg (nearest town)
Activities // Hiking, trail riding, mountain biking
Best conditions // Summer means fine weather
Little extras // Enjoy a cup of coffee or a gourmet dessert on the inn's terrace, typical of the Tyrol.

'I set my van down on the banks of the Wolfgangsee, loomed over by the Schafberg mountain. . .the hypnotising deep blue of the water . . . won't let me leave until the next morning.'

Opera House – but it will be the Hofburg, palatial home of the Habsburgs for 600 years, that will be the highlight of my visit. Here you can see the opulent Imperial Apartments and the Sisi Museum, dedicated to the fascinating life of 19th-century empress, Elisabeth.

Compared to many European metropolises, Vienna truly has a soul. Perhaps it's because its history is so closely linked to illustrious composers – Schubert, Haydn, Strauss and Mozart spent most of their lives here. Their memory is still palpable in most neighbourhoods, and a treat on any trip to the city is hearing an occasional snatch of music in a cafe, church or street corner. **AD**

Opposite: Basilica of Our Lady of the Pillar, on the banks of the Ebro in Zaragoza, Spain.

MORE LIKE THIS
GO WITH THE FLOW

THE SHANNON (IRELAND)

Ireland's longest river, the Shannon, cuts through the central Irish plain from north to south, its course dotted with small fishing ports. Six *loughs* (lakes) mark your progress towards the Atlantic through a little-visited region, the Lakelands, where birdsong resounds in the reed beds and peat bogs. Visit the Shed Distillery in Drumshanbo on the shores of Lough Allen to discover the secrets of Irish gin. The next day, head south and stop off in the welcoming town of Athlone, straddling the Shannon near Lough Ree, where you can explore the lush green banks. After a visit to the 12th-century castle, head for Nenagh, a town also boasting an impressive fortress. The nearby Dromineer boating centre on Lough Derg is the perfect place to enjoy the water before heading off to the mouth of the Shannon in Limerick.

Start // Lough Allen
Finish // Limerick
Distance // 241km (150 miles)
More information // ireland.com

THE EBRO (SPAIN)

Following the course of the Ebro means experiencing a succession of varied landscapes – mountains, forests, rice paddies – as well as interesting towns to stop in. Logroño, capital of La Rioja, is famous for its richly ornate cathedral, as well as Calle Laurel, where you can enjoy a glass of local wine accompanied by some *pinchos* (tapas). Southeast, in the province of Navarre and still on the banks of the Ebro, Tudela is also worth a visit for its Plaza de los Fueros, the hub of this historic city. Follow the river for a few kilometres to discover beautiful Zaragoza, with its marked Moorish influence and notable religious buildings, including the Basilica of Nuestra Señora del Pilar. Another city with a rich architectural heritage, Tortosa in Catalonia, is the gateway to the mountainous Els Ports Natural Park and the Ebro Delta near L'Ampolla, home to hundreds of birds.

Start // Logroño
Finish // L'Ampolla
Distance // 398km (247 miles)
More information // spain.info

THE RHINE

This road trip takes you through some exceptional regions, sometimes rolling and picturesque, sometimes vast and wild. For your first encounter with the Rhine, head to Switzerland and the heart of Basel. You can then follow the river slowly, parking your van here and there. The Rhine marks the Franco-German border for 200km (124 miles) – beautiful villages and nature parks are part of this area, including the Taubergiessen Nature Reserve and the island of Rhinau opposite, on the French side, which is a delight for birdwatchers. The journey continues with castle after castle – plan a visit to Karlsruhe, sometimes described as a German Versailles. Cologne's architecture is not to be outdone, with the towers of its immense Gothic cathedral dominating the river. End your adventure in the Netherlands, near Rotterdam, in the Rhine Delta, a wetland that brings together several rivers, including the Meuse.

Start // Basel
Finish // Rotterdam
Distance // 824km (512 miles)
More information // germany.travel

SWITZERLAND FROM LAKE TO LAKE

Western Switzerland's lakes Geneva and Neuchâtel are an ideal destination for lovers of contrasting landscapes and appealing cities.

José, my travelling companion, and I have just crossed the border into Switzerland from France and arrived in Geneva, at the western edge of the country. We're here to linger around the region's two great lakes, Geneva (aka Léman) and Neuchâtel, on the borders of the Alps and the Jura Massif.

Darkness has already fallen by the time we enter Geneva, and we're dazzled by the myriad signs glittering all around us. We decide to head for the outskirts to spend the night, and find a parking space by the lake without difficulty. Early next morning, we're able to see the great lake itself in daylight. A thin layer of mist envelops the sugar-pink water, snow-capped peaks in the background. We put on our hats and gloves, and set off on a walking tour of the old town. St Peter's Cathedral, with its grey stonework and tall, green spire, is a particular highlight. We also stroll through the botanical gardens, in search of a touch of the exotic and, above all, a little warmth. Numerous tropical plant species are preserved in wonderful greenhouses here, all open to the public. Finally, we wander to the banks of Lake Geneva to admire its famous water fountain, the *Jet d'Eau*. At 140m (459ft) high and spouting 500 litres (110 gallons) per second at 200kph (124mph), it's a spectacular sight and has been a city landmark since the late 19th century.

Seeing the exorbitant prices in Geneva, we're pleased we already stocked up on provisions before leaving France. Fortunately, Lausanne, 60km (37 miles) away on Route 1 along the north shore of the lake, is a little more affordable. We meet with two friends who put us up for a few days, allowing us to explore the surrounding area in good company, and quickly fall under the spell of this city, known as the 'Pearl of Lake Geneva'. The Cité hill, a medieval quarter with many bars and restaurants, is a must-see. Dominating the town, it's home to an imposing Gothic cathedral, as well as St Maire Castle, a marvellous 14th-century building, cube-shaped and crowned with brick and red tiles. Below us, we can see the lake and the Alps in the distance. Opposite is France.

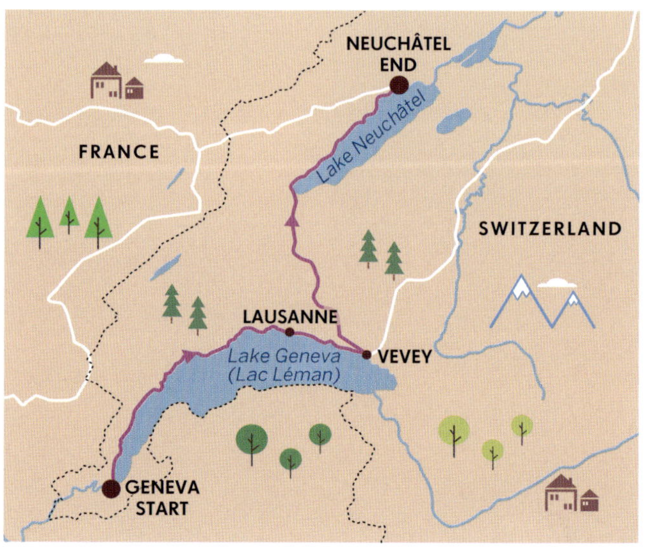

We're taking advantage of our visit to the capital of the Vaud Canton to try an unmissable speciality, Swiss fondue, or *fondue moitié-moitié*, made with Gruyère and Vacherin cheeses. After a hearty meal, a tobogganing session just outside Lausanne is the perfect way to burn off a few calories and get some fresh air.

Our road trip through the land of cheese and chocolate continues in Vevey, a small lakeside town just 18km (11 miles) from Lausanne. There's a huge and intriguing fork, 8m (26ft)high, planted right in the middle of Lake Geneva near the town, which we learn belongs to the Alimentarium, a museum that presents food in a playful way. We walk along the shores of the lake to the cries of a battalion of seagulls. The town is peaceful, the sun shines brightly, and we admire the pastel shades of the pier set in sharp relief against the surrounding mountains.

We almost forget that it's the middle of winter – until the evenings when, back in the van, we hold a daily competition to find the best outfit for the night, usually made up of fluorescent ski socks, a fleece hat and several layers of clothing. When we wake up and are dragged out of bed by the first light, we count the hours until the sun makes us a few degrees warmer. The morning ritual is unchanging: scrape the windscreen on the outside, but also on the inside, then put the coffee pot on the fire to warm us up as much as possible. The little-known joys of life in a camper.

We leave the canton of Vaud for Neuchâtel, near the lake of the same name, a drive of around 90km (56 miles) along

HALF-AND-HALF FONDUE

Among Switzerland's most famous dishes, the *fondue moitié-moitié* (half-and-half fondue) leaves no traveller hungry for more. Made with equal parts Gruyère and Vacherin cheeses, to which white wine is added, this is a convivial meal, ideal after a day in the snow. The most discerning gourmets rub their *caquelon* (fondue pot) with garlic first, and cut cubes from day-old bread so that they stay on the forks better.

Below: Lake Geneva. Above: Swiss fondue. Opposite: Château de Neuchâtel. Page 127, from top: Lavaux vineyards and Lake Geneva; Lake Neuchâtel.

'A thin layer of mist envelops the sugar-pink water and snow-capped peaks in the background.'

vine-covered hillsides. The historic, spread-out town has charm enough to rival many other Swiss tourist destinations. A walk along the cobbled streets leads to the foot of the castle and nearby collegiate church, an elegant architectural ensemble that overlooks the water. Built on a rocky spur, the medieval fortress is particularly remarkable. Its pale, rectangular walls contrast with a bronze-coloured roof, spiked with peaks. Neuchâtel also has many picturesque streets, and a number of pretty squares where you can sit on a cafe terrace and watch the world go by. But it's on the shores of the lake that the most enjoyable moments are to be found. The water is still and transparent, swans swim in peace and quiet, and locals and visitors amble along the banks. Once again, the distant mountains looms on the horizon, and I fall in love with the view. I don't know at the time, but one day I'll be settling down just a stone's throw from this magnificent region. **AD**

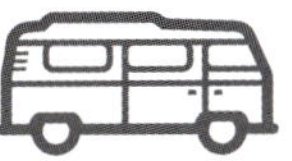

ROAD MAP

Start // Geneva
Finish // Neuchâtel
Distance // 167km (104 miles)
Recommended duration // 3-to-5 days
When to go // Summer, for swimming
Culinary specialities // Fondue, chocolate in a multitude of forms

THE PERFECT SLEEP SPOT

Description // Col de la Tourne, with views of the Alps
GPS coordinates // 46.98781658408268, 6.792258533979785
Access // Easy, by road (10km/6.2 miles from Lake Neuchâtel)
Facilities // None
Traffic // Little evening traffic
Little extras // The hike signposted from the car park leads to a magnificent viewpoint over Lake Neuchâtel (short, well-marked walk, but steep).

Opposite, from top: Old town of Biel; Passwang landscape; Road near Saint Ursanne.

MORE LIKE THIS
SWISS TRIPS

THE JURA MOUNTAINS

Wait for fine weather to visit the Swiss section of the Jura Mountains. Start your itinerary in the medieval town of St Ursanne – the old St Jean Bridge spanning the Doubs River and the sumptuous cloister give the town a special cachet. Drive to Doubs Nature Park for some relaxation on the banks of the small Etang de la Gruère, with its precious flora. Continue past the watchmaking centre of La Chaux-de-Fonds up to Tête de Ran, leave the van and follow the easy, panoramic trail that attracts snowshoeing and paragliding enthusiasts. Some 25km (15 miles) away – accessible from Les Brenets – Saut du Doubs waterfall marks the border with France. Get lost along the *sentier des contrebandiers* (smugglers' trail) and the Doubs River basin, before driving on to Lake Taillères in the Brévine Valley, where you'll find a car park (with WC) perfect for overnighting.
Start // St Ursanne
Finish // Lake Taillères
Distance // 109km (68 miles)
More information // myswitzerland.com

A TOUR OF LAKE LUCERNE

Lake Lucerne offers a concentration of Swiss landscapes. This loop begins at the foot of the mountains, in Lucerne, a historic city of medieval architecture. Protected by ramparts, its colourful old town is bordered by the Reuss River, which is crossed by a splendid wooden bridge. The southern shores of the lake have many attractions, including the Bürgenstock, a peak from the foot of which various hiking trails lead to beautiful views. Next, drive along the shore and stop at Tell's Chapel, on the eastern shore of the lake at Sisikon. Its remarkable frescoes make reference to folk hero William Tell. Stay close to the blue-green water further north, on the winding 2B, and enjoy the various trails and vantage points on Mt Rigi, before making a slow return to Lucerne.
Start/Finish // Lucerne
Distance // 108km (67 miles)
More information // myswitzerland.com

NORTHERN SWITZERLAND

A trip to northern Switzerland wouldn't be complete without a stopover near Lake Biel, lined with hillsides, lovely villages and well-maintained trails. You can also explore the town of Biel itself – the brightly painted streets of the historic centre, with their arcades and fountains, are a sight to behold. Not far away, pretty Solothurn, on the banks of the Aare River, conceals an admirable clock tower. A wander through the old town is a lovely way to spend a few hours. Drive on into Thal Nature Park, covered with green hills and full of hikes and farmhouses. Here you'll find a secluded spot for a night in the forest. Finally, visit Lenzburg Castle, a huge 12th-century fortress built on a rocky spur, and Habsburg Castle, whose massive, crenellated tower overlooks a vineyard.
Start // Biel
Finish // Habsburg
Distance // 112km (70 miles)
More information // myswitzerland.com

FROM WALLONIA TO LUXEMBOURG

A road trip from the medieval towns of Wallonia to the castles of Luxembourg.

I mentally trace a route on a road map between Namur, the capital of Belgium's Wallonia region, and Luxembourg. From medieval city to castle, from plateau to valley, my plan is to follow the course of the Meuse River, before reaching the Ardennes and the banks of the Semois, in southern Wallonia, and then the Grand Duchy of Luxembourg.

Starting point of the drive, Namur lies at the confluence of the Sambre and Meuse rivers. Napoleon nicknamed its citadel the 'termite mound of Europe' due its immense network of underground passages, which can now be visited with a guide. This is where the monumental *Searching For Utopia* sculpture now stands, a golden turtle overlooking the city of which it has become an emblem. Namur's Place d'Armes has the town's most remarkable building – the Neorenaissance old stock exchange, behind which the belfry rises. I almost trip over a set of bronze statues representing two companions accompanied by two snails, symbolising the renowned slowness of the local people.

Back at the wheel, I follow the course of the Meuse along the N92 to get to Dinant. The route through the valley is green and winding. Through the window, I can admire the river interspersed with small islands, the trees and cliffs offering a varied spectacle and the banks lined with castles and gorgeous Mosan-style villas. Arriving in Dinant, I discover a very attractive, colourful village wedged between the river and a huge cliff. I also discover that it's very easy to park here during the day. The view from Avenue Colonel-Cadoux, on the water's edge, is perfect for photos, as are the bulbous bell tower of the imposing collegiate church and the 19th-century, cliff-top fortress. Beer lovers can visit Maison Leffe, a museum dedicated to the beverage that was brewed in a local abbey as early as 1240 (these days, Leffe is produced in Leuven). As for me, giving in to my sweet tooth, I break my teeth on some *couques de dinant*, extremely hard cookies made from honey and flour.

Next stop is the medieval town of Bouillon, 63km (39 miles) south on the N95 road, through forests made magical by autumn. This is another charming place, located in a

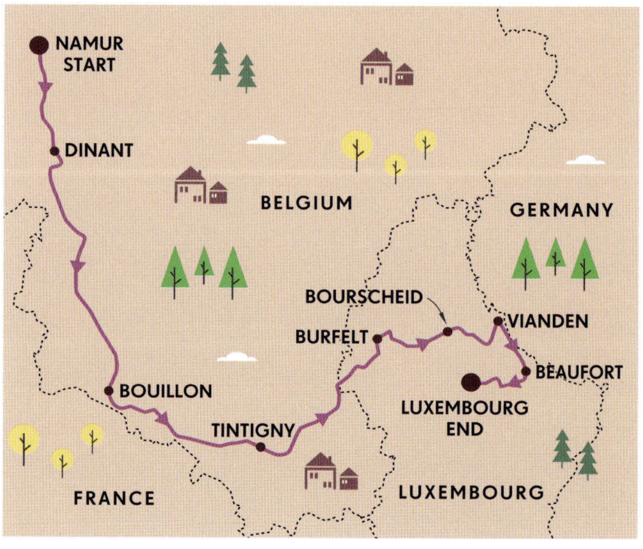

TOUR OF THE VALLÉE DES SEPT-CHÂTEAUX

The CR105 road between Mersch and Koerich is known as the 'Valley of the Seven Castles'. This 25km (16 mile) route takes in a succession of fortresses from different eras, through forests and villages. Ansembourg and Septfontaines castles are not open to the public, but there are a number of lookouts from which to view them.

'I take the camper to Bouillon's lookout and contemplate the view of the town embraced by the river.'

magnificent green setting and surrounded by the Semois River. Below the castle, the walk along the riverbanks to the Cordemoy Bridge is very pleasant. I take the camper to Bouillon's lookout and contemplate the view of the town embraced by the river. To get there, I opt for a shortcut on the map called 'Rue de la Belle-Étoile' (beautiful star street), seduced by the name. Soon though, the initially steep dirt road becomes a narrow, muddy track. I squeeze against the trees, seeing a ravine on the left, the branches scratching the bodywork. A cupboard in the van, poorly closed, opens and gradually empties its objects on the floor with each pothole jolt. According to the GPS, there are only a hundred metres to go. 'Come on, we're almost there!' I say out loud. Suddenly, I hit the brakes. A huge branch blocks the way – it's impossible to go any further. I switch on the hazard lights and put the vehicle into a long reverse. Finally, I'm back on a more sensible approach to the lookout via Rue de la Bichetour. Once at my destination, I start by picking up all my belongings scattered across the floor. Fortunately, nothing is broken – I avoid carrying fragile objects in the camper, preferring kitchen utensils made of bamboo, wood, stainless steel and recycled plastic.

After 49km (30 miles) along the French border on the N84, I arrive at Vieille Hage Farm in Tintigny after dark to spend the night. I love waking up and discovering a new place – you never know what to expect, and this time it's a nice surprise. Outside, I can see brown and white cows grazing in the green meadow. Absolute calm. After buying farm-fresh eggs and milk directly from my hosts, I set course for Luxembourg, where I plan to explore the Ardennes forest of Oesling (or Éislek), a region in the north of the Grand Duchy. The N87 passes through small towns and fields. On leaving one village, I'm shocked to see a 'Luxembourg' sign – I crossed the border without realising it.

In Burfelt, I join a forest trail lined with wooden statues, reaching a beach on the Sûre River which provides the perfect setting for

Opposite: Château de Beaufort. Above: Luxembourg City. Below: At the foot of the Bouillon lookout. Page 133: Citadel and collegiate church of Notre-Dame de Dinant.

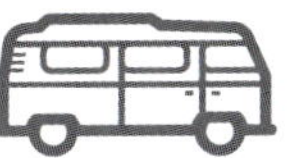

ROAD MAP

Start // Namur
Finish // Luxembourg
Distance // 281km (175 miles)
Recommended duration // 6-to-10 days
When to go // Late summer, after school holidays
Culinary specialities // *Biétrumé de Namur* (a delicious melting caramel), *kuddelfleck* (a Luxembourg dish based on breaded and fried tripe or beef stomach), *couques de dinant* (hard biscuits)

THE PERFECT FARM SPOT

Description // Vieille Hage Farm in Tintigny, a small campsite with a warm welcome
GPS coordinates // 49.648250, 5.508398
Light pollution // None
Access // Dirt road
Facilities // Barbecue, water, electricity and toilets
Parking // 8 pitches
Little extras // In a field surrounded by nature, with a beautiful view of the pastures; very quiet; possibility of buying eggs and fresh milk directly from the owners.

a picnic break. Higher up, a lookout offers a sublime view of the Haute-Sûre Reservoir. The sun is going down and I'd like to sleep here, but I'm not sure it's allowed. Resigned to leaving, I'm about to go when suddenly a herd of deer appear and flee across the fields. Moments later, I come across two foxes.

My exploration of Luxembourg takes on the air of a journey back in time, as I discover the forts that dot the landscape. The hardest part is knowing which ones to choose. I start with 11th-century Bourscheid, followed by 11th-14th century Vianden, and ending with Beaufort, a mix of medieval ruins and a Renaissance-style castle. Finally, it's time for the capital, Luxembourg City, 36km (22 miles) to the south via the CR121. I park on Rue Münster, close to the old centre, and head off on foot. The city is small and a great way to see it is along the Wenzel Circular Walk, which offers glimpses of its 1000-year history, including the impressive rocky promontory of the Bock and the Corniche, which overlooks gorges and well deserves its nickname of 'Europe's most beautiful balcony'. **AL**

Opposite, from top: Turaida Castle, Latvia; Stolzenfels Fortress, Germany.

MORE LIKE THIS
THE CASTLE COLLECTION

RHINELAND-PALATINATE (GERMANY)

On the roads of Rhineland-Palatinate, discover a concentration of castles in a natural setting. Start this epic journey in Eltz, whose 12th-century fortress lies in the middle of a forest. Take Route 262 to Bürresheim Castle (12th century), located in a landscape of wooded mountains and streams. Then set off to conquer the 67km (42 miles) of the UNESCO-listed Upper Middle Rhine Valley – between Koblenz and Bingen am Rhein, routes 9 and 42 follow the river as it winds its way between hill-top castles and steep vineyards, creating an enchanting scene. Highlights include the 18th-century Prince-Elector's Castle in Koblenz, the Neogothic fortress of Stolzenfels, Marksburg Castle, the ruins of Rheinfels Castle (13th century), Pfalzgrafenstein Castle, built on an island in the middle of the Rhine, and romantic Rheinstein Castle.

Start // Eltz Castle
Finish // Rheinstein Castle
Distance // 151km (94 miles)
More information // germany.travel

TRÁS-OS-MONTES E ALTO DOURO (PORTUGAL)

In the far north of Portugal, 'beyond the mountains' as its name suggests, lies the Trás-os-Montes e Alto Douro region, home to handsome villages, nature parks and castles. Take time to visit Vila Real and its Fundação da Casa de Mateus, a splendid Baroque palace with lush gardens. After a stopover at the hot springs of Vidago and Chaves, park your camper for the night at the entrance to Montesinho Natural Park. Check out Bragança Castle, built in the 15th century and home to a military museum, stock up on olive oil, sausages and cheeses at the town's market, then head south on the N219 – you can visit the medieval castles of Algoso and Mogadouro before losing yourself in the Douro's wine valleys.

Start // Vila Real
Finish // Douro Valley
Distance // 272km (169 miles)
More information // visitportugal.com

VIDZEME (LATVIA)

Vidzeme, the northeastern region of Latvia, isn't short of castles. First stop though is the capital, Riga, on the banks of the Daugava River. Explore its historic heart where the imposing yellow castle, built between 1330 and 1353, is the Latvian president's residence. Then set off for Sigulda, home to the brick castle of Turaida ('God's garden' in the ancient Livonian language). From the top of its tower, there's a magnificent view over the Gauja Valley. Follow the E77 road to Cēsis and the Wenden fort, the best-preserved Teutonic Order castle in the country, whose basements can be visited by kerosene lamp. Follow the P30 to Cesvaine Palace, built in Anglo-German style, and end the drive 50km (31 miles) north at Stāmeriena Castle, rebuilt in Neorenaissance style.

Start // Riga Castle
Finish // Stāmeriena Castle
Distance // 242km (150 miles)
More information // vidzeme.com

A CARNIVAL COMBINATION

This bucolic itinerary goes through the heart of the Black Forest, along the banks of the Rhine and into lively towns, with carnival as a common thread.

It's carnival season (*Fastnacht* in German) and I'm off to explore southwest Germany, northern Switzerland and Liechtenstein. This tri-country combination promises to be full of authentic experiences and, accompanied by two friends, Nathalie and José, the plan is to travel through parts of the Black Forest and up the Rhine, visiting bustling towns and taking part in the festivities wherever we can.

First stop is Freiburg im Breisgau which Nathalie, who is German, knows well, having lived there for several years – I nominate her as guide for the day. The city's Little Venice district has pretty bridges spanning canals with the reflections of buildings shimmering in the water. Nathalie then leads me into the Markthalle, a covered market that brings epicureans together around flavours from the four corners of the globe. We buy a few falafels and enjoy them in front of the cathedral, gazing up at the Gothic, terracotta-coloured building with its large stone tower. The visit is rounded off with a climb up the Schlossberg, a wooded hill from which we enjoy a 360° panorama of the town, the Black Forest and even the Vosges Mountains.

Drawn to the countryside just outside Freiburg, we leave the city to spend the night in the heart of the Black Forest, the tree-covered mountain range that stretches 140km (87 miles) from Baden-Baden to the Rhine. We focus on the range's southern part, driving for around 50km (31 miles) to the Feldberg, its highest point (1493m/4898ft). As the day draws to a close, we park on the edge of a grove of fir trees, alone in the middle of glorious nature, listening for the slightest sound: the breeze in the leaves; the hoot of an owl; the song of a few birds. Lulled by this sylvan symphony, we slowly abandon ourselves to the arms of Morpheus – there's nothing like the peace of the forest to send you to sleep.

Basel marks our return to civilisation, after 70km (43 miles) on the B317 in a thick fog. This first foray into Switzerland, a stone's throw from the German and French borders, is all about elegance. The city's medieval quarter is particularly attractive, starting with the central square, Marktplatz, where a frescoed red sandstone town hall watches over the large market every morning. Nearby, Basel's Gothic minster is equally impressive with its twin spires and fern-green, poppy-red and golden-yellow glazed roof tiles.

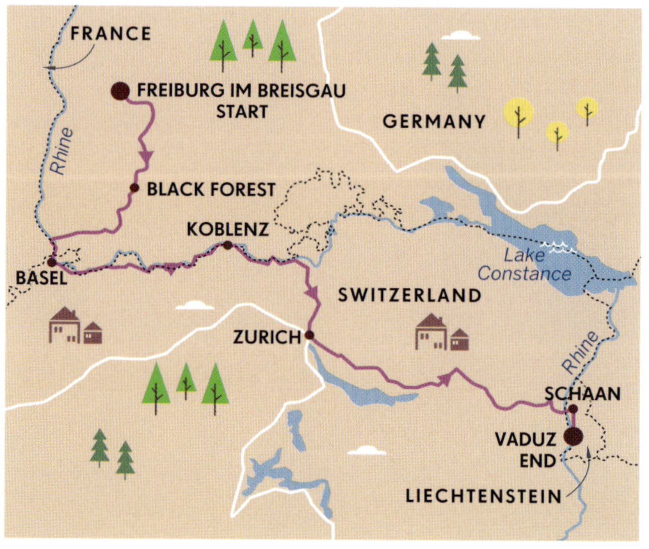

Nathalie's trip comes to an end here, and I'm now hosting José in the T4, in what we call our mobile flat-share – José knows the vehicle like the back of his hand, having lived in it for several months. We cross the Rhine again to reach the German side of the river, following the wooded, pastoral 34 to Koblenz. Numerous villages are on our route, which we visit as we drive along. What they all have in common is that they actively celebrate Carnival. In each of them, garlands and colourful flags offer a cheerful sight on these dull late-winter days. It's in the inns, however, that you feel the human warmth the most, leaning against the solid wood counters, a pint of lager in hand.

It's back to Switzerland for the next stop on our road trip – Zurich. The city's mainly known as a major financial centre, but we're surprised to discover a place full of charm. The skyline of the country's largest conurbation is quite distinctive: on either side of the Limmat River, beautiful churches face each other, including the Grossmünster (the Romanesque cathedral, with two symmetrical towers) and the Fraumünster (elegant and slender, with a copper roof and remarkable stained-glass windows). The rest of Zurich is a mix of wide avenues with luxurious boutiques and narrow streets with a concentration of artists and antique dealers.

On a whim, we decide to set off for Liechtenstein, intrigued by this principality we rarely hear about. We reach it in about 100km (62 miles), on a road lined with mountains and two large lakes, and choose to stop at Schaan. In this German-speaking

THE BLACK FOREST

The Black Forest in Germany's southwest extends over 6000 sq km (2317 sq miles). This patchwork of landscapes (pastures, peaks, forests, vineyards, lakes), criss-crossed by a multitude of trails, delights outdoor enthusiasts. In winter, there's plenty for skiers to do and summer sees water sports enthusiasts head for the region's largest lakes: Schluchsee and Titisee.

Above: Vaduz Castle. Opposite: To Freiburg im Breisgau. Below: Liechtenstein. Page 139, from top: Black Forest; Basel Old Town; Zurich.

'Alone in the middle of glorious nature, listening for the slightest sound: the breeze in the leaves; the hoot of an owl'.

region, Carnival is far from over – in fact, this Mardi Gras is in full swing giving a joyful boost to our visit. The locals, all in costume, greet us in German, smiling broadly. Some happily throw handfuls of sweets at us from a parade of motorised floats. The euphoria is contagious and this proves to be one of the best moments of the trip.

We can't leave Liechtenstein without seeing the castle of Vaduz, the capital. Only 3km (2 miles) from Schaan, the 'city' has a population of just 5000. Above the deserted main street – all the merrymakers are at Schaan's Carnival – an impressive fortress, with crenellated ramparts, has been home to the Princely Family of Liechtenstein for a century (though the building is much older). The sober walls, brightened only by windows with colourful shutters, leave little room for enchantment. However, the vineyards below and the surrounding mountains add charm to the picture. To make the most of this alpine landscape, we take to the fields, letting the camper transport us through the meadows. Freedom belongs to those who let themselves get lost. **AD**

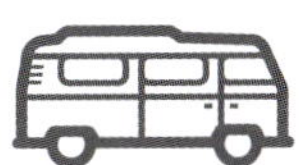

ROAD MAP

Start // Freiburg im Breisgau
Finish // Vaduz
Distance // 296km (184 miles)
Recommended duration // 7-to-10 days
When to go // Autumn, for the Black Forest's flamboyant colours, or Carnival, for celebrations galore
Culinary speciality // *Weisswurst* (a white sausage from southern Germany made with veal, pork, parsley and lemon)

THE PERFECT PICNIC SPOT

Description // Lusthäusle viewpoint, in the Black Forest
GPS coordinates // 47.87272571416583, 7.849580341702525
Access // Easy, via the L123 road
Activities // Hiking and contemplation
Visitor numbers // Few off-season visitors
Little extras // Share a gourmet moment with friends on the benches of a little hut, facing a pretty valley.

Opposite: Urho Kekkonen National Park, Lapland, Finland.

MORE LIKE THIS
FOREST ITINERARIES

NORTHERN FINLAND

Travelling to Finland in autumn provides the opportunity to see the taiga (subarctic forest) in all its glory. It's from the small town of Kajaani, surrounded by lakes and conifers, that you'll venture into the country's north in your vehicle. The E63 takes you through the centuries-old forests that surround Luosto, past numerous stretches of water along the way. Nearby, visit the Lampivaara amethyst mine, then head for Urho Kekkonen National Park, where you can hike deep into unspoilt nature. Finland's third-largest lake, Inari, is the next stop, near its namesake town, a paradise for fishers and kayakers. Finally, drive along the E75 through the taiga, where you'll find several car parks for an overnight stay, before heading for the shores of beautiful Lake Mantojärvi, a stone's throw from Utsjoki on the Norwegian border.

Start // Kajaani
Finish // Utsjoki
Distance // 817km (508 miles)
More information // visitfinland.com

FROM BERLIN TO ROSTOCK (GERMANY)

Leave the hustle and bustle of Berlin behind and escape along Route 11, deep in the woods, to the Schorfheide-Chorin Biosphere Reserve. This large protected area has plenty of trails and numerous ponds where you can enjoy a picnic in the sunshine after a few hours hiking. Experience another off-grid moment in the Norduckermärkische Seenlandschaft, this time by bike. Then grab the steering wheel and head for Malchow, a peaceful village in the middle of the Mecklenburg Lake Plateau. Allow yourself time to soak up the surrounding forest, where you'll feel cut off from the world. The icing on the cake is a few kilometres beyond Rostock at the Western Pomerania Lagoon National Park, populated by a rich collection of fauna, between clumps of trees and the Baltic Sea.

Start // Berlin
Finish // Rostock
Distance // 369km (229 miles)
More information // germany.travel

VELEBIT (CROATIA)

If you're in the mood for some wilderness immersion, grab the wheel of your camper and head deep into Croatia, to Krasno. Surrounded by fir trees, this town is the gateway to the Northern Velebit National Park, a region with a pristine ecosystem. Between May and November, you can enjoy these craggy landscapes after buying your entrance ticket at Velebit House, Krasno's information office. Follow the winding, wooded road to the summit of Veliki Zavižan for a hike offering excellent views. Leave the park and continue to Štirovača, a remote reserve surrounded by forest. Stretch your legs amongst the trees before parking along the Dunjevac stream for the night. In the morning, climb up to the old tower of Perušic for a bird's-eye perspective of the wooded hills, then finish at Karlobag on the coast, stopping at the Baške Oštarije lookout on the way.

Start // Krasno
Finish // Karlobag
Distance // 168km (104 miles)
More information // np-sjeverni-velebit.hr

DUTCH GETAWAY

From modern architecture to traditional windmills, from the Gouda cheese market to Amsterdam's museums, take a springtime tour of the Netherlands.

My friend Max and I have agreed to meet up in Rotterdam. Our plan? A week criss-crossing two of the Netherlands' coastal provinces: South Holland and North Holland. Preferring not to venture too far into the traffic of the country's second-largest city – which is also one of the ten most important ports in the world – I park the camper van in Noordereiland, an island neighborhood just a 15-minute walk from Rotterdam's centre.

Max soon arrives. He puts his backpack in the van and we set off to explore the streets of what looks like a laboratory for contemporary architecture. This design aesthetic was born after WWII, during which Rotterdam was almost entirely destroyed by bombing. With the exception of a few emblematic buildings, the local authorities have resolutely looked to the future, meaning even today, Rotterdam is a playground for forward-thinking architects.

We start with Kijk-Kubus, designed by Piet Blom in the 1980s. Leaning at 45°, these 38 yellow cube houses pique our interest and we're able to satisfy our curiosity by touring the show home, furnished with almost as much ingenuity as my camper van (I may be biased). Just behind these unusual houses, Oude Haven and its traditional boats offer a striking contrast. This mix of styles follows us as we continue through the impressive covered market (Markthal) then the Maritime Museum district, and gives the city its charm.

But it's time to move on to Camping and Hall Landhoeve, just 28km (17 miles) to the east, where we have a reservation for the night. Once we've parked on our spot, we rent bikes and pedal off to the Kinderdijk windmill park. Nineteen of these were designed to drain water from the canals. The beauty of the park captivates us – it's not for nothing that it's a UNESCO World Heritage Site. The late hour prevents us from visiting the interior of the windmills, so we cycle along, contemplating the landscape as it takes on the colours of the setting sun.

Next morning, I wake up with backache after a night on the hard cot, while Max is still asleep in my soft bed. I decide that it would probably be a good idea to alternate our sleeping arrangements every evening. I prepare the coffee and let him sleep while I head off for a shower. Today, we're off to Gouda, a few kilometres to the north. The region is, of course, famous

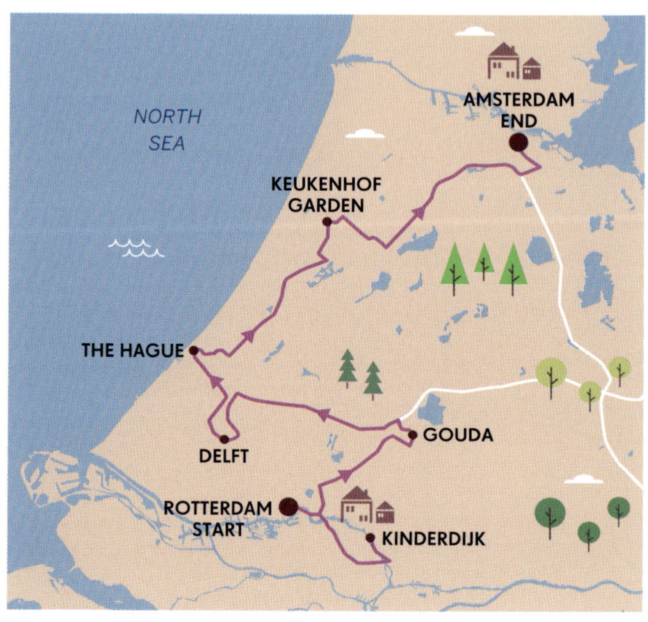

© Achim Thomae | Getty Images

for its cheese, sold at a market held in front of the town hall every Thursday morning from April to September, with the large, yellow wheels of deliciousness stacked on the ground. I also discover another local speciality, *stroopwafel*, biscuit-like waffles filled with molasses syrup.

For a change, we've booked a night in a guesthouse for our next stop, Delft. The following day, we walk through the town, famous for its blue pottery and Vermeer paintings, to the sound of the church bells. We fall for its old canals with their flower-filled quays, ancient buildings, stone facades and cobbled streets.

Up next is The Hague, on the North Sea, where the intention is to spend a lazy afternoon on the beach. Like Amsterdam and other major urban centres, The Hague has established a 'Milieuzone', a low-emission zone with no access for diesel vehicles. This type of area is equipped with cameras that scan offenders' licence plates. Wisely, I park my old diesel camper on the outskirts of town and we take public transport to

'We pedal carefree through the fields, intoxicated by the scent of flowers.'

Scheveningen Beach where surfers, beach volleyball courts and a Ferris wheel on the pier are all to be found – add a *Baywatch* lifeguard tower and you could be in California.

We then head northeast. stopping about halfway between The Hague and Amsterdam at the famous Keukenhof garden. This huge floral showground, with over seven million plants – tulips, daffodils, hyacinths – is packed with tourists from all over the world. On our way out, we rent bicycles and the staff provide us with a map showing four cycle routes ranging in length from 5 to 25km (3-16 miles). We pedal carefree through the fields, intoxicated by the scent of flowers.

The last stage of our trip brings us to Amsterdam, where we've booked a pitch at Camping Gaasper. Three days are all it takes to get a good sense of the capital, which has so much to offer. In addition to its history and world-class museums, it boasts a flower-filled setting and a feeling that life is good. But perhaps what makes it unique is the omnipresence of water – there are 165 canals and 1300 bridges here – and of bicycles. It's hard not to love a place where everyone asserts their choices and aspirations without fear of being judged. There are countless cycling possibilities from the city, whether to Haarlem's famous De Adriaan windmill, the Zaanse Schans windmills or the fishing village of Marken in Waterland. In the Netherlands, perhaps more than anywhere else, the bicycle is the ideal extension of the camper van. **AL**

THE ANNE FRANK HOUSE

In Amsterdam, on the banks of the Prinsengracht canal, stands the Anne Frank House. The WWII home of the author of the famous diary is particularly moving. This is where the young girl and her family hid during the Nazi occupation of the Netherlands, in rooms hidden behind a bookcase.

Opposite, from top: Rotterdam; Tulip field at Zaanse Schans. Page 145: Windmills at Kinderdijk.

ROAD MAP

Start // Rotterdam
Finish // Amsterdam
Distance // 191km (119 miles)
Recommended duration // 7-to-10 days
When to go // April to mid-May to combine Gouda cheese shopping with flowering bulbs at Keukenhof
Culinary specialities // *Stroopwafel* (waffle cookie), Gouda cheese

THE PERFECT CHEESE MAKER

Description // De Kaaskamer cheese dairy in Amsterdam
GPS coordinates // 42.637801, 11.889072
Access // Nice pedestrian area Negen Straatjes neighbourhood
The menu // Dutch cheeses selected from the best farms in the country
Little extras // Taste a wide selection and take advice from the cheese maker

Opposite, clockwise from top: Uffelse mill, Limburg; De Hoge Veluwe national park, Gelderland; Van in a Groningen street.

MORE LIKE THIS
NETHERLANDS CONTINUED

FRISIAN COUNTRY

Located at the northern tip of the Netherlands, the province of Friesland is full of surprises. This land of *polders* (reclaimed land), lakes and peat bogs offers a complete change of scenery – even the road signs are in Frisian, the locally official language, alongside Dutch. For a camper van loop, depart from Leeuwarden, capital of Friesland, after visiting its modern museum which showcases the province's culture. In August, boating enthusiasts will want to stop off at Sneek for its regatta of old sailing ships. Then it's off to Stavoren, a port on the shores of IJsselmeer lake. Follow the shores of this former North Sea gulf to Makkum and Harlingen, with their canals and old brick warehouses. Before returning to Leeuwarden, explore Dokkum and its traditional mills, then make a detour to Lauwersmeer National Park for lots of avian action.

Start/Finish // Leeuwarden
Distance // 215km (134 miles)
More information // holland.com

LIMBURG

To explore Limburg's countryside at the wheel of your van, head for the southern edge of the Netherlands where this province is an enclave between Germany and Belgium. Crossed by the Meuse River, Maastricht boasts medieval architecture and a rich cultural scene. Take in the city from Fort Sint Pieter before exploring the region's proud historic towns and villages hidden between meadows and orchards: Thorn and its whitewashed houses; Roermond and its cathedral. Along the way, swap the camper for a bike and ride through the vast Brunssummerheide Nature Reserve, a land of moorland and heather. Before ending your tour in De Maasduinen National Park, with its impressive dunes (and quicksand), take a break in the gardens of Arcen Castle and stretch your legs in Venlo, a town with ancient buildings on the banks of the Meuse.

Start // Maastricht
Finish // De Maasduinen National Park
Distance // 141km (88 miles)
More information // holland.com

GELDERLAND

Situated in the east of the country, Gelderland is the Netherlands' largest province. To experience its De Hoge Veluwe National Park, you can either stay in your vehicle for a half-day safari observing the animals (boar, deer, mouflons) or borrow one of the bicycles available to visitors and enjoy the silence of this area of heather and shifting dunes. On the edge of the park, Arnhem, lapped by the Rhine, has open-air museum offering an excellent introduction to Dutch traditions. Then head to Groenlo, the historic town of the Achterhoek region, a rural, wooded area with some 30 vineyards, which is a pleasure to drive through. Stop off at Zutphen and Doesburg, beautifully preserved medieval towns. This is the traditional heart of the Netherlands. Finish in Apeldoorn, 20km (12 miles) north of De Hoge Veluwe park, to buy a few souvenirs at the Saturday market or in the shops in the town centre.

Start // De Hoge Veluwe National Park
Finish // Apeldoorn
Distance // 157km (98 miles)
More information // holland.com

HIGHLIGHTS OF LAKE CONSTANCE

Winning lakeside landscapes and exceptional historic towns.

What a pleasure to finally reach the shores of Lake Constance after several hours on the road from France. There I meet up with Nathalie, a German friend who lives in Überlingen and with whom I'm planning to take the camper around this immense lake on the borders of Switzerland, Austria and Germany. From Überlingen, we start our loop from the west. I fully trust Nathalie's recommendations, especially since, as I usually travel alone, I'm happy to be guided by someone who knows the area inside out.

Before we set off on our road trip, however, we'd like to celebrate our reunion in style, and, fittingly, it's Carnival season. Behind the apparent serenity of Lake Constance lies a completely different atmosphere, generated by *Fastnacht*, a lively, Carnival tradition from German-speaking Switzerland. And so we find the brightly painted streets of Überlingen alive with parades, in a state of total celebration. Aside from the festivities, many historic buildings catch my eye, but according to Nathalie, nothing beats a long walk along the quays. The view of the lake's still, cerulean waters proves her right.

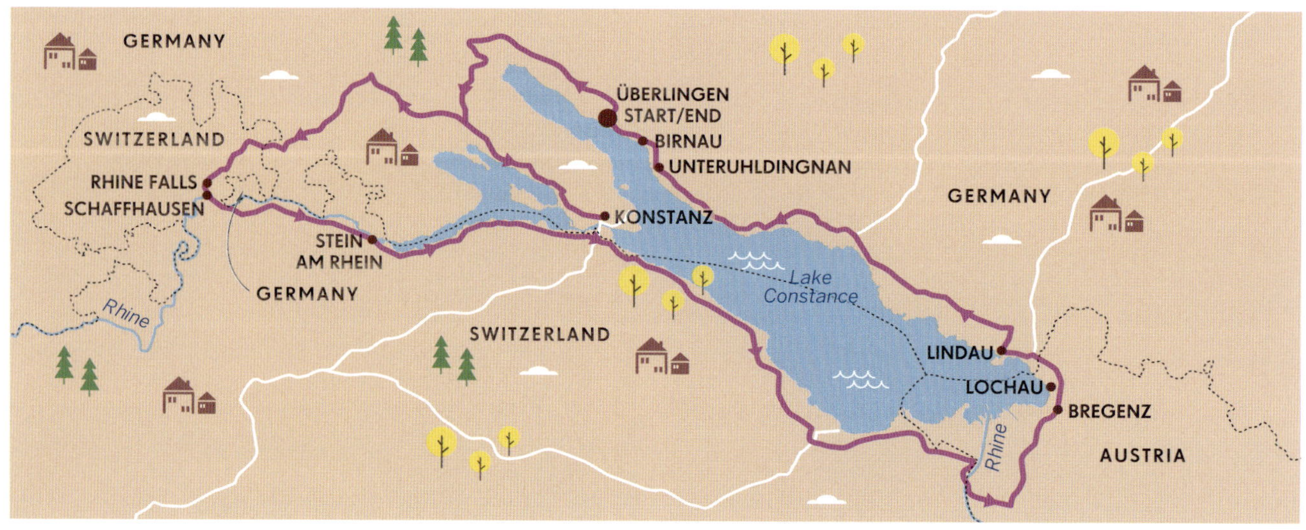

THE RHINE FALLS

The Rhine Falls, between Neuhausen am Rheinfall in Germany and Flurlingen in Switzerland, are one of the largest in Europe, with a cascade 23m (74ft) high and 150m (492ft) wide. Above the falls, the Laufen Castle hotel-restaurant enjoys an exceptional setting. Several car parks provide easy access.

© Sven Fuchs | Shutterstock

Soon we're behind the wheel. The first wow moment on this voyage takes place just 50km (31 miles) south as soon as we arrive in Konstanz – this is the largest conurbation on the lake but has the most incredibly peaceful atmosphere. Nathalie takes me on a tour of the Altstadt (old town), with its cobbled streets, historic shopfronts. and imposing minster, clad in white stone and rising 76m (249ft) high. We stroll through the heart of the city and our slow route takes us close to the port and its pretty jetty, a popular meeting place for seagulls. Here again, our attention is drawn by the crystal-clear lake.

Back in the van, we take a quick detour from the lakeshore to visit the Rhine Falls on the Swiss side, not far from Schaffhausen. The Rhine flows through Lake Constance, continuing its course from the lake's western end. The violent flow of the waterfall the river forms here, between Neuhausen am Rheinfall and Flurlingen, makes it one of the largest in Europe, and the volume of water spewed out by the cataract is as deafening as it is impressive – a worthwhile side trip.

We then follow the Rhine for 20km (12 miles) to reach the lower part of Lake Constance (aka Untersee) at Stein am Rhein, our next stop. Half-timbered houses covered in frescoes brighten up the streets of this Swiss town's centre, an architectural set piece which, to our great delight, takes us back to medieval times.

It's time to look for a place to sleep, so we follow Route 13 along the south shore of the lake towards Austria. We'd like to set up near a beach, but can't find any authorised overnight parking on the waterfront, meaning we're forced to head inland. Not a bad idea, as it turns out. As we make our way along the road, we spot a hill in the middle of the fields, offering a beautiful view of the lake. A perfect place to stay.

Next day we clock up kilometre after kilometre on the way to Austria and the town of Bregenz, on Constance's southeastern edge. The capital of Vorarlberg is a great place to stock up on provisions as prices here are much lower than in Switzerland. The city is also a great place to sightsee, wandering through the historic section of the town, centred around the massive Baroque St Martin's Tower. Bregenz, it turns out, is a jewel of a place, positioned between lake and mountains (the Pfänder, 1062m/3484ft, is the best known), and a walk along the pier rounds off our stay.

Back to Germany, and specifically Lindau, another pearl in Lake Constance's crown. Its lively, multihued streets give me a boost of energy, added to by the fact that Carnival is being

Opposite: Überlingen. Above: Lindau. Below: Unteruhldingen open-air museum. Page 151: Sunset over the lake.

celebrated here too, and the entertainment is in full swing. A small marina lies protected by jetties jutting out from Lindau into the lake. At the end of one jetty, a newer lighthouse overlooks the azure expanse of water and gives a privileged view back towards the city and its Mangturm, an ancient lighthouse with a roof of green and amber tiles.

Now all we have to do is follow Route 31 back to our starting point, reluctantly counting down the hours we have left. We stop off at Unteruhldingenan open-air museum, 50km (31 miles) from Lindau, where reconstructions of small wooden houses built on stilts with thatched roofs show how life was lived back in the Neolithic and Bronze ages.

Just a few kilometres away, Birnau's pilgrimage church marks the final stop on our journey. This colossal salmon-walled building, surrounded by vineyards, gazes out over the lake. From the outside, it looks fairly ordinary, but as soon as you push open the door, you realise what an architectural feat this is. The nave is decorated with lace-like stonework and paintings, making it a masterpiece of Rococo art – and a great way to end the trip. **AD**

'As we make our way along the road, we spot a hill in the middle of the fields, offering a beautiful view of the lake. A perfect place to stay.'

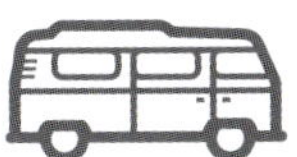

ROAD MAP

Start/Finish // Überlingen
Distance // 287km (178 miles)
Recommended duration // 5-to-7 days
When to go // Summer for swimming, Carnival for festivities
Culinary specialities // *Käsespätzle* (small pasta-like flour and egg dumplings with herbs and cheese)

THE PERFECT PICNIC SPOT

Description // Just off Lake Constance, in Lochau (Austria)
GPS coordinates // 47.527220294982506, 9.747932390880157
Access // Pay parking along route 190
Activities // Vanlifers with bicycles will appreciate the nearby bike path.
Visitor numbers // Very busy in summer; quiet in low season
Little extras // A long walk along the shore, before hitting the road again

Opposite, from top: Montalcino, Italy; Rothenburg ob der Tauber, Germany.

MORE LIKE THIS CHARMING TOWNS

THE ROMANTIC ROAD (GERMANY)

The Romantic Road is one of the most attractive routes in Bavaria, leading from magnificent castles to picturesque towns. Start your drive in the streets of Würzburg, opposite the impressive Residence, a Baroque palace. Then head south to experience the magic of the medieval town of Rothenburg ob der Tauber, before visiting the town of Nördlingen, built in a meteorite crater and surrounded by circular ramparts. Next up is Augsburg, one of Germany's oldest cities. Admire the 16th-century Fuggerei, the oldest social housing complex in the world. Further down the road, follow the shores of the Forggensee Reservoir to Füssen, home to a number of extraordinary castles including famous Neuschwanstein, built by Ludwig II of Bavaria.
Start // Würzburg
Finish // Füssen
Distance // 335km (208 miles)
More information // bavaria.travel

VILLAGES OF TUSCANY (ITALY)

For a taste of Italy's *dolce vita*, organise a camper trip to the sublime Tuscany region. From Florence, take the alternative route to Siena (SR222), and lose yourself in the hamlets and vineyards of the Chianti region. You'll be able to taste exceptional wines and easily find a place to sleep. Take a detour to some of Tuscany's most beautiful villages: San Gimignano and its centuries-old towers; Volterra and the ruins of its Roman theatre; and Monteriggioni with its imposing fortifications. After strolling through Siena's Piazza del Campo and taking in the sights of the city, drive to nearby Val d'Orcia, and follow the winding hills planted with olive groves, vineyards and cypress avenues. Visit the village of San Quirico and, before heading home, relax in the thermal waters of the Bagni San Filippo.
Start // Florence
Finish // Bagni San Filippo
Distance // 245km (152 miles)
More informatione // visittuscany.com

ZEELAND PROVINCE (NETHERLANDS)

In the southwest of the Netherlands, Zeeland is made up of islands and peninsulas at the mouths of the Scheldt, Rhine and Meuse rivers. From the scenic port of Breskens, cross the mouth of the Scheldt via the N62 tunnel to Middelburg, the province's attractive capital, surrounded by canals – the Markt and many 18th-century houses are well worth a look. At the western tip of the Walcheren Peninsula, Westkapelle welcomes you with its beautiful beaches and magnificent lighthouse. Not far away, you'll find the warm atmosphere of Domburg, an old village nestled between dunes and forest. Then it's on to the characterful town of Veere, with its cobbled streets and picturesque monuments. Finally, cross the spectacular N57 bridge over the Oosterschelde Dam to Zierikzee, where you can admire its harbour, home to old sailing ships, mills and ramparts.
Start // Middelburg
Finish // Zierikzee
Distance // 135km (84 miles)
More information // holland.com

ROAD TRIP TO THE HEART OF SWITZERLAND

Journey from the Swiss capital to the mountains of the Valais.

Snow has enveloped the camper in a heavy white blanket overnight. It's dawn and the light is still subdued. Outside sounds seem muffled. José and I didn't expect the thermometer to drop so far below zero on our trip through Switzerland, from historic towns to pristine landscapes, in the cantons of Bern, Fribourg, Vaud and Valais. But here we are, the cold and snow giving us and the van the opportunity to test our resilience.

Bern, the Swiss capital, is the first stop on this expedition and we're having trouble finding a parking space – a not uncommon problem when driving this kind of vehicle. After a long search, we end up parking in the suburbs and set off to explore the 'city of a hundred fountains' on foot. Said fountains are delicately sculpted potable water sources, emblems of medieval times, which brighten up the streets of the old town, itself a UNESCO World Heritage Site, with its 6km (4 miles) of arcades. From the Zytglogge clock tower, whose animated figures put on an entertaining show, to the Federal Palace, a superb building with a vast dome dominating the Bundesplatz, we go from surprise to surprise, much to our delight. Equally charming are the snatches of conversation in French, German and, more rarely, Italian we notice. The city is evidence of Switzerland's multilingual make-up. Sadly we don't hear anyone speak its fourth official language, Romansh.

After this fine introduction, we drive 30km (19 miles) to the neighbouring canton, stopping off at its namesake capital, Fribourg. This medium-sized medieval town sits on the Sarine, a river spanned by one of the oldest footbridges in the country, the picturesque Bern Bridge, with wooden railings and a tiled roof. Numerous churches point their steeples towards the sky across the city. The most impressive is undoubtedly the Gothic cathedral of St Nicholas, overlooking the river from its rocky spur. Renowned for the quality of its Art Nouveau stained glass, the building also features a colossal 76m (249ft) tower, visible for miles around.

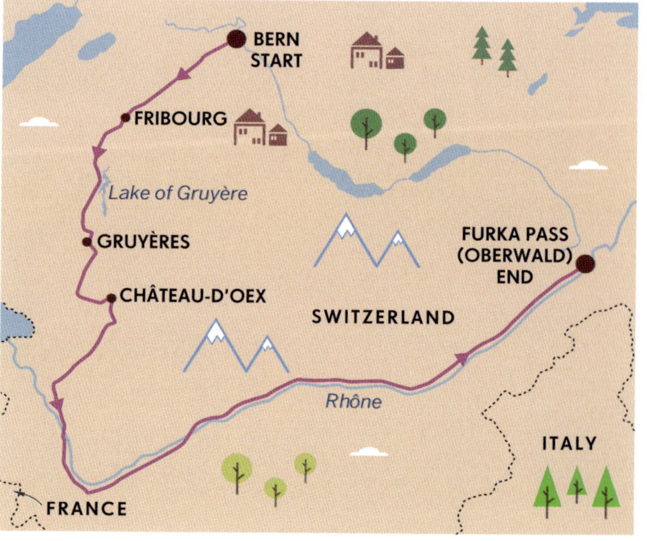

'The sight of multiple hot-air balloons rising above the Pays-d'Enhaut district with a backdrop of the sparkling Pre-Alps is magical.'

Having decided to take our time, we make a few short side trips to explore the region in greater depth. Route 12 heads south for 35km (22 miles), skirting the immense Lake of Gruyère, before reaching the town of Gruyères, birthplace of the famous Swiss cheese. A tasting session confirms it: the celerated cheese deserves its delicious reputation. The medieval streets of Gruyères' centre aren't bad either, huddled below a massive, impregnable-looking fortress and St Théodule Church with its imposing bell tower, worth a look for the view of the mountains looming in the distance.

Our route now takes us to Château-d'Oex in the canton of Vaud, just 25km (16 miles) along Route 9. This large village of 3000 souls hosts the annual International Balloon Festival – and luckily for us, this week-long event is taking place when we arrive. The sight of multiple hot-air balloons rising above the Pays-d'Enhaut district with a backdrop of the sparkling Pre-Alps is magical. We watch the multicoloured floating marvels silhouetted against the sky, wide-eyed, before gasping at a paragliding aerobatics demonstration, followed by the loops of a small plane. This unexpected but wonderful experience is a highlight of the trip.

Moving on, we arrive in the Valais, driving past Martigny, Sion and Brig, crossing the entire Swiss Rhone valley, heading east. It's certainly not the most attractive part of the trip. Apart from a few orchards on the hillsides, there are many industrial plants along the N9, particularly around Visp. We eat up the kilometres as quickly as possible and head for the Furka Pass, flirting with an altitude of 2429m (7969ft).

Time and again, we've gazed longingly at photos of this mythical stretch of road, where the famous Gletscher hotel-restaurant sits on a hairpin bend. We know that this is one of the most beautiful drives in the Swiss Alps, and can't wait to get to grips with this snake of tarmac. Unfortunately, our luck runs out – the pass is closed and we learn that we must load the camper onto a train at Oberwald Station if we wish to continue our adventure in this direction. The journey will take 20 minutes and leaves us at Realp, on the other side of the mountain. We hesitate for a moment over buying a ticket, then decide to turn around. It's always good to have something to come back for. **AD**

WINTER IN A CAMPER VAN

In winter, it's essential to insulate the cabin well, and bring enough blankets and warm clothes. Equip your vehicle with chains or snow tyres, a shovel, a scraper and wiper fluid suitable for frost. And don't forget to protect your water pipes – don't fill your tanks completely, or turn them off.

Opposite, clockwise from left: Château-d'Oex International Balloon Festival; Gruyères; Bern. Page 157, from top: Alpine landscape in Gruyères; Lac de la Gruyère.

ROAD MAP

Start // Bern
Finish // Furka Pass
Distance // 277km (172 miles)
Recommended duration // 5-to-7 days
When to go // Summer for sun; winter for skiing
Culinary specialities // Gruyère cheese

THE PERFECT PHOTO SPOT

Description // 360° view from the tower of Fribourg Cathedral (closed in winter)
GPS coordinates // 46.8064098851494, 7.163213724662242
Access // Park near the town centre, walk to St Nicolas' Cathedral and climb the 365 steps leading up to this fabulous panorama.

Opposite: Cheese weighing building in Edam, Netherlands.

MORE LIKE THIS
CHEESE ROUTES

THE NETHERLANDS

The pastures of the Krimpenerwaard, where dairy cows graze, are the ideal place to start this cheese-focused foray. From here, it's a short drive to Gouda, heart of the Netherlands' Cheese Valley. The historic city is home to the wonderful St John's Church, which dominates the town, but it's probably at the market that you'll experience your finest moments. Don't miss the Goudse Waag Museum to discover the secrets of pressed curds, before getting back in your camper van. Drive through fields to the attractive canals of Leiden for a spot of spicy cumin farmhouse cheese, full of character. Follow the A4 around Amsterdam to the charming town of Edam, on the shores of the IJmeer lake. Tour the 18th-century cheese warehouses and sample the flavours of the little red balls. Finally, check out Alkmaar's cheese market, 30km (19 miles) away, the largest in the country.

Start // Gouda
Finish // Alkmaar
Distance // 134km (83 miles)
More information // holland.com

SWITZERLAND

Begin your Swiss cheese adventure in Villars-sur-Ollon with an unforgettable hike to a high-altitude restaurant where you can enjoy a raclette lunch. Time your trip for the first Sunday in May, and the medieval town of Gruyères will reward your planning with its cheese festival. It's easy – and appealing – to get there on a short drive along the shores of Lake Geneva. To taste the famous *fromage à pâte cuite* (pressed cheese) and fondue-staple Vacherin, and understand how they are made, continue to Les Invuettes dairy, close to Charmey. Spend the night by nearby Lake Murten, then take the road to Bellelay and visit the abbey and museum of Tête de Moine, a delicious cheese shaped into rosettes – as beautiful as it is delicious. Finish in Affoltern im Emmental, at the village's cheese dairy, where you'll learn all you need to know about this holeyest of cheeses.

Start // Villars-sur-Ollon
Finish // Affoltern im Emmental
Distance // 262km (163 miles)
More information // myswitzerland.com

ITALY

Turophiles (cheese lovers) are spolit for choice in Italy, so it's best to focus on one area. This itinerary concentrates on the country's north, beginning in Emilia-Romagna. Near Parma, the birthplace of both ham and Parmesan, the village of Basilicagoiano is home to Caseificio Santo Stefano, a dairy where you can see the cellars where Parmigiano Reggiano matures. Further north, Lombardy is the stronghold of Gorgonzola – near Milan, try different varieties of this blue cheese at various cooperatives, including Caseificio Angelo Croce in Casalpusterlengo. You can overnight nearby on the banks of the Po. On the home stretch, head for Piedmont and the province of Cuneo, whose culinary heritage is universally acclaimed. Knock on the doors of Giolito Fiorenzo Formaggi to discover the distinctive taste of Bra cheese, before journeying into tomme, ricotta and mascarpone territory.

Start // Basilicagoiano
Finish // Bra
Distance // 265km (165 miles)
More information // italia.it

IN FLANDERS' FIELDS

Discover the great cities of Flanders, from Bruges to Ghent, Brussels to Antwerp, with their well-preserved architecture and engaging atmosphere.

For this road trip in northern Belgium, I'm joined by a Parisian friend, Simone, who has never travelled in a camper van before. She dreams of visiting the great cities of Flanders – so let's go. First stop is Bruges, nicknamed the Venice of the North. We park the vehicle in the free Boogschutterslaan car park, a 15-minute walk from Bruges' historic centre. As I do every time I leave the van alone, I place any valuables in the backpack I'll be taking with me, then put away anything lying around and draw the curtains to avoid attracting the attention of passers-by – some people recommend leaving the curtains open to show that there's nothing to steal.

Once ready, we head for the Kruispoort (Holy Cross Gate). From the bridge over the canal, we can see the wooden windmills of the Sint-Janshuismolen Park.

The old town is immediatelly appealing, with beautiful old brick houses and romantic canals where swans glide. It's like travelling back to another era. After a cruise on the canals, we make our way to the Markt, Bruges' central square, whose colourful facades are topped with gabled roofs. The square hosts an interesting market on Wednesday mornings, in the shadow of its imposing, 13th-century Gothic belfry, which regularly plays its carillon. We'll end our visit at the Begijnhof, a sort of village

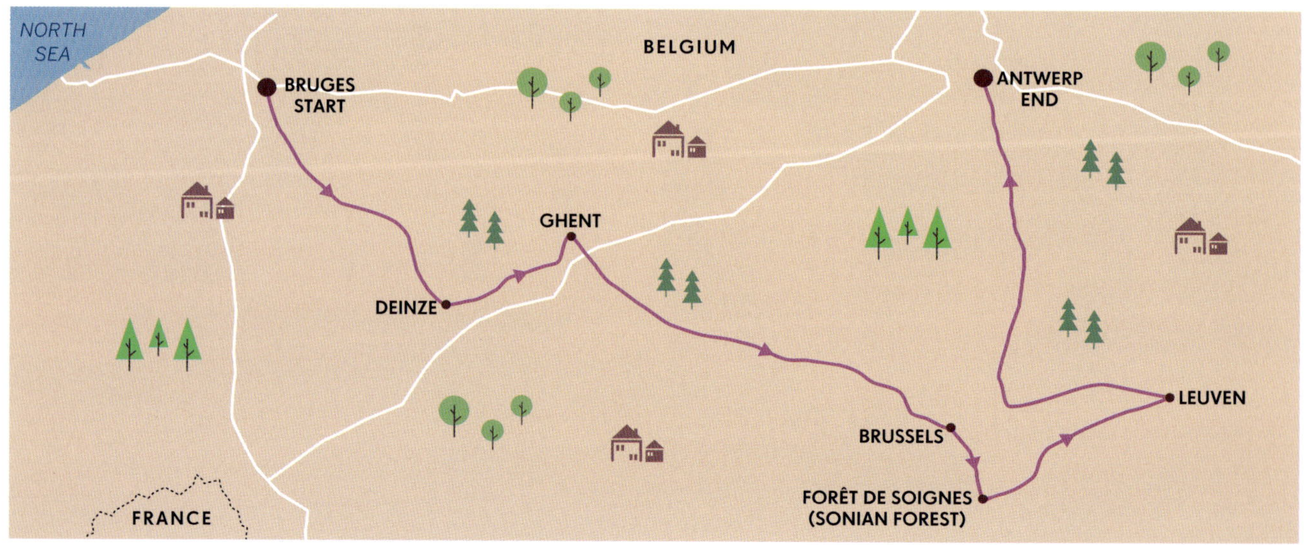

© Ekaterina Belova | Adobe Stock, for the two photos below © Alexandra Lam

EV 892 EX

THE SONIAN FOREST

Situated close to Brussels, the Forêt de Soignes (Sonian Forest) has become a 'cathedral of beech trees' over the years, covering almost 4400 hectares and shared between Belgium's three regions. Recognised as a Special Area of Conservation, it is part of the Natura 2000 network and a UNESCO World Heritage Site. The forest has never been cleared: its terrain has remained in its natural state for hundreds of years!

'The old town is immediately appealing, with beautiful old brick houses and romantic canals where swans glide.'

within the city, cut off by a moat. A small stone bridge leads to these traditional living quarters for pious, unmarried or widowed women, where a large courtyard-garden with tall trees is surrounded by some thirty white-fronted houses.

In the evening, we leave Bruges and head east on the E40 to a nature spot, Noorderwal, near Deinze. It's nice to have a co-pilot and we chat the whole way, but at the same time, my van isn't really set up for two people and once we've stopped, it takes a certain amount of gymnastics not to step on each other's toes. We soon adjust though, dividing up tasks so as to make the most of this small space.

The next day, Ghent, 25km (16 miles) away, is calling. The city centre is a Low Emission Zone (LEZ) meaning my diesel-powered vehicle is banned and must be parked outside this zone. So we leave the camper in the free Bourgoyen car park and take the bus into the old town. Ghent, with its canals, belfry and medieval architecture, resembles Bruges, but is more modern and less touristy. We walk through the streets following an art trail, then enjoy *cuberdons*, a traditional Belgian confection in the shape of a cone, sitting among the students on the Graslei quay. Our agenda also includes a look at the torture instruments in the castle of the counts of Flanders, and finishes with an evening bike ride along the illuminated streets and canals.

The following morning we're back on the E40, heading for the capital, Brussels. This region is also an LEZ, so I choose the free Stalle car park, with no height limit and located next to a tramway line. All roads in Brussels lead to the extraordinary Grand Place where we're impressed by the richness of the facades, including the Gothic town hall topped by a belfry, the Neogothic King's House and the various guildhalls, with their intricate, exhibitionist details. A few streets away, we laugh at the sight of the city's mascot, the Manneken-Pis in his frequently-changing costume. After window-shopping at Galeries Royales Saint-Hubert, we enjoy *wafels* on the lawn of the Cinquantenaire Park, commemorating Belgium's independence. You can't leave the capital without seeing the Atomium, a futuristic structure built in 1958 that glows with 3000 lights as soon as night falls.

My camper isn't fitted with solar panels so it's the alternator that recharges the batteries when I'm on the move. To be self-sufficient in power, I need to drive enough and regularly, but since we've been in Belgium, my faithful old van hasn't covered many kilometres. We therefore choose to spend the night at Camping 3CB, on the eastern outskirts of Brussels, where we can connect to an electrical terminal and replenish our water supply.

A noisy truck wakes us – the joys of camping – but we make the most of the early start by cooking a hearty breakfast and enjoying it on the picnic table that's been gathering dust in the boot. I don't often use it when traveling alone, preferring to keep things simple. After this feast, we drive 5km (3 miles) south to the Tervuren car park in the verdant Forêt de Soignes (Sonian Forest) and set off on a gentle jog among beech and oak trees, some of them two hundred years old. What a pleasure it is to be in the middle of nature with birds singing.

Before heading off to Antwerp, we make a detour to Leuven, 20km (12 miles) east, to admire its incredible Gothic town hall, a veritable stone lacework masterpiece of 236 statues, and enjoy a beer on a terrace in the lively Oude Markt.

Antwerp itself is a dynamic port and trading city. To avoid the LEZ, we leave the van in a paid car park for motorhomes, near the Parc des Expositions metro station. Our tour of the city begins at Rubens' house, then we walk past boutiques, restaurants and art galleries to reach the Grand Place, home to the monumental cathedral, and finish with a visit to the old port and the trendy Museum aan de Stroom district. It's with sadness that I say goodbye to my friend on the platform of the city's Central Station – but we both look forward to repeating this successful trip. **AL**

Opposite: Lake of Love in Bruges. Below: Ghent. Page 163, from top: Grand-Place de Bruxelles; Forêt de Soignes; Rue de Bruges.

ROAD MAP

Start // Bruges
Finish // Antwerp
Distance // 225km (140 miles)
Recommended duration // 5-to-7 days
When to go // Christmas, for decorations and markets
Culinary specialities // *Wafels* (waffle cookies), chocolate, *cuberdons* (cone-shaped sweets), beer, mussels and *frites*

THE PERFECT FISHING SPOT

Description // Beautiful spot on the banks of the Lys River
GPS coordinates // 50.980364, 3.510738
Light pollution // Low
Access // Dirt track (muddy in wet weather)
Facilities // None
Visitor numbers // A few other fishers along the canal
Little extras // Quiet and shaded

Opposite: Gdańsk, Poland.

MORE LIKE THIS
BRICK GOTHIC WONDERS

NORTHWEST POLAND

Your Polish Brick Gothic road trip starts in Gdansk, one of the country's most remarkable Hanseatic cities. The region boasts many monuments and places steeped in history. Drive along the DW211 through the Kaszubski Park Krajobrazowy forest, then follow the E28 road along the Baltic Sea to reach the West Pomeranian Voivodeship in the northwest of the country. Venerable buildings line the route including St Mary's Church in Sławno, Szczecin's former town hall, the 15th-century Ratusz Staromiejski, and the Marian collegiate church of Stargard Szczeciński, arguably Poland's finest Brick Gothic church. In Myślibórz, you can overnight by a lake or on the edge of a forest.

Start // Gdansk
Finish // Myślibórz
Distance // 463km (288 miles)
More information // eurob.org

NORTHERN GERMANY

Germany, home of Brick Gothic, boasts a wide variety of the style's architectural highlights, both religious (village churches, cathedrals) and secular (town halls, gates and ramparts), along a route you can follow, driving through rural landscapes where the red of the buildings contrasts with the green of the meadows. To start, look for the small round or square marks adorning some of the bricks on traditional houses in Lüneburg. Further north, Lübeck is notable for the Brick Gothic towers of its St Mary's and St Peter's churches. Continue eastwards on the B105, which runs alongside the Baltic Sea and passes through several towns representative of Brick Gothic, such as Rostock, Ribnitz-Damgarten, Wismar and Stralsund – the latter two are World Heritage Sites.

Start // Lüneburg
Finish // Stralsund
Distance // 352km (219 miles)
More information // eurob.org

DENMARK

Wherever you are in Denmark, you're never more than 50km (31 miles) from the coast – meaning you can happily dine in the back of your van, enjoying an enchanting view of a beach or the softness of a clear summer night by the sea. Along with seaside attractions, the country's many cultural highlights include plenty for fans of Brick Gothic architecture. To discover these jewels, begin close to capital Copenhagen at Roskilde – its cathedral, the most important in the country, was one of the first in Scandinavia built in brick and the crypts and vaults bear witness to a thousand years of Danish history. Haderslev Cathedral dates to the 13th century and boasts a fine organ and excellent acoustics within its Brick Gothic walls. Finally, don't miss the Cistercian abbey and church of Løgumkloster.

Start // Roskilde
Finish // Løgumkloster
Distance // 274km (170 miles)
More information // eurob.org

THE GERMAN ALPINE ROAD

This Bavarian gem of a drive goes through a fairy-tale landscape between lakes and mountains.

When I was little, I loved stories about princesses in majestic castles lost in bewitching mountain landscapes. Driving along the German Alpine Road is like bringing those childhood stories to life. This winding scenic route links the astonishing castles of King Ludwig II of Bavaria with the marvellous South Bavarian mountains.

Neuschwanstein Castle, world-famous for its romantic medieval architecture, occupies a breathtaking site. The building is considered one of the models for the 'Sleeping Beauty' palace created by Walt Disney. You can visit the interior, with its opulent decor inspired by Wagner's operas, but I prefer to discover the various exterior views of this impressive castle, perched 200m (656ft) above sea level. Despite the many tourists with the same idea, I'm still delighted by the panorama from the Marienbrücke.

My fairy-tale trip continues east with Linderhof Palace, the smallest of Ludwig II's fantasy buildings and yet the most sumptuous. The formal gardens and their water features are inspired by those of Versailles, while among the estate's follies, a Moroccan house and a Moorish pavilion demonstrate non-European influences, and the Venus Grotto has been laid out like a set from Wagner's *Tannhäuser*. Linderhof was the only castle completed during Ludwig II's lifetime, and the monarch loved to spend time here.

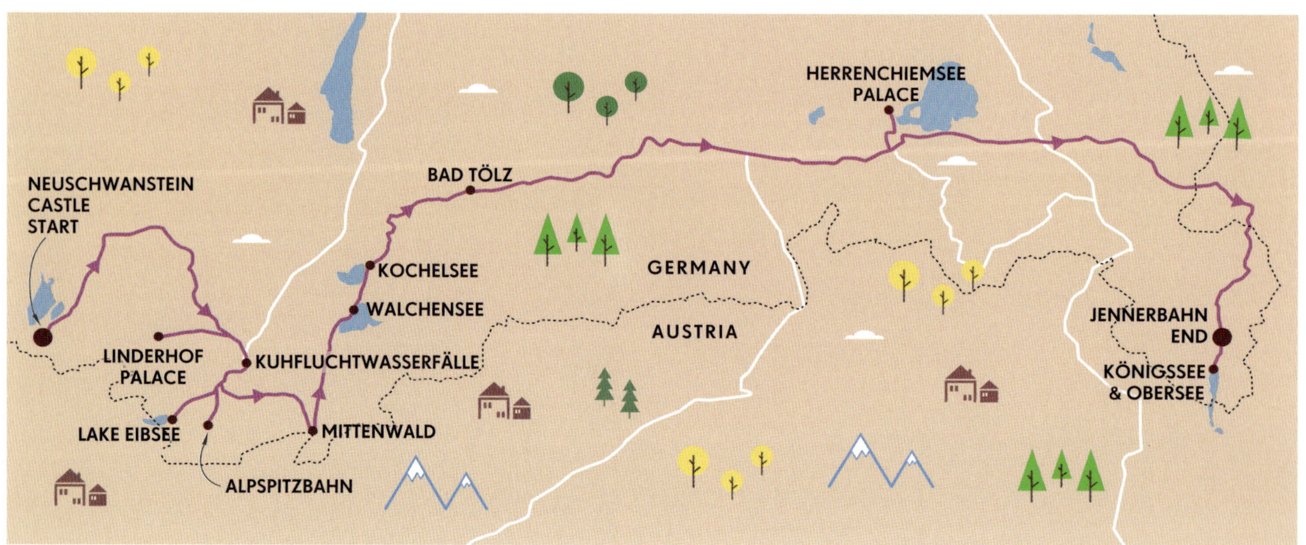

I return to the camper van, waiting for me in the car park, planning to spend the afternoon in the Partnach Gorge, some 30km (19 miles) away. As I refuel in Farchant, an attendant informs me that access to the gorge is temporarily closed due to falling rocks. He recommends instead a hike to the Kuhfluchtwasserfälle, waterfalls in the Ester Mountains above Farchant. A few minutes later, I'm locking the van at the start of the walk. After 45 minutes on a signposted path lined with benches, shelters and wooden sculptures, I reach the beautiful waterfalls and continue on a steeper, more challenging path that leads to an incredible view of the verdant Farchant Valley.

Back at the vehicle, it's time to look for a place to sleep. Unfortunately, there aren't many nice spots authorised for overnight stays in the area, and campsites are prohibitively expensive. So I stop in a public car park, 10km (6 miles) to the south, in Grainau. It's going to be cold so I install the thermal insulation curtains, turn on the gas heater for a few hours, then turn it off when it's time to slip into bed with a hot water bottle.

Early in the morning, a thin layer of frost covers the windows. I turn on the heating again and the water heater and wait in the warmth of my bed. Feeling sore after yesterday's hike, I do some stretching outside. I've decided to take it easy today – when you're travelling alone, it's important to take care of yourself and watch out for small signs of injury or illness.

Just 4km (2.5 miles) away, I take the Alpspitzbahn cable car to the summit of Osterfelderkopf, 2050m (6726ft) above sea level. A steel platform, named AlpspiX, juts out over a 1000m (3281ft) void, offering spectacular views. The most beautiful peaks in the Bavarian Alps are here, including, on my left, the Zugspitze, Germany's highest peak at 2962m (9718ft). I take the time to stroll around and continue the adventure by climbing a little higher.

After this breath of fresh air, it's time to return to the foothills for an 8km (5 mile) walk around Lake Eibsee, whose smooth surface reflects the Zugspitze. The turquoise hues of the water are mesmerising. I then take the B2 road to the town of Mittenwald, 30km (19 miles) away. This quaint village, whose main street is bordered by a stream, is home to a beautiful church and plenty of pretty houses with exteriors covered in frescoes, sometimes with a trompe-l'œil effect. The Karwendel Massif, which marks the border with Austria, rises in the background, as if watching over the village. It's possible to get there by cable car, but I prefer to visit the Leutasch Gorge on foot before heading to the Walchensee and Kochelsee lakes, where I plan to spend the night.

The next day is dedicated to the last and largest palace built by Ludwig – Herrenchiemsee, the 'Bavarian Versailles', located on a large island in Lake Chiemsee. On the way (about 100km/62 miles via the B472), I stop off in the old town of Bad Tölz to try a traditional Bavarian breakfast, *Weisswurstfrühstück*, white sausages made from veal, pork and spices, served with a

FALLER-KLAMM-BRÜCKE

Not far from the Austrian border, 15km (9 miles) south of Lenggries, the Faller-Klamm-Brücke is a road bridge built in 1957 over Lake Sylvenstein. The view is unobstructed and engrossing. The turquoise water contrasts with the lush vegetation of the hills behind, making the forest landscape feel a bit like Canada. Two car parks allow you to extend your time here with a picnic or a swim.

Below: Weisswurstfrühstück. Above: Faller-Klamm-Brücke. Opposite: Herrenchiemsee Castle. Page 169, from top: Neuschwanstein castle; Königssee.

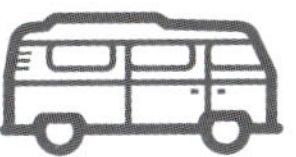

ROAD MAP

Start // Neuschwanstein Castle
Finish // Jennerbahn
Distance // 344km (214 miles)
Recommended duration // 10-to-12 days
When to go // Late summer/early autumn for the tree colours
Culinary specialities // *Weisswurstfrühstück* (white sausage and pretzel), *knödel* (potato dumplings), *leberkäse* (kind of meatloaf)

THE PERFECT SLEEP SPOT

Description // Large flat gravel lot surrounded by forest
GPS coordinates // 47.477024, 11.236279
Light pollution // None
Access // Easy
Facilities // None
Parking // 10 pitches
Little extras // Possibility of walking or cycling. Close to the Austrian border.

'It's time to return to the foothills for a walk around Lake Eibsee, whose smooth surface reflects the Zugspitze.'

pretzel. Stomach full, I park at Chiemsee's pier from where boats leave for the castle, whose Hall of Mirrors and gardens are further reminders of the Bavarian king's admiration for the home of Louis XIV. Ludwig only spent around ten days in the palace, however, dying before its completion and having spent more on it than on Neuschwanstein and Linderhof combined.

My German Alpine Road journey ends in style at lovely Königssee, a lake surrounded by high cliffs. A wide range of activities is on offer and I choose to take an electric boat across the water to the pilgrimage church of St Bartholomew. Then, taking to the skies on the Jennerbahn cable car, I contemplate the German peaks one last time at the end of my trip. **AL**

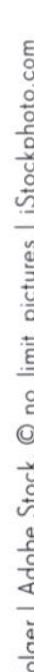

Opposite: Incles green valley, Principality of Andorra.

MORE LIKE THIS
MOUNTAIN HIGH

THE TATRAS (SLOVAKIA)

The Tatras, in the inner Carpathian mountain range, are ideal for hiking. Park your camper van near the breathtakingly beautiful glacial lake of Štrbské Pleso. From here, hike north through the forest (approximately three hours) to Popradské Pleso, another attractive lake. If you're feeling fit, continue with the tough ascent of Sedlo pod Ostrvou (1966m/6450ft), from where you'll have a fantastic view of Lake Poprad, surrounded by the Mala Basta and Kopky peaks. Drive on to Belianska Cave, famous for its stalactites, water features and acoustics. Continue with the Treetop Walk Bachledka, a canopy-high route over some 600m (1969ft) of footbridges through the forests of Pieniny National Park.

Start // Štrbské Pleso
Finish // Treetop Walk Bachledka
Distance // 137km (85 miles)
More information // slovakia.travel

HARZ REGION (GERMANY)

Travelling through the mountainous landscape of Harz National Park means venturing into a land of of legends. Start this loop to the north of the park in the pretty towns of Goslar, Wernigerode and Quedlinburg. All three feature traditional half-timbered architecture. Then move on to Hexentanzplatz, a plateau overlooking the Harz Valley that is an ancient Saxon place of worship and the subject of many superstitions. Treat yourself to a hike through thick deciduous and coniferous forests, between rock piles and cliff faces. Immerse yourself in the silence of the peat bogs, before visiting the Barbarossa Cave, the largest anhydrite rock cave in Europe. Then head north to discover Mt Brocken, 1141m (3743ft) high. Park your vehicle and climb a streamside path to enjoy views over the region, before completing this loop in Goslar.

Start/Finish // Goslar
Distance // 254km (158 miles)
More information // nationalpark-harz.de

PRINCIPALITY OF ANDORRA

In the heart of the Pyrenees, the Principality of Andorra is a wonderful corner of nature that can be discovered by camper van. Park at Grau Roig and gaze at the mountains that frame the Pessons Cirque. The lakes that dot the area can be explored on foot. Then it's on to the Incles Valley, with its traditional houses and green meadows where horses and cows graze. Return to the road and park at Engolasters Lake, before setting off on foot into the Madriu-Perafita-Claror glacial valley, a road-free, World Heritage-listed pastoral jewel. The 800m (2625ft) ascent is gentle, climbing through a landscape of rock faces, alpine meadows, glaciers and lakes. Drive to picturesque villages such as Pal and Ordino, and end your stay with a climb to the three Tristaina lakes.

Start // Pessons Cirque
Finish // Tristaina Lakes
Distance // 81km (50 miles)
More information // visitandorra.com

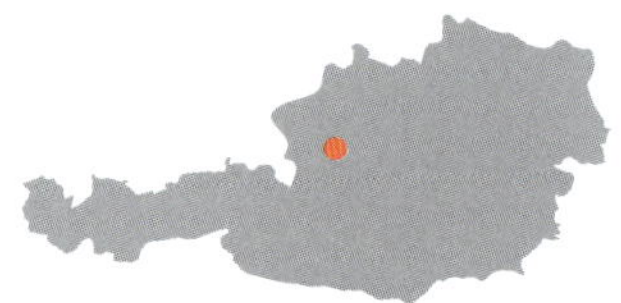

AUSTRIAN NATURE ESCAPE

Take a drive through lakes and mountains, discovering nature's grandeur along the awesome Grossglockner High Alpine Road.

I'm planning my Austrian road trip from the Graz public library. I could be doing this from the camper, but I love the smell of books, and as I gather information and map out my itinerary, my mind is already travelling – a foretaste of the adventure to come. I know I'll never be able to see it all, so I make choices, especially as I want to leave room for the unexpected, taking advantage of the freedom my rolling home gives me. The gist of the plan though is simple – a green escape between lakes and mountains, from Graz to the alpine landscapes of the Hohe Tauern National Park.

On my way to Grüner See, a lake 80km (50 miles) northwest of Graz, is the spellbinding region of Styria, Austria's green heart. Through the van window, I can see cows sunning themselves in the pastures. From the starting point for hikes to the lake, deep in the mountains, I set off through the forest, surrounded by birdsong, when reflections begin to dance in the trees. This is the Grüner See, and what a sight it is – a vast mirror where the landscape splits into two. Its pure water comes from the melting snow of the mountains around it ,meaning in spring the lake is at its highest level and submerges everything in its path: trails, benches, pontoons. Come the end of summer and the water is receding, disappearing completely in winter.

After a picnic surrounded by nature, I drive west again to the Hallstättersee, another lake, this one in the southern Salzkammergut region. After 100km (62 miles) on the A9, it's time for a break at the Wörschach Gorge whose footbridges wind through strange rock formations and past magnificent waterfalls. Then it's less than an hour to the lake. From the town of Obertraun onwards, the road follows a fabulous route on which specially designed areas allow you to stop and enjoy the panorama of this stretch of water surrounded by mountains. Finally, I park in Hallstatt – in a large private car park which has a sort of letterbox for dropping off donations. – have dinner and settle into bed with a book.

Next morning, a familiar pounding on the roof wakes me up – I don't have to open the curtains to know it's raining. With a grimace, I motivate myself to get out anyway where the smell of wet nature is actually a delight, encouraging a smile under my umbrella. That said, my plan to visit the Five Fingers lookout to take in its view over Hallstättersee has been washed away by the downpour. Even so, I have to admit that the mist lends a mysterious charm to the village, calm and peaceful in the

STRECHAU CASTLE

To the southeast of Linz, Styria's second-largest castle, 11th-century Strechau, stands on a rocky spur, accesible through the gate of the former bastion. Guided tours reveal some of the fortress' furnished rooms, including the beautifully frescoed ballroom, and some farmhouses. There's also a fine collection of vintage cars from Austrian brand, Steyr.

'As I gather information and map out my itinerary, my mind is already travelling – a foretaste of the adventure to come.'

absence of tourists. I make my way through the narrow streets among the chalets built into the mountainside. You've got to have strong leg muscles to live on the highest slopes here. In a pastry shop, I taste my first *Schaumrolle*, a puff pastry roll filled with whipped cream, then end my exploration of Hallstatt with the ossuary, containing over 600 hand-painted skulls, inscribed with the date of death and the name of the deceased.

Not far from the lake, the old salt mines or the Dachstein Cave with its sparkling ice formations are possible stops, but I chose to head straight for Werfen and another ice cave, the world's largest accessible ice cave in fact. After 70km (43 miles) on Route 166, I reach the shuttle and cable car that take visitors to a platform where the footpath to the cave begins. Only the first kilometre of the cave's 42km (26 miles) is open to the public but that's enough for this cathedral of ice to work its magic.

The mythical Grossglockner High Alpine Road, highlight of Hohe Tauern National Park, is next on the itinerary – and I can't wait. For 48km (30 miles), it's a succession of vertiginous waterfalls, peaks over 3000m (9843ft) and lakes. To see the sunrise over the mountains from the Edelweissspitze observation tower, I sleep in the car at the entrance to the park, next to the toll booth. The following day, I present my ticket, purchased online, and receive a map in return. The route starts with numerous hairpin bends up to the pass, the wide, pleasant road blending harmoniously into the landscape. The camper is coughing a bit, but I know it's good for the drive. The first rays of sunshine light up the lovely winding road I've travelled and the many peaks that surround me. With the whole day ahead, there's no need to rush. Every bend offers breathtaking views, so I slow down to make sure I don't miss any of the scenery: Fuscher Törl Pass; Fuscher Lake. There are museums and restaurants along the way too, but nothing beats the pleasure I get from cooking for myself at Hochtor Pass, the road's highest point at 2505m (8219ft).

Opposite: Grüner See. Above: Heiligenblut church. Below: Schaumrolle. Page 175: Grossglockner route.

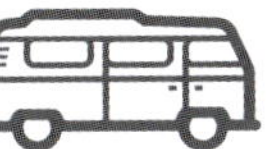

ROAD MAP

Start // Graz
Finish // Heiligenblut
Distance // 400km (249 miles)
Recommended duration // 7-to-10 days
When to go // The Grossglockner High Alpine Road is open from May to November, weather permitting
Culinary specialities // *Apfelstrudel* (apple, raisin, walnut and cinnamon pastry), *schaumrolle* (puff pastry roll with whipped cream)

THE PERFECT SLEEP SPOT

Description // Beautiful, picturesque campsite in Heiligenblut
GPS coordinates // 47.037201, 12.8385
Light pollution // Camping lights
Access // Easy, by road
Facilities // Showers and toilets, wi-fi, electricity, washing machine, water and drainage.
Parking // 50 pitches
Little extras // A warm welcome and a good restaurant, free choice of lawn location, superb mountain views.

Coming out of a tunnel, I turn right towards the Kaiser-Franz-Josefs-Höhe observation platform and am left speechless as I approach the Pasterze, the longest glacier in the Eastern Alps. The Grossglockner route ends with the tall spire of the church in Heiligenblut, where I spend the night in a campsite, dreaming of natural wonders and prolonging the joys of the day. **AL**

Opposite: Pulkkilanharju bridge, Finland.

MORE LIKE THIS
CLASSIC ROUTES

LAKE PÄIJÄNNE (FINLAND)

Enjoy a journey on one of Finland's most scenic roads, along Lake Päijänne. Bookended by the towns of Lahti to the south and Jyväskylä to the north, this is the country's second-largest lake, stretching some 135km (84 miles). Take Route 314 along the densely wooded eastern shore to discover charming villages and countless hiking trails and to cross the narrow, 8km-long (5 miles) Pulkkilanharju Bridge. Your mobile home will be surrounded by water on both sides. Park at the end of the bridge and take your inflatable canoe out to visit KelvennelsIand, made up of craggy rocks and sandy eskers (glacier-formed formations). Spot protected birds and bivouac at one of the many campfire sites on the road to Jyväskylä.

Start // Lahti
Finish // Jyväskylä
Distance // 181km (112 miles)
More information // nationalparks.fi/paijannenp

THE WILD ATLANTIC WAY (IRELAND)

Take an unforgettable trip from Donegal to Downpatrick Head on part of Ireland's Wild Atlantic Way. Strips of land extending proudly into the ocean will appeal to surfers and wilderness enthusiasts alike. Leave Donegal for Bundoran, the country's surfing capital, then drive to the Mullaghmore Peninsula, where you can admire (not-open-to-the-public) Classiebawn Castle and perhaps spot whales and dolphins. Continue along the coast and park on Streedagh Beach for a meal overlooking the ocean. Then it's time for some history at Lissadell House, on Sligo Bay, a Neoclassical manor house where Irish revolutionary Constance Markievicz lived. Finish with the breathtaking cliffs of Downpatrick Head – but not until you've tried a surf session on Strandhill Beach.

Start // Donegal
Finish // Downpatrick Head
Distance // 193km (120 miles)
More information // ireland.com

THE OUR VALLEY (BELGIUM)

A camper is ideal for touring the Our Valley, a 100km (62 mile) loop through rolling countryside dotted with forests. From the commune of St Vith, take your time following the signposted road to discover quaint villages and their heritage, such as the 18th-century carved cross at Amel. There are plenty of other opportunities to take a break: do some forest-bathing on the Heppenbach art and nature trail; try mare's milk at the Kessler farm in Honsfeld; visit Burg-Reuland Castle; admire the Gothic chapel of St Hubert Chapel in Weweler. Continue to the Monument of Europe, where Germany, Luxembourg and Belgium meet, then take a short foray across the plains of the Grand Duchy to visit the Luxembourg hamlet of Weiswampach before returning to St Vith.

Start/Finish // St Vith
Distance // 100km (62 miles)
More information // ostbelgien.eu

CENTRAL AND EASTERN EUROPE

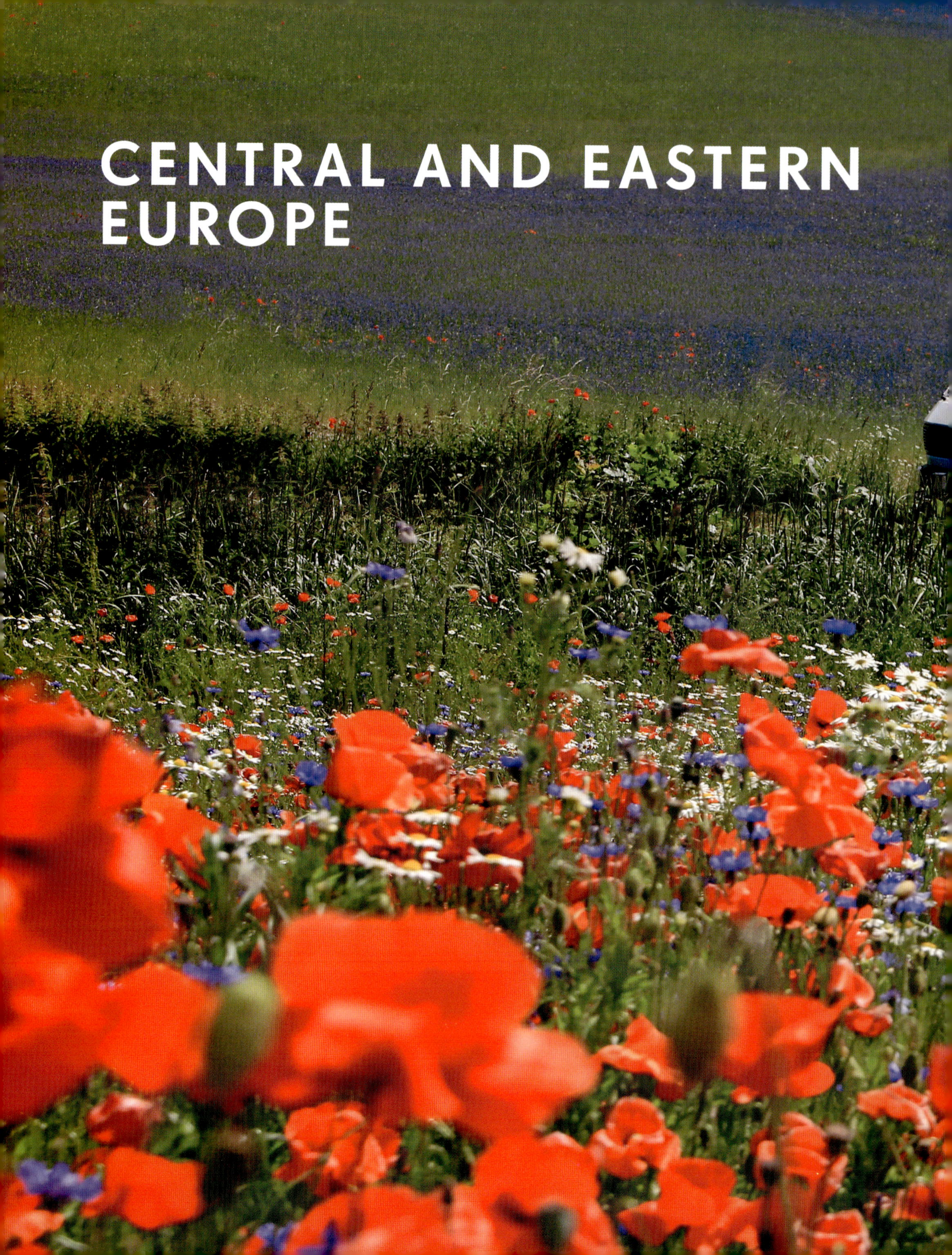

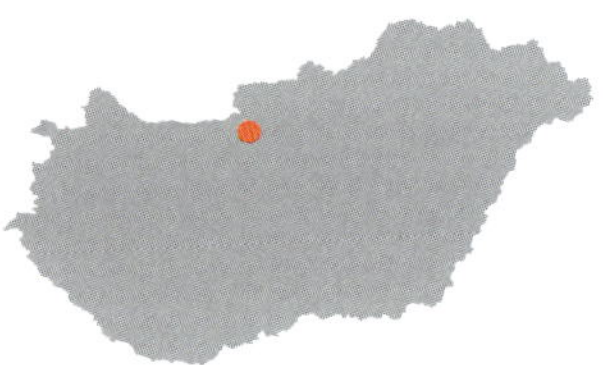

DISCOVERING HUNGARY

There's a lot to discover in western Hungary, from Lake Balaton to Hollókő and the country's capital, Budapest, 'Pearl of the Danube'.

It's from Croatia that I enter Hungary, for a road trip that will take me from the southwest of the country to Hollókő, not far from the Slovak border. My first stop is Héviz, where I intend to enjoy the benefits of Europe's largest thermal lake. The country is rich in hot springs and 'taking the waters' is a long-standing tradition here which I'm keen to follow.

When I arrive at the lake, the air temperature is 10°C (50°F), and steam forms a cloud on the surface of the water. Equipped with a towel, I step out into the cold in my bikini. A sign indicates that the water is 34°C (93°F) inside the pavilions, and 28°C (82°F) outside. The slight smell of sulphur I notice is characteristic of natural hot springs. What isn't so characteristic is the gentle caress I'm surprised to feel on my legs – the lake, 38m (125ft) deep, is home to harmless fish which are brushing against me. It's getting dark, and as the other guests begin to leave, I'm left alone outside, enjoying the peaceful lake and the sunset until the very last moment. Once dried off, it's back to the camper for a quiet drive along route 71 to one of many spots on the north shore of immense Lake Balaton.

With a surface area of 592 sq km (229 sq miles), Balaton is Europe's largest freshwater lake, its shores lined with around 130 beaches offering all kinds of water sports. I stop off at the ancient volcanic island of Tihany, which today forms a small peninsula in the lake. A Benedictine abbey, surrounded by a pretty village, has an exceptional view, while the rest of the peninsula is a nature reserve where hills alternate with marshy meadows. In the afternoon, I continue northeast along the lake, the autumn sun reflecting off its surface.

After about 40km (25 miles), and having left Balaton behind, I reach the village of Hajmáskér. An impressive building draws the eye here, a monumental barracks built at the end of the 19th century, now totally abandoned. Looking at its ruined towers, you can imagine the heyday this architectural marvel must have enjoyed under the Austro-Hungarian Empire. I like to visit, with due caution, disused places like this, in the spirit of urban exploration, but their decaying atmosphere always leaves a bitter taste. I comfort myself in the nearby town of Székesfehérvár with a good goulash, the beef and paprika stew which is the soul of Hungarian cuisine. *Jó étvágyat*! Enjoy your meal!

After a night on the edge of Sárpentele Forest Park, I wake up with the urge to follow its 2km (1.5 mile) fitness trail before planning my itinerary for the rest of the day. On the map, I

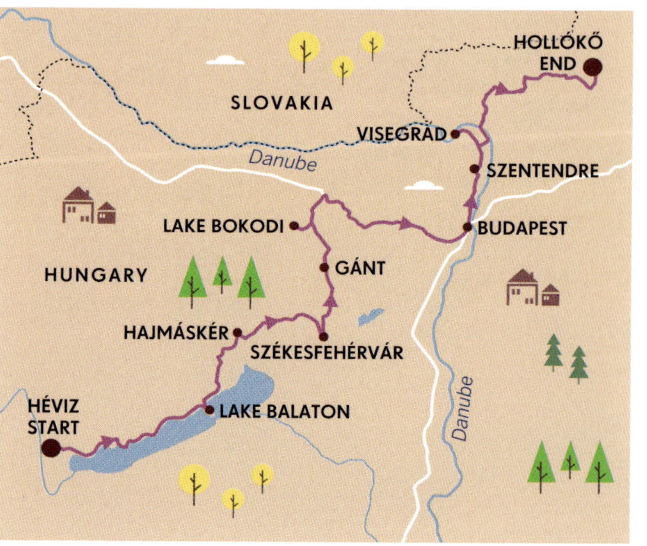

© Andras_csontos | Adobe Stock, © Alexandra Lam

notice the floating village of Lake Bokodi, some 60km (37 miles) to the north, and decide to head straight for it. Crossing green plains that go on as far as the eye can see, suddenly, around Gánt, an unreal red landscape gets my attention. I immediately turn around, venturing down a small dirt road until I seemingly arrive on Mars. It's actually a former bauxite quarry, whose undulating red slopes contrast sharply with my white camper van. Unfortunately, the quarry's museum is closed, but I spend several hours marvelling at this otherworldly landscape, delighted by this unexpected discovery.

Finally continuing on my way, I reach the floating village of Lake Bokodi at the end of a bumpy road. Small, colourful fishing huts on stilts are linked to each other and to the mainland by wooden walkways. Only a factory chimney in the background detracts from the tranquillity of this picturesque place.

I'm only an hour from Budapest on the M1 motorway now, but before getting back behind the wheel, I use an app to check the air quality in the capital that day – in the event of a smog alert (issued 24 hours or even 48 hours in advance), access to certain major Hungarian cities may be prohibited to the most polluting vehicles.

On arrival in the capital, I park the van near the Danube, in the car park (for which a charge is made during the day) of the Gellért Baths, the famous Art Nouveau thermal baths. Temperatures have been dropping since this morning, but fortunately there's nothing easier in a camper than opening your wardrobe and finding a change of outfit. Well wrapped up, I hasten to the top of nearby Gellèrt Hill where the Liberty Monument stands, a tribute to the Soviet soldiers who fell in the liberation of Budapest in 1945. Unfortunately, the clouds deprive me of a sunset over the city.

My evening exploration continues along the banks of the river. Numerous sights are illuminated, including the spectacular parliament building, topped by a dome and bristling with spires. Away from the Danube, the old Jewish quarter is home to some of Hungary's most popular underground party venues, *romkocsmák* ('ruin bars'), such as Szimpla Kert, an eccentric pub housed in a huge building featuring graffiti, cast-iron bathtubs and works of art.

There's plenty to do in Budapest and my second day is spent visiting its different neighbourhoods, religious buildings, traditional cafes and covered market. Leaving the capital, I hit the road again, heading into the Danube Bend region, north of the city. First port of call is Szentendre, some 20km (12 miles) away, which has been home to an artists' colony since the 1920s. Various museums house collections of ceramics, sacred art and design – enough to keep you busy for a whole day. Next up is Visegrád and its medieval fortress which dominates a loop of the Danube. Then it's on to my final destination, the tiny village of Hollókő, a bastion of traditional Hungarian culture close to the Slovakian border. **AL**

THE HUNGARIAN PARLIAMENT BUILDING

The seat of Hungary's National Assembly (Parlament or Országház) sits on the eastern bank of the Danube in Pest. This national landmark, completed at the beginning of the 20th century, is 268m (879ft) long and has 10 courtyards, 29 staircases and 691 rooms. Its Neogothic towers are intentionally reminiscent of London's Palace of Westminster.

Below: Former bauxite quarry near Gánt Gánt. Above: Budapest parliament. Opposite: Village on Lake Bokodi. Page 183, from top: Tihany Abbey and Lake Balaton; Sárpentele Forest Park.

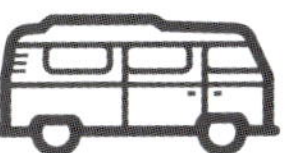

ROAD MAP

Start // Héviz
Finish // Hollókő
Distance // 514km (319 miles)
Recommended duration // 7-to-10 days
When to go // Autumn for the beautiful colours
Culinary specialities // Goulash, *kürtöskalács* (spit-roasted cake), *lángos* (fried bread)

THE PERFECT SLEEP SPOT

Description // Quiet campsite on the banks of the Danube with mountain views, west of Visegrád
GPS coordinates // 47.81619, 18.86032
Light pollution // None
Access // Easy
Facilities // Fully equipped campsite
Parking // 10 pitches
Little extras // Bike paths along the Danube in the immediate vicinity, with the option of taking the train to visit Visegrád Castle.

'I reach the floating village of Lake Bokodi . . . small, colourful fishing huts on stilts are linked to each other and to the mainland by wooden walkways.'

Opposite, from top: Badacsony mountain; Rural landscape in Hungary.

MORE LIKE THIS
HUNGARY IN DEPTH

THE PUSZTA PLAIN

Before taking your camper across the vast horizons of the Puszta, the pastoral plain that stretches across eastern Hungary, start with a visit to Kecskemét, its capital. Enjoy the smell of the apricot trees and appreciate the bewitching architecture, particularly the town hall with its salmon-coloured facade and mosaic roof, before driving to peaceful Lake Tisza whose banks are ideal for a picnic break. Then follow Route 33 into Hortobágy National Park. Try to visit this vast patchwork of steppes and pastures, punctuated by thatched-roof villages, in autumn for the spectacle of the crane migration. The road trip's final stop, Debrecen, is the country's second-largest city and best known for its large, pale-yellow, Neoclassical church. On the outskirts, various car parks in the immense public garden of Great Forest Park welcome you for a night amid greenery.

Start // Kecskemét
Finish // Debrecen
Distance // 231km (144 miles)
More information // hnp.hu

AROUND BADACSONY MOUNTAIN

The Badacsony basalt massif borders the northwestern shore of Lake Balaton and is famous for its dry white wine. Get your visit off to a flying start by exploring the Szentbékkálla Sea of Stones on foot, a fascinating geological landscape of polished pebbles and strange, gigantic rock formations. Nearby, climb the heights of Mt Badacsony where an immense viewpoint offers 360° views of the surrounding countryside. You won't regret the effort. Then return to your camper and head for Lake Balaton. You'll find plenty of places to park for the night in a peaceful setting with a view over the water, including near Szépkilátó. A few kilometres west, don't miss the huge Baroque Festetics Palace in Keszthely, while further north lie the ruins of the Sümeg fort. Looping south a stop at Csobánc Castle, from which you can see Lake Balaton, will bring you full circle.

Start // Szentbékkálla
Finish // Csobánc Castle
Distance // 98km (61 miles)
More information // visithungary.com

IN THE HEART OF THE CSONGRÁD-CSANÁD

The Csongrád-Csanád region lies in the very south of Hungary, not far from the Serbian and Romanian borders. Crossed by the Tisza and Maros rivers, Szeged is the cultural capital of the Great Plain, worth a stop for its Art Nouveau buildings. Then get back behind the wheel and follow Route 47 to Hódmezővásárhely, a village of Baroque houses renowned for its pottery. Nearby, the marshes and reedbeds of Mártély offer a pleasant interlude with nature. On the outskirts of this town, park by the river for the night. Next cross the Pusztaszer floodplains to Ópusztaszer Heritage Park for a trip back to the 890s CE – the era of the Hungarian conquest of the Carpathians, as witnessed by the unusual stone yurts. Finally, set course for Mórahalom to wallow in its thermal waters, before meeting the buffalo of Nagyszéksós Reserve.

Start // Szeged
Finish // Nagyszéksós Reserve
Distance // 117km (73 miles)
More information // visithungary.com

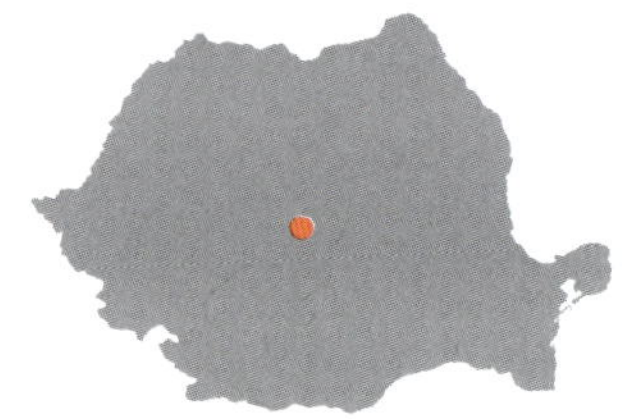

TRANSYLVANIA ROAD TRIP

Travel to the edge of the Carpathians across the legendary lands of Transylvania.

While my T4 prefers straight, level roads, I think I'm more partial to mountain routes which take you around bend after bend, up into the clouds. My travel partners Gina and José won't contradict me on this point. Having arrived from Bulgaria a few days earlier, we headed for the Carpathian Mountains to get a bit of height. The plan is to cross Transylvania from southeast to northwest, stopping here and there in the region's prettiest towns. Fortresses, historic cities and rugged landscapes will all feature in our adventure through the heart of Romania.

Our trip begins in Sinaia, a little jewel nestling at the bottom of the Prahova Valley, halfway between the Bucegi and Baiu mountains. The 'Pearl of the Carpathians' is home to two castles: Peleș, with its pointed towers reaching for the sky; and Pelișor, a less imposing fortification whose exterior is reminiscent of an Alpine chalet. We also visit the town's monastery, built in the late 17th century as a tribute to Egypt's Mt Sinai. This architectural ensemble includes two churches in milky and ochre tones, and gave its name to the town. The three of us have fallen for Sinaia and are looking forward to the rest of the journey after this auspicious start.

Following Route 1 northwards for 50km (31 miles), we enter Brașov, a town that attracts plenty of tourists who, like us, have come to lose themselves in the Carpathians. Many of the buildings are well worth a visit, including the sober, slender and immaculately white St Nicholas Orthodox Church, the Black Church, a huge Gothic cathedral built of grey stone and covered with a brown roof, and the town hall opposite, with its pale yellow facades supporting the clock tower.

The real reason we've come this far though is to see Castle Dracula, officially known as Bran Castle, which lies some 30km (19 miles) to the southwest. The castle is very busy, which makes us reluctant to buy a ticket. Parked under the fortress, a little online research reveals that many rooms are not open to the public. What's more, we learn that the infamous Vlad the Impaler, inspiration for Count Dracula, probably never even stayed here. We're extremely disappointed. So we turn our backs on the thick walls and crimson-tiled turrets, as picturesque as they are, and prepare a feast in the back of the camper. A tin of lentils, a little couscous, a few slices of bread and some sheep's milk cheese – a menu that is unanimously

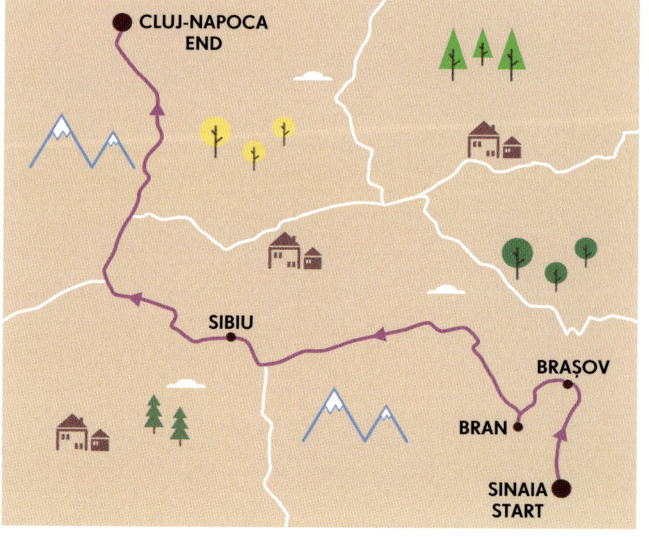

'The 'Pearl of the Carpathians' is home to two castles: Peleș, with its pointed towers reaching for the sky; and Pelișor . . . whose exterior is reminiscent of an Alpine chalet.'

appreciated by our small team, and which is the ideal meal for avoiding cooking and washing up.

Lunch over, the trip continues westwards to Sibiu, one of Transylvania's largest cities, 140km (87 miles) away. En route, we come across a stream lined with large pebbles and are tempted to enjoy a quick dip in the water (takes care of showering for the day), even if that water comes from the surrounding rocky peaks and is as icy cold as it is clear.

Bodies refreshed, we head for Sibiu, Romania's cultural hub thanks to the numerous festivals – opera, cinema, theatre – it hosts each year. This former Saxon stronghold is also a city renowned for its elegance, where pastel-hued houses line the various beautifully cobbled squares of the upper town. In the background, the Făgăraș Mountains are a looming reminder that the Carpathians are not far away.

We have to follow part of this mountain range to get to the city of Cluj-Napoca, our ultimate stop, and, contrary to our usual habits, we opt for the freeway (A1 then A10, for 175km/109 miles) – Romania is large and the camper van is beginning to show signs of wear and tear, so we decide to make the drive as easy as possible. It takes just two hours to reach the country's second-largest city, and another one of its most important cultural centres. From Baroque to Rococo to Neogothic, the ancient walled city of Cluj is full of architectural wonders. On Union Sq, the heart of the city, a swarm of pigeons is bustling about and the cafe terraces are packed. We didn't expect so much life and are delighted to have stopped here, lingering for a while around St Michael's Catholic Church, with its red roof and sand-coloured stonework, one of Romania's most impressive Gothic buildings. With no fixed route in mind, we explore the surrounding area and arrive at Muzeului Sq. Its medieval appeal, many restaurants and pedestrianised streets complete the pretty picture Cluj, and Romania in general, have presented us with. This country is far from being the rather austere place we'd imagined it to be. **AD**

THE LEGEND OF DRACULA

Bram Stoker's 1897 *Dracula*, the story of an immortal vampire with a thirst for fresh blood, was inspired by Vlad III the Impaler, 15th-century Prince of Wallachia. Nicknamed Drăculea ('son of the dragon'), Vlad, if not a vampire, was a bloodthirsty tyrant whose record of violence is shocking.

Opposite, clockwise from left: Sinaia monastery fresco; Peleș castle; Pelișor castle. Page 189, clockwise from top: Sibiu old town; T4 in the woods; Bran castle.

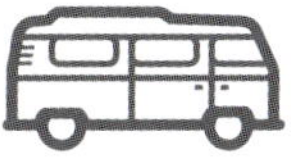

ROAD MAP

Start // Sinaia
Finish // Cluj-Napoca
Distance // 395km (245 miles)
Recommended duration // 5-to-7 days
When to go // Late spring or summer, for milder weather than the rest of the year
Culinary specialities // *Papanași* (cottage cheese fritters covered with red fruit jam)

THE PERFECT SLEEP SPOT

Description // Wild location in Tureni Gorge, 31km (19 miles) before Cluj-Napoca
GPS coordinates // 46.605934233411446, 23.7119547251663217
Access // Easy, via E81 then 72 from Turda
Activities // Hiking
Visitor numbers // These gorges are much less touristy than the neighbouring Turzii Gorge.
Little extras // Direct access to the Tureni Reserve

Opposite, from top: Brno, Czech Republic; Casino de Constanța, Romania.

MORE LIKE THIS
GO EAST!

A TRIP TO SLOVAKIA

In the heart of Slovakia, the historic town of Banská Bystrica, at the foot of the mountains, is an excellent place to immerse yourself in the local culture. Sample its gastronomy in one of the restaurants in the central square, with its refined architecture, before driving along routes 66 and 72 to get to Muránska Planina National Park. Largely covered by forest, this vast area of rough terrain boasts a multitude of signposted trails, allowing you to get up close to its rich biodiversity. Next, visit Košice, the country's second-largest city. Particularly fine are the old town with its St Elisabeth's Cathedral, the impressive Jakab Palace and the pastel paintwork of the buildings' facades. End your journey on the shores of the Vel'ká Domaša reservoir, where you can fall asleep right next to the water.

Start // Banská Bystrica
Finish // Vel'ká Domaša reservoir
Distance // 289km (180 miles)
More information // slovakia.travel

AROUND EASTERN ROMANIA

Embark on an adventure to the end of Europe, beginning in the lovely Romanian town of Constanța, on the shores of the Black Sea. Its large beach and pleasant harbour make it a favourite spot for vanlifers visiting the Dobroudja region. Head north to the fishing village of Jurilovca, surrounded by several lagoons and separated from the sea by a thin strip of sand. A little further on, you'll come to Tulcea, the gateway to the Danube Delta. Get closer to the port and take a boat trip for birdwatching (ibis, pelicans). Finally, you can drive along the St George, a branch of the Danube that winds its way to Murighiol in the marshlands of the southeastern delta, waving at the local fishers as you go.

Start // Constanța
Finish // Murighiol
Distance // 186km (116 miles)
More information // romaniatourism.com

GETAWAY IN THE CZECH REPUBLIC

It's hard not to fall for the timeless charm of Brno and its warm atmosphere. Between its medieval fortress and its old town hall tower, you'll find a condensed version of the best the Czech Republic has to offer. The second leg of the journey is just as charming. The small university town of Olomouc boasts wonderful religious buildings, as well as large parks where you can stroll freely. Disconnect from the world for a day or two in the neighbouring Morava Plain – its remote woodlands provide plenty of perfect spots for a sweet night in a camper. When you're ready to move on, head east on Route 1 and make a brief foray into the wetlands along the Oder River. Finally, park in Ostrava and take a walk through the maze of pedestrian streets in its historic centre, visiting the sand-coloured Romanesque cathedral on the way.

Start // Brno
Finish // Ostrava
Distance // 242km (150 miles)
More information // visitczechrepublic.com

FROM SAXON SWITZERLAND TO BOHEMIAN PARADISE

Journey through the mountainous region between Germany and the Czech Republic, discovering gorges and fantastic rock formations.

Don't let their names fool you. Saxon Switzerland and Bohemian Switzerland can be found in Germany and the Czech Republic respectively, located in the Elbe Massif, which extends on both sides of the border. Starting from Dresden, capital of the German state of Saxony, this route crosses the massif and then continue southeastwards to the Bohemian section, all linked by a succession of exceptional rock formations.

The city of Dresden, surrounded by hills and criss-crossed by the meandering river, is sometimes referred to as 'Florence on the Elbe'. It was largely destroyed by bombing in 1945, but a long and painstaking rebuilding process has restored many of its monuments. I stroll through the Baroque old town, visiting the famous Frauenkirche – a church destroyed and rebuilt identically fifty years later – as well as the green vault of the Residenz Palace, home to the treasures of the kings of Saxony, and the famous Opera House. I also make a detour to the Kunsthofpassage to see Heike Böttcher's musical blue house, which 'sings' when it rains.

Retrieving the camper, I look for an overnight spot south of the city, towards Saxon Switzerland. Using the satellite map on my phone, I find a large deserted field and settle in for the night. But just as I'm falling asleep, I'm rudely awakened by the arrival of two other vans – a group of young people with dogs have come out to drink and smoke. Soon, my vehicle is vibrating to the rhythm of their music, blasting out of speakers, and I'm left with no option but to leave this rave and, in my pyjamas, at 2am, look for a quieter location for what's left of the night.

In the morning, first stop is the pretty market town of Königstein, 38km (24 miles) southeast of Dresden on a bend in the Elbe, surrounded by rolling forests. Bicycles can be rented here so visitors can take advantage of the cycle path that follows the river, but the area is best known for the 13th-century fortress, perched on a rocky plateau. It can be reached by a 45-minute walk, but, tired after my interrupted night, I choose to drive up

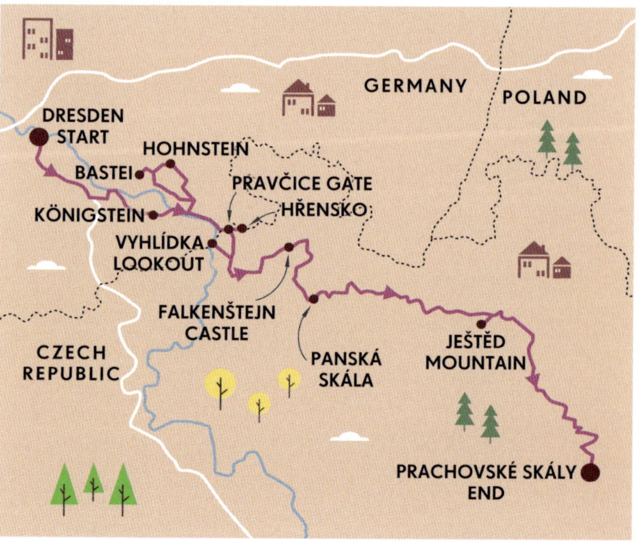

to the fortress' car park – it's well worth a visit, especially for the great view from the top of the ramparts.

Leaving town, the B172 and K8723 lead to Hohnstein, a village on the opposite bank of the Elbe. Sitting in a natural setting, it offers an attractive mix of half-timbered houses, cobbled streets, a small yellow church and a cliff-top castle. After a walk through the village, I grab a bite to eat and enquire about walking options. The tourist office directs me to the Bastei site. Leaving the van at the car park, I set off on a tour of the Schwedenlöcher Gorge. The steep passage through the valley and the trails up and down through the forest are both a challenge and a wonder. As for the walls of the gorge, they're the playground of many climbers.

The incredible Bastei Bridge connects several vertical rock formations and resembles a natural fortress. It's crowded but provides a phenomenal view of the Elbe Valley. Of the three vantage points from which to view the bridge, my favourite is the one at Ferdinandstein, which takes in the whole site (best avoided if you're afraid of heights though, as you have to walk along a precipice on a narrow path to get to it). Back in the camper, I head for Ferienhof Mandry, a farm stay where I've booked a pitch for the night and where I receive a warm welcome.

Leaving Germany in the rearview mirror, the next day it's on to the Czech Republic and Bohemian Switzerland National Park. I take the B172 road eastwards. For drivers, there's one detail that makes crossing the border a notable experience – in the Czech Republic it's compulsory to turn on your dipped headlights, day and night. After 19km (12 miles), I reach Hřensko, a small town with quaint houses that's a starting point for many hikes.

My first expedition will be to the majestic Pravčice Gate, the largest natural sandstone arch in Europe. I park at the Mezní Louka car park and take the Gabrielina Stezca, a flat path which, after an hour's easy walk through the forest, brings me to the famous sight's lookout. There's an admission charge but the vantage point gives you a clear view of the arch and surrounding rock columns. I head back down to Hřensko where I visit the Kamenice Gorge, extending the walking tour with an excursion in a rowing boat.

After taking in a number of other fantastic viewpoints in the national park – the Vyhlídka lookout, overlooking the Elbe, and the ruins of Falkenštejn Castle, sitting above the forest and rock columns – I leave Bohemian Switzerland. Some 24km (15 miles) later, I arrive at Panská Skála, near the town of Kamenický Šenov in northern Bohemia. More extraordinary rock formations await me here, reminding me of the Giant's Causeway in Northern Ireland – hexagonal basalt columns, up to 15m (49ft) high, formed 30 million years ago as a result of volcanic activity.

Less than an hour away, via route 13, I stop in the highest car park on Ještěd mountain, famous for its summit topped by

CLIMBING IN SAXON SWITZERLAND

Saxon Switzerland offers excellent climbing opportunities. With 1106 separate sandstone formations and over 20,000 routes, it's Germany's richest open-air climbing area. Many of these routes are protected as part of the national park, and climbers must rely on their own belay devices and make sure they have the right equipment.

Below: Basalt columns at Panská Skála. Above: Panorama of tthe Pravčická Gate. Opposite: Facades of Dresden. Page 195, from top: Bastei bridge; Forest near Prachovské Skály.

'The steep passage through the valley and the trails up and down through the forest are both a challenge and a wonder. As for the walls of the gorge, they're the playground of many climbers.'

a kind of UFO. This hyperboloid building worthy of a science-fiction film serves as both a hotel and a TV antenna. I discover that it's possible to spend the night in the car park as long as I leave before 9am the next day – perfect. From where I've parked it's only a few steps to the top of the mountain to take in the view. Across the vast panoramaaround me, my gaze wanders southeast, where my adventure in this Bohemian idyll will continue, with promises of more dense forests and dramatic rocks before I arrive in my end-of-the-line destination, Prachovské Skály. **AL**

ROAD MAP

Start // Dresden
Finish // Prachovské Skály
Distance // 255km (158 miles)
Recommended duration // 7-to-10 days
When to go // Spring or autumn for beautiful colours
Culinary specialities // *Dresdner Christstollen* (traditional marzipan cake with dried and candied fruit), *bramborová* (potato, mushroom and carrot soup).

THE PERFECT SLEEP SPOT

Description // Ferienhof Mandry, a farm in the heart of Saxon Switzerland
GPS coordinates // 50.909175, 14.142696
Light pollution // Low
Access // Easy, by road
Facilities // Cold water, electricity and drainage included in the price; other equipment available as an option
Parking // 3 pitches with compulsory reservation via ferienhof-mandry.de
Little extras // Holidays on a farm in the middle of the fields, with a multitude of animals including horses and alpaca. Warm family welcome; fresh local produce available for purchase; horseback riding.

Opposite, from top: Belogradchik fortress, Bulgaria; Aghia Triada monastery, Meteora, Greece; City of Stones, Adršpach, Czech Republic.

MORE LIKE THIS
ROCKS AND HARD PLACES

THE BROUMOVSKO REGION (CZECH REPUBLIC)

The 'City of Stones' in Adršpach, not far from the Polish border, forms an astonishing 3.5km (2 mile) long trail at the foot of high walls and rock formations. Stepping through the Gothic gate built at the entrance to the site in the 19th century, you feel as if you've entered another world. Head to the waterfalls and a crystal-clear lake where you can embark on a boat trip. Continue on to the stone city of Teplice and detour to the Ostaš Nature Reserve – in addition to the spectacle of the rocks themselves here, there's the dizzying view from the top of the cliff and memorable sunsets. Finally, end your stay in East Bohemia at the long ridge of the Broumov Walls, the starting point for excellent hikes to other geological sights.

Start // Adršpach
Finish // Broumov Walls
Distance // 27km (17 miles)
More information // broumovsko.cz

METEORA (GREECE)

From the middle of the Thessalian Plain rise the gigantic rock formations of Meteora. This UNESCO World Heritage Site was once home to as many as 24 monasteries balanced on the peaks or built into the rock faces. Begin with a picnic with a view at the top of the Meteora lookout, above the small town of Kalambaka. Then take your time discovering different roadside viewpoints. Of the five monasteries and one convent still occupied and open to the public, don't miss those of Great Meteoron, Varlaam and Agios Nikolaos Anapafsas. Sleep in the shadow of the Meteora at the Vrachos campsite in Kastraki. Nearly 17km (11 miles) of trails provide access to the monasteries, which are impossible to reach by road. To finish on a refreshing note, head for Lake Plastiras, 63km (39 miles) to the south, for an invigorating swim.

Start // Meteora View
Finish // Lake Plastiras
Distance // 88km (55 miles)
More information // visitmeteora.travel

BELOGRADCHIK (BULGARIA)

In the far northwest of Bulgaria's Vidin region, Belogradchik is an impressive geological landscape, with large masses of singularly shaped sandstone ranging from yellow to red. Start at the namesake fortress, which dates back to Roman times but has been rebuilt several times, from where you can enjoy a breathtaking view of the western slopes of the Balkan Mountains. It's at the wheel that you'll best be able to appreciate these 30km (19 miles) of rock formations in their entirety, parking where you fancy to take a stroll among the boulders. Stop off in the vineyards of Borovitza, then continue your geological exploration with the Venetsa Cave, with its remarkable calcite decorations, followed by the Kozarnika Cave, occupied since the Lower Palaeolithic. Finally, discover Neolithic cave paintings in the Magura Cave.

Start // Belogradchik Fortress
Finish // Magura Cave
Distance // 72km (45 miles)
More information // bulgariatravel.org

BULGARIA FROM LAND TO SEA

From the country's interior to the shores of the Black Sea, this itinerary winds its way through mountains and interesting towns.

Crossing the Greek border, we enter Bulgaria. From the very first kilometres of our journey, which will take us across the country to the Black Sea, it's clear we've entered a very different world. My friends José and Gina seem as surprised as I am to discover how much remains of the Soviet era for a start. Massive, drab buildings adorn the suburbs of Blagoevgrad, a medium-sized university town where we make our first stop.

Experience has taught us not to be fooled by first impressions though, and we decide to set off in search of a livelier, more picturesque area in the city centre. Parking the camper, we're anxious to comply with any local regulations so we inspect the surrounding area carefully: there are no signs of any kind, and none of the cars parked nearby have any kind of disc or sticker. Satisfied we're ok, it's time to explore the heart of Blagoevgrad on foot. The Varosha district, with its old stone houses and

BURGAS

The country's leading port and a major seaside resort, this ancient Roman city is one of the must-see stops on any road trip around Bulgaria. On the to-do list: strolling the lively downtown streets and from the maritime garden to the lighthouse; water sports (jet-skiing, kayaking) and wellness activities; and major events, including an international folklore festival in summer.

'In the centre, gleaming church domes and minarets coexist harmoniously, while enticing scents . . . waft through the streets.'

cobbled streets, is the one that appeals most to us. Delighted by our visit, we return cheerfully to where we'd parked the camper – and discover that the left front wheel is locked in a metal clamp. Impossible to remove. A man comes up to us and translates the notice left on our windscreen: we have to call a premium-rate number. A few minutes later, another individual approaches, keys in hand, and offers to give us back our freedom in exchange for a few bucks. A thrill of relief confirms that our adventure can restart.

A hundred or so kilometres pass quickly as we speed along the A3 towards Sofia, skirting the Rila Massif. As dusk descends, we opt to sleep just outside the capital for Gina's first night in the van, choosing a remote, forest location by Lake Pancharevo. We find a car park with an all-encompassing view of the water and surrounding snow-capped mountains. Our friend has a gigantic smile on her face. Which is fortunate, because with three of us squeezed into a Volkswagen Transporter made for two, you'd better be in a good mood. Bedtime requires a little organisation, with everyone tidying away their things properly. José is very considerate and insists on sleeping on the floor, in his duvet, under the bed. Personal comfort has given way to camaraderie, conviviality and sharing.

Sofia is only 12km (7.5 miles) from the lake, and we set off to explore early next morning. This is the second time I've visited the city, and I can't get enough of it. Top attraction is the Alexander Nevsky Cathedral, with its verdigris and gold domes, one of the most important Orthodox places of worship ever built (it was constructed in memory of the Russian soldiers who died for Bulgaria's independence). Elsewhere, the capital's Central Mineral Baths, geometric streets, onion-dome churches and Ottoman mosques are all fascinating in their own way.

We continue the urban part of our itinerary in Plovdiv, 140km (87 miles) from Sofia on the A1 and bordered by wooded hills and cultivated fields. The country's second-largest city, elegant and architecturally rich, has no reason to envy its bigger sibling. In the centre, gleaming church domes and minarets coexist harmoniously, while the enticing scents of *kürtöskalács* (sweet cylindrical spit cakes) and *döner* (kebabs) waft through the streets. Plovdiv is a modern city but one that has preserved traces of its past within its walls – a splendid Roman theatre is the finest example.

Back on the road, routes 64 and then 6 run south past Central Balkan National Park to Shipka. On the heights above this small town, at the foot of the mountains, stands a superb Orthodox monastery, white and bright pink, topped with golden

Opposite: Chipka monastery. Left: Plovdiv street. Below: Traditional fabrics. Page 201, from top: Roman theater in Plovdiv; Black sand beach in Byala.

onion domes. Inside, a thousand icons with golden details fill the sanctuary. Looking for a parking place for the night, we get back behind the wheel. We haven't planned our itinerary, preferring to let ourselves be carried along by whatever takes our fancy – which means on this occasion we end up staying at a service station, having found nothing better. The employees warn us that vehicles in the area are regularly robbed, but, luckily, a secure, fee-charging enclosure adjoins the rest area. We salute someone's bright idea and pay up.

The following day, it's on to Burgas and the Black Sea, 200km (124 miles) east – the eastern edge of Europe. We head straight for the long sandy beach and then straight into the Black Sea.

The next stage of our programme is straightforward enough – drive north along the coast. By the side of the E87, a traveller sticks out his thumb and we welcome him aboard. The four of us hit it off to the extent that we're invited to spend the evening with him and a few of his friends on a 'secret' beach near Byala. We park the camper at the top of a cliff and follow him to the cove where we settle in, alone in the world, for the rest of the night. To the sound of the swell and the music of our guitars, we share a few glasses of wine, reconnecting with the pleasure of simple things and the joys of fraternity. **AD**

ROAD MAP

Start // Blagoevgrad
Finish // Byala
Distance // 644km (400 miles)
Recommended duration // 5-to-7 days
When to go // Spring or autumn, for Black Sea swimming without the crowds
Culinary speciality // *Taratora* (cold soup made with yogurt, cucumber, walnuts, spices and olive oil)

THE PERFECT PICNIC SPOT

Description // Parking with direct view of the Black Sea in Aheloy
GPS coordinates // 42.639301536443533, 27.648288203419O3
Access // Easy, by road
Activities // Fishing, walking or sunbathing
Visitor numbers // Quiet area
Little extras // Sunset over the sea

Opposite: Møns Klint cliff, Denmark.

MORE LIKE THIS
TOES IN THE WATER

ZEALAND (DENMARK)

In eastern Denmark, the chalk cliffs of Møns Klint merge into the Baltic Sea in an eye-catching natural wonder. Its beach attracts travellers curious to discover this exceptional site, and within walking distance is Havrelukke car park, with a fire pit and picnic tables (no overnighting). Next, follow the E47 for a quick trip to the city of Roskilde, located on the edge of a fjord on Zealand, the country's largest island. It's home to many natural and cultural gems, including a Viking Ship Museum containing five Viking vessels. Head to the centre of capital Copenhagen for a wander through its lively streets, before driving on to the magnificent Frederiksborg Castle, reflected in the waters of a lake. To sleep by the sea, head a little further north to the village of Tisvilde and its colourful huts.

Start // Møns Klint
Finish // Tisvilde
Distance // 217km (135 miles)
More information // visitdenmark.com

THE ALBANIAN COAST

Less busy than its Balkan neighbours, Albania is an ideal destination for travellers who like their seaside free of crowds. As you explore the port town of Durrës, you'll be struck by its many archaeological remains. Take a swim on the city beach before heading south to Karavasta Lagoon. You can take a camper van around this protected reserve, surrounded by forest, enjoying maximum peace and quiet. Get out your binoculars and with a bit of luck you'll be able to spot some Dalmatian pelicans. The SH4 will take you to a second exceptional natural site, Narta Lagoon, which has two beautiful beaches and an interesting Byzantine monastery. Continue on the SH8, a winding coastal road offering great views, all the way to Saranda. Climb up to the lighthouse of this seaside resort at the end of the day for a sunset to remember.

Start // Durrës
Finish // Saranda
Distance // 293km (182 miles)
More information // albania.al

NORTHERN PORTUGAL

If you love the pleasures of the beach and visiting towns with character, the Portuguese coast is for you, especially its quieter northern stretches around Caminha. On the banks of the Minho River, this peaceful place faces Spain across the water and has an old-fashioned charm. After enjoying its attractions, take the N13 south along the Atlantic. You'll pass a number of beaches where you can put your towel down, such as Vila Praia de Âncora – the further you head from the town, the more deserted the sands will be. Then head for the mouth of the Lima River in Viana do Castelo, a remarkable town with a magnificent historic centre and pretty marina. Continue to Póvoa de Varzim, a lively nightlife resort that is a popular summer destination, and finish with some big city action in Porto.

Start // Caminha
Finish // Porto
Distance // 105km (65 miles)
More information // visitportugal.com

FROM THE HEART OF POLAND TO THE BALTIC SEA

From Warsaw to Gdańsk, take a tour of Poland's major cities.

D*zień dobry*, hello. *Tak* is yes. *Nie* is no. *Prosze* means please, and, to say thank you, *dziękuję*. I'm revising my Polish vocabulary – though I'm not quite sure of the pronunciation – as knowing a few useful words is the least I can do as I prepare to embark on a road trip through the major cities of central and northern Poland.

First stop is the Furmańska camper van park in Warsaw. A car park with no facilities, but with the advantage of being a stone's throw from the old town. I lock the van, withdraw a few zlotys from an ATM and am ready for a day in the Polish capital. The multimedia Fountains Park on the banks of the Vistula River is a great place to begin my explorations, before heading for the historic centre. Before crossing the Barbican, a sturdy Gothic edifice marking the northern entrance to the old town, I'm greeted by the statue of Marie Curie, Warsaw's most famous woman – though she had to swap her home town for Paris to pursue her work on natural radioactivity. Arriving at the market square, it's hard to believe that the superb colourful facades of the Renaissance, Gothic and Baroque buildings there are not original. Everything you see today was meticulously rebuilt after 85% of the city was destroyed during WWII. It's a magnificent example of reconstruction, justly listed as a UNESCO World Heritage Site.

I continue my time travel in Zamkowy Sq, home to the Royal Castle, another replica of an 18th-century original. The weather's fine so I sit down on the terrace of Zapiecek, a restaurant where the *pierogi*, large, tasty steamed dumplings, are well worth sampling. The afternoon is spent at the Warsaw Rising Museum, where rare photos, films and personal accounts detail the German occupation of the country from 1939 onwards and the story of the 1944 uprising, which was doomed to failure for lack of international support. As night falls, I take a municipal bicycle to see the Palace of Culture and Science, an impressive 237m (778ft) skyscraper 'gifted' by Stalin to the Polish people.

The next morning, Łazienki Park, south of the capital, calls. It's early autumn, the leaves on the trees have taken on golden

© David Johnston | Adobe Stock

hues and these royal gardens laid out in the 18th century look resplendent. I contemplate the architecture of the park's palace, reflected in the water of an ornamental lake, then after this breath of fresh air, I take the A2 southwest. A long straight stretch of 136km (85 miles) through agricultural plains leads me to Łódź, Poland's third-largest city, remarkable for the bold architecture of its industrial wastelands transformed into cultural or commercial centres. I walk along Ulica Piotrkowska, Łódź grandest boulevard. This pedestrian shopping street lined with Art Nouveau buildings and chic restaurants was another victim of WWII destruction, but was also rebuilt and has been the beating heart of the city since the 90s.

I leave Łódź to overnight 70km (43 miles) to the west, on the peaceful banks of Jeziorskomeer lake, surrounded by nature. I unfold my picnic table, dine with my feet in the sand and think about how the places I've visited over the past few days have made me realise how lucky I am to be free, in good health and born in a country at peace.

Early next morning I'm on the A2 motorway again, heading northwest towards Poznań because I don't want to miss the twelve strokes of noon. I arrive just in time in front of the city's Renaissance town hall clock where, once a day, its mechanism stages a duel between two little goats. The show is short but unusual enough to keep onlookers entertained. The Rynek (old market square) is surrounded by restored Baroque and Neoclassical houses, now home to boutiques, cafes and restaurants. I sit on the terrace of one for a drink before ambling around an island northwest of the centre where the monumental Ostrow Tumski cathedral is encircled by two arms of the Warta River. The day finishes in the crooked forest of Krzywy Las, home to 400 oddly-shaped pine trees. The trunk of each tree is mysteriously bent at 90°, some 40cm (16 inches) above the ground. It's thought that the pines' strange forms have been intentionally created by human hands.

The following day I'm heading north across the plains of Wielkopolska (Greater Poland) province, via the S5 road. It's 255km (158 miles) to Toruń, where I leave the camper in a car park at the entrance to the town and set off to discover this wonderful place with its medieval ramparts. Not very popular with tourists, Poland's gingerbread capital is one of the few places in the country to have been spared the bombings of WWII. I've got into the habit of starting my urban explorations with the Rynek, and Toruń's market square differs somewhat from the others I've seen, with its red brick buildings. I climb the 96 steps to the Gothic tower of the town hall and enjoy a bird's-eye view of the medieval quarter. Then it's a street-level stroll through the city, admiring the Baroque stucco facade of the Under the Star townhouse, gaping at the astonishing frogs and violin-playing child sculptures adorning a fountain and stopping in front of the house where Nicolas Copernicus was born.

ST MARTIN'S CROISSANT

A regional speciality is the tasty *rogal świętomarciński* croissant, garnished with white poppy seeds. Its recipe is listed in the EU's protected designations of origin register, meaning St Martin's croissants can only be produced in Poznań and Wielkopolska, according to a specific recipe. Every year, for the national 11 November holiday, over a million are made. *RogalŚwi̧etomarcińskiare consumed.*

Below: Inside the van. Above: Malbork Castle. Opposite: Poznań. Page 207: Krzywy Las forest.

'The next day, a final detour to Malbork, famous for its brick castle – the gigantic proportions of this jewel of Teutonic Order architecture . . . take my breath away.'

I drive north again, with Gdańsk in my sights, and stop off in the Tuchola Forest, one of the country's largest, dotted with lakes, and where large expanses of heather bloom in autumn. The next day, a final detour to Malbork, famous for its brick castle – the gigantic proportions of this jewel of Teutonic Order architecture, built in the 15th century, take my breath away. Half an hour's drive brings me to Gdańsk where tomorrow I'll devote an entire day to discovering this Baltic port steeped in history. The Royal Way, lined with refined architecture; the Market Square (Długi Targ); Ulica Mariacka, one of Poland's most beautiful streets; and last, but not least, the Museum of the Second World War, the city's main tourist attraction. The itinerary promises to be a busy but rewarding one. **AL**

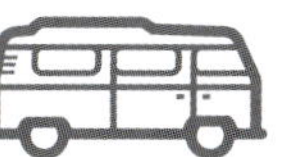

ROAD MAP

Start // Warsaw
Finish // Gdańsk
Distance // 882km (548 miles)
Recommended duration // 10-to-12 days
When to go // During the festive season, when Christmas markets and decorations light up the cities
Culinary specialities // *Pierogi* (dumplings), *zapiekanka* (baguette filled with mushrooms and cheese), *sernik* (white cheese and raisin cake).

THE PERFECT SLEEP SPOT

Description // Municipal motorhome site in Zborowo, by the lake
GPS coordinates // 52.375622, 16.625976
Light pollution // Low
Access // Easy — by road
Facilities // Cold water, toilets, electricity and playground.
Parking // 12 pitches
Little extras // You can spend up to two nights free of charge. To camp longer, contact the town hall.

Opposite, from top: Rose field near Karlovo, Bulgaria; Tulips in Amsterdam, Netherlands.

MORE LIKE THIS
FLORAL ESCAPADES

HYACINTH FORESTS, BELGIUM

This is a trip on which you'll want the camper windows wide open. Start south of Brussels, in the Hallerbos Forest, where at the end of April fragrant blue hyacinths bloom in their millions, best viewed (and smelled) along the many marked trails. Then head east on the N272, between meadows and the Woods of Brabant, to reach the Brakelbos and Muziekbos forests. Less frequented than Hallerbos, they sport carpets of bluebells in springtime. The journey continues south into Wallonia, via the N56, to Ghlin Wood, an ideal place to stretch your legs on foot or mountain bike. More wild hyacinths can be found further south, in the Bois du Grand Bon Dieu, a haven of tranquillity dotted with astonishing wooden sculptures. Don't forget to bring binoculars as you may well come across deer on your journey.
Start // Hallerbos Forest
Finish // Bois du Grand Bon Dieu
Distance // 150km (93 miles)
More information // hallerbos.be

THE ROSE VALLEY (BULGARIA)

Between the Balkan Mountains on one side and the Sredna Gora range on the other, the narrow roads of the Rose Valley promise an olfactory overload. Between May and June, fields of roses cover this fertile land, the world's leading producer of rose oil. Choose Kazanlak, the 'Rose Capital', as your base. In addition to a museum dedicated entirely to the flower, the town comes alive on the first weekend in June with an intoxicating Rose Festival. Villages such as Rozovo and Rajena also organise rose-themed events on certain weekends. All these festivities are usually accompanied by harvesting, parades and traditional dances. While exploring the Rose Valley, stop off at Ostroucha to admire the princely tomb built by the Thracians 4000 years ago – proof that this suave, peaceful spot was already popular long before the roses arrived.
Start // Kazanlak
Finish // Karlovo
Distance // 85km (53 miles)
More information // rosefestivalkazanlak.com

THE KINGDOM OF THE TULIP (NETHERLANDS)

A must-see to get your Dutch floral tour off to a good start is Amsterdam's floating flower market, in the heart of the city's canals. Buy a few bulbs, then make the 45-minute drive west to Keukenhof garden, where from April to mid-May an incredible display of tulips looks so impressive it's hard to believe they aren't artificial. Drive along the North Sea – with a pause to breathe in the fresh air – to Alkmaar, a charming town famous for its Friday cheese market. Then take your camper on the Houtribdijk, a 32km (20 mile) dike that closes off an ancient North Sea inlet. Across the water, in central Flevoland province, is Lelystad, the start of the 'flower bulb circuit' and home of the country's largest tulip fields. Plan to cheat on your four-wheeler, as there's nothing like cycling to fully enjoy this multicoloured region.
Start // Amsterdam
Finish // Lelystad
Distance // 163km (101 miles)
More information // holland.com

CENTRAL EUROPE CIRCUIT

Loop through the heart of the continent on a drive through Slovakia, Austria, the Czech Republic and Hungary.

Scribbling on a map, I sketch out a circuit linking the capitals of four Central European countries in a clockwise direction: from Bratislava to Vienna, along the Danube, through Bohemia to Prague, through traditional Slovak mountain villages to the warmth of Hungarian hot springs, before returning to my starting point. A few months later, I'm setting off on this epic van tour.

It all begins in Bratislava, capital of Slovakia. I park in a huge free car park on the banks of the Danube, next to the Sad Janka Kráľa public garden, and walk across the Nový Most bridge to the centre of the city. I stroll through the pretty streets, pushing open the doors of the churches for a peek inside, and reach the town hall square where a street artist offers to draw my portrait for free. I play along, sitting down and pulling out my own sketchbook to return the favour. Josef, the artist (and sitter), can't believe I'm travelling alone and he's full of questions. Once he's finished drawing, he offers to be my guide and so I continue my visit in his company until, as the day draws to a close, it's time to say a fond farewell – tonight I plan to cross the border to the Austrian capital, just 70km (43 miles) away.

Two nights camping on the outskirts of Vienna let me experience the city's Habsburg palaces, traditional cafes and bustling markets during the day. My journey then continues eastwards along the famous Danube, a route which is

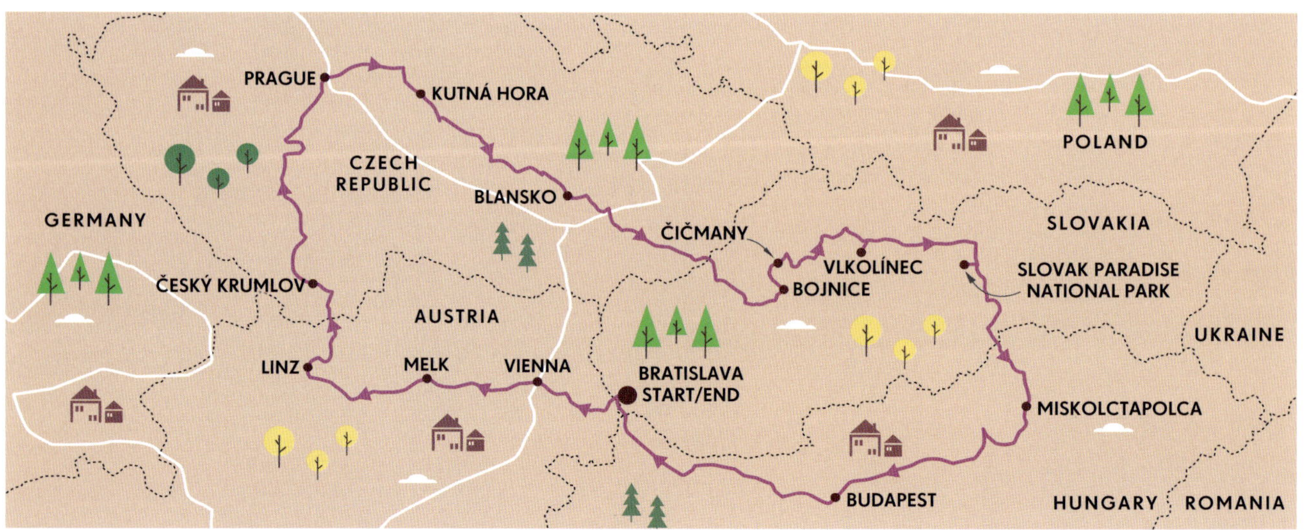

particularly spectacular in the Wachau Valley, where the river passes scenic villages, orchards and vineyards and numerous castles. Opposite Emmersdorf, I'm drawn by the Baroque Benedictine abbey of Melk, high above the river – so much so that I park the camper and visit the exuberantly decorated abbey church (all cherubs, polished marble and golden swirls), the imperial apartments and the splendid library. Continuing up the Danube, shortly before Linz, another abbey, St Florian's, demands a stop. It's a still-active monastery, founded in the 9th century and later remodeled in the Baroque style, featuring a grandiose library with a frescoed ceiling.

After Linz, the itinerary turns north and soon takes me to southern Bohemia in the Czech Republic. Night is falling when I park in the castle car park in Český Krumlov. When I wake up, I hurry to get ready to go out as I hear the first cars arriving in the neighbouring squares. The autumn colours are as lovely as this small medieval town itself, nestled in a loop of the Vltava River. Its cobbled streets, old houses covered in carvings and, a few steps from the old town centre, puppet museum all catch my eye. At the latter I take a tour and reconnect with my childhood. Then it's back to the camper and off to Prague, just over 200km (124 miles) away on Route 20. I take a break halfway along the road, near the town of Zduchovice, a nice place to exercise stiff limbs in the dappled woods of Větrov. The view from Vyhlídka Solenice of the horseshoe-shaped bend of the Vltava, surrounded by greenery, is breathtaking.

It's nearly 9am and I've slept in a car park near Prague's historic centre. When I arrive, Old Town Sq is packed to the rafters. Some kind of demonstration? No, it's just the crowd waiting for the astronomical clock to chime so that the march of the Apostles can begin as the statue of Death rings a bell. Oppressed by the mass of tourists, I cross the Charles Bridge and find a quieter side of the city on the Vlatava's other bank.

An hour's drive east brings me to Kutná Hora and its marvellous, immense, Gothic church of St Barbara whose airy vaults are covered with lace-like stonework. After a walk through the streets of this mining town, I ponder the strange beauty of the Sedlec Ossuary, a church entirely decorated with bones. Continuing on my way, I enter the region of Moravia and stop off at Blansko in the Moravian Karst, a pretty, hilly, wooded region of canyons and caves. A circuit takes you to the bottom of the Macocha Gorge, 138m (453ft) deep, created by the collapse of a large cave ceiling.

Bojnice Castle's elaborate battlements and cylindrical towers mark my return to Slovakia. Built in the 12th century, the fortress was redesigned in the Romantic style in the 20th century by the Pálffy family and houses their rich collections. A completely different atmosphere awaits in Čičmany and Vlkolínec, two

LEDNICE CASTLE

This Neogothic castle in the Czech Republic was once the Liechtenstein royal family's summer residence. The interior is elaborately decorated, while the surrounding park features a greenhouse of exotic plants, a Venetian fountain, a Roman aqueduct, and a minaret.

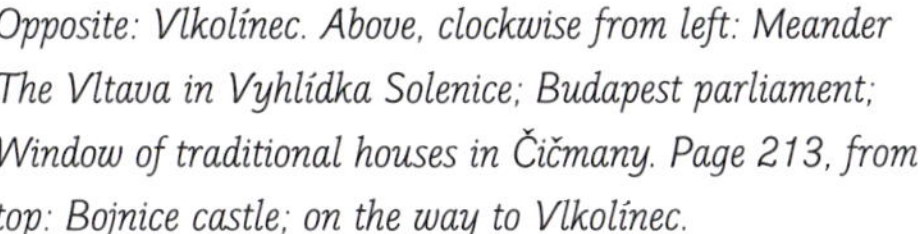

Opposite: Vlkolínec. Above, clockwise from left: Meander The Vltava in Vyhlídka Solenice; Budapest parliament; Window of traditional houses in Čičmany. Page 213, from top: Bojnice castle; on the way to Vlkolínec.

traditional villages lost in the mountains. The former is famous for its dark wooden houses, painted with white motifs inspired by local embroidery and lace. The second is made up of more wooden houses typical of mountainous regions.

I continue east. Through the windows, vast plains and fir forests unfold, with the Tatra Mountains to the north. I reach my next stop, Slovak Paradise National Park, after 100km (62 miles). Located to the north of the Metalliferous Mountains, it's home to numerous hiking trails for all levels, with waterfalls, caves and steep gorges to reward your exertions.

After this immersion in nature, I head for the northeast of Hungary, where more wonderful discoveries are in store – the 30°C (86°F) waters of Miskolctapolca's subterranean thermal baths, Eger's surprising conical rocks, the salt mountain of Egerszalók – before returning to the Danube and the splendours of Budapest. From the Hungarian capital it's a short drive to finish where this Central Europe circuit began, back in Bratislava. **AL**

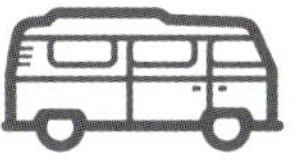

ROAD MAP

Start/Finish // Bratislava
Distance // 1780km (1106 miles)
Recommended duration // 12-to-15 days
When to go // Any season; early mornings are quieter in the capital cities
Culinary speciality // *Trdelník* (a type of spit-roasted cake traditional in Central Europe, prepared with dough wrapped around a stick and filled with sugar before being baked over a wood fire)

THE PERFECT SLEEP SPOT

Description // Camp Pacho, near Bojnice Castle in Slovakia, open April to September
GPS coordinates // 48.781179, 18.683606
Light pollution // Low
Access // Easy, by road
Facilities // Fully equipped
Parking // 24 pitches
Little extras // The campsite adjoins a restaurant and hotel. There are bungalows and lawn pitches.

Opposite, from top: Visegrád citadel, Hungary; Baba Vida fortress, Bulgaria.

MORE LIKE THIS
ALONG THE DANUBE

THE CRADLE OF THE DANUBE (GERMANY)

A plaque in the town of Donaueschingen, the start of this trip, reads: 'Here the Danube is born'. The river flows over 687km (427 miles)from its source here in Germany's Black Forest to the Austrian border, and along its banks you'll come across places full of charm and steeped in history. From Donaueschingen, head east for 31km (19 miles) to Tuttlingen, where you can visit the Burg Honberg fortress, the steam locomotive museum and, nearby, the Danube Sinkhole, where the river disappears for a few kilometres underground. Drive to Beuron Abbey, Sigmaringen Castle (last refuge of France's wartime Vichy regime in 1944-1945) and the Upper Danube Nature Park. Last stop: Ulm's Gothic cathedral and its spire, the tallest in the world at 161m (528ft).

Start // Donaueschingen
Finish // Ulm
Distance // 167km (104 miles)
More information // tourism-bw.com

AROUND BUDAPEST (HUNGARY)

Budapest owes its nickname of 'Pearl of the Danube' to the many architectural highlights along its riverbanks: Buda Castle; Matthias Church; the Citadel; Gellért Baths; the Fisherman's Bastion; the Hungarian Parliament. Once you've had your fill of the capital's treasures, discover what the sourrounding area has to offer. Route 10 takes you to Esztergom and its basilica, Central Europe's largest. Not far away, the ruins of the royal castle bear witness to the city's status as a capital in the Middle Ages. Back in your camper, drive along the Danube on route 11. From Visegrád's citadel, look out over a bend in the Danube below. Discover the museums and galleries of pretty Szentendre, then finish in Gödöllő and its palace, famous for having been one of Empress Sissi's favourite haunts.

Start // Budapest
Finish //Gödöllő
Distance // 134km (83 miles)
More information // hungary.com

THE DANUBIAN PLAIN (BULGARIA)

A road trip across the Danubian Plain in the northern part of Bulgaria reveals an off-the-beaten-track side of the river that few tourists see. Begin in the town of Vidin with the Baba Vida Fortress, the only Bulgarian castle to have survived the Ottoman conquest intact. Then head east, following the course of the river (and the Romanian border). Birdwatch in Persina Nature Park, which has eleven small islands and 200 avian species. The river reaches the southernmost point of its long course at Svishtov, a pleasant terraced town on a green hill. The architectural heritage of Ruse, the last stop on this itinerary, transports you back to the Danube and Bulgaria of the Belle Époque.

Start // Vidin
Finish // Ruse
Distance // 403km (250 miles)
More information // bulgariatravel.org

SOUTHERN POLAND SIGHTSEEING

See southern Poland's highlights on a journey from Wrocław to the Carpathian Mountains via Krakow.

To explore southern Poland is to revel in the country's architectural charms while also reliving Europe's darkest hours and the history of the Nazi occupation.

This autumn road trip begins in the old town of Wrocław, capital of Lower Silesia. Focused on a gorgeous market square, the centre is brimming with restaurants and bars, busy with students on the move. After this great introduction, I take the camper southwest to reach two must-see sites. The first, in

Świdnica, is the Church of Peace, a UNESCO World Heritage Site built entirely of wood in 1656 and boasting Baroque ornamentation inside. The second is the Vang church, a curious wooden building dating from the 12th century, brought from Norway and reassembled piece by piece in Karpacz, an exclusive ski resort in the Karkonosze Mountains of the Sudetenland.

My day ends on the plain in Książ, a pretty town in the middle of the woods, famous for its magnificent castle, one of the best preserved in Poland. From medieval to Baroque, the building juggles styles, and the tour includes a huge underground network built on Hitler's orders in 1943, with little-known intentions. Looking for a place to sleep, I decide on a large plot in the middle of nowhere, just a few minutes' drive from the castle. My heating has broken down, so I'm hoping my duvet and hot water bottle will suffice. But sadly no. The cold wakes me in the middle of the night so I pull out all the stops, putting on a beanie and pulling the top of the duvet over my head – it's like being in a sarcophagus. I resolve to buy a small oil heater the next day, and to rent a camping pitch with electricity.

I'm gradually leaving the Sudeten Mountains behind me and moving on to the urbanised, industrialised plains of Upper Silesia. I take a break at Moszna Castle, built in the mid-17th century and looking like something out of a fairy tale. Instead of trying to count its 365 rooms and 99 towers and turrets, I walk through its appealing gardens.

As I drive along the A4 motorway, I'm preparing myself for a complete change of vibe, having booked a ticket for a 1pm tour of the Auschwitz II-Birkenau concentration camp. As part of a group of 25 people, I embark on an emotional tour of horror, bursting into tears at the entrance to the barracks. In the late afternoon, an icy mist descends on the site, adding to the desolation.

It's hard to describe all the feelings this visit evokes. With a heavy heart, my hands clenched on the steering wheel and my mind elsewhere, I let the van speed off towards Kraków. At the Smok campsite, located in a leafy suburb 4km (2.5 miles) from the old town, I'm relieved to find a bit of life again. But I choose to stay in the camper to recover from the day's experiences, alone and in silence.

Another sunny day, and after a warmer night, I'm feeling a bit better. Having booked three nights at this campsite, I leave the van each morning and take the bus to the city centre. I make friends with two boastful Frenchmen I meet by chance and find myself smiling again. Until late in the evening, we explore the medieval old town, amazed by the grandeur of the buildings around the main market square – one particular highlight is the flamboyant decoration of St Mary's Basilica (Kosciol Mariacki), a Brick Gothic masterpiece.

After a lie-in next morning, I set about the chore of doing the laundry, which is inevitable when you live and travel long distances in a converted vehicle. Top tip: put dirty clothes in a closed container filled with water and detergent and let the

THE WOODEN CHURCHES OF LITTLE POLAND

Six churches in the Lesser Poland region have been designated World Heritage Sites for their age and the quality of their preservation. They use horizontally arranged logs, a technique practised since the Middle Ages in eastern and northern Europe. To see their soaring roofs and murals, visit the villages of Dębno, Binarowa, Sękowa, Blizne, Lipnice Murowana, and Haczów.

Below: Wroclaw Market Square. Above: Archangel Michael Church in Dębno. Opposite: barszcz. *Page 219, from top: Morskie Oko; Vang church in Karpacz.*

jolts of the road produce a washing machine-like action to get things clean.

My new French friends join me in the camper to visit the Wieliczka Salt Mines, 15km (9 miles) south of Kraków. Excavated in the 13th century to mine white gold, this labyrinth stretches 245km (152 miles) and is 327m (1073ft)deep. Between chapels sculpted entirely from salt and underground lakes, the guided tour lasts around two hours and is time well spent.

After my third night at the Kraków campsite, it's time to hit the road again, direction the Carpathians, on the Polish-Slovak border. I take the S7 to resort town Zakopane where I've booked a room with a local, but not before a detour to the small village of Dębno to admire the Church of Archangel Michael. This astonishing architectural feat was constructed of larch wood in the 15th century without a single nail.

The landscape becomes increasingly mountainous as I head to Zakopane and temperatures drop. Sitting in the foothills of the Tatras, the town's 19th-century wooden villas have been transformed into museums and hotels. A favourite with skiers in winter, the resort is also the starting point for many summer hikes in the Carpathian Mountains. I crown my trip with a hike to Morskie Oko (Eye of the Sea) – one of the five most beautiful lakes in the world according to the *Wall Street Journal*. The granite peaks of the High Tatras can be seen in the background, a promise of future excursions. **AL**

ROAD MAP

Start // Wrocław
Finish // Morskie Oko
Distance // 720km (447 miles)
Recommended duration // 10-to-12 days
When to go // Any time – if your van is equipped for snow
Culinary specialities // *Barszcz* (beetroot soup), *zurek* (soup made from a variety of vegetables, rye flour and caraway, served with smoked bacon or hard-boiled eggs)

THE PERFECT SLEEP SPOT

Description // Camping Forteca, on a small lake southeast of Wroclaw; open April to October
GPS coordinates // 50.755922, 16.69579
Light pollution // Low
Access // Easy, by road
Facilities // Fully equipped, on-site restaurant
Parking // 40 pitches
Little extras // Convenient for excursions to the Sudetenland.

Opposite, clockwise from top: Mountain landscape in Scarisoara, Romania; Predjama castle, Slovenia; Entrance to Scariosara cave, Romania.

MORE LIKE THIS
A PASSION FOR CAVES

LOVECH'S CAVES (BULGARIA)

Bulgaria's karst soil holds almost 4500 caves, and this road trip will take you on a tour of those in the province of Lovech. Near the village of Karpachev, the first cave, Stalbitsata, takes on a mystical air when the sun shines on it. Take Route 301 to the second, Devetashka, one of the country's largest, with 2.5km (1.5 miles) of galleries and a 35m-high (115ft) entrance. Drive due west across the Devetashko Plateau to attend a choir concert in Saeva Dupka Cave, renowned for its acoustics. To the north lies Prohodna, where the 'Eyes of God' are formed from two natural openings in the vault. Take a detour to Karlukovo to admire the curious stone houses planted with grass, then head for the Besedkata lookout: take a seat on a bench and enjoy the view of the meandering Iskar River.

Start // Stalbitsata Cave
Finish // Besedkata viewpoint
Distance // 134km (83 miles)
More information // bulgariatravel.org

SLOVENIAN CAVES

Slovenia is home to extraordinary caves, some of which are listed as UNESCO World Heritage Sites. First stop, Križna, has more than 20 underground lakes, visited by boat. Cross the Cerknica Plain towards Postojna Cave; its 24km (15 mile) subterranean network can be explored by train. Then visit Predjama Castle, built in the 13th century in a huge rock cavity, and drive 30km (19 miles) along the E61 to Divača Cave, with its beautiful stalactites. Next door, contemplate the geological splendours of Vilenica Cave before being plunged for a few seconds into complete darkness. Finish on a high note with the phenomenal Škocjan Caves – you'll walk along the edge of a 100m-deep (328ft) canyon where the Reka River roars.

Start // Križna Cave
Finish // Škocjan Cave
Distance // 90km (56 miles)
More information // slovenia.info

ROMANIA'S CAVES

Take time to discover the incredible variety of Romania's underground treasures. In the Rosia de Bihor mining area, Farcu (Crystal) Cave is aptly named as its calcite formations sparkle in the light. Back in the driver's seat, head for Méziad Cave, whose spacious chambers contain colonies of bats and an array of mineral formations including stalactites, stalagmites, columns and curtains. Retrace your steps back to route 764. Just 40km (25 miles) away, enter Apuseni Natural Park, carved into gorges and deep valleys. Take a detour to Bear Cave, where the skeleton of a cave bear over 15,000 years old has been found. Finally, drive to Gârda de Sus and take the narrow road to the village of Ghetari, from where the ascent to Scărișoara, one of the country's largest ice caves, begins.

Start // Farcu Cave
Finish // Scărișoara Cave
Distance // 158km (99 miles)
More information // parcapuseni.ro

NORTHERN EUROPE

A GRAND TOUR OF THE UK AND IRELAND

Take a turn through rolling countryside and wilderness, with lovely stops at famous towns.

The sweet scent of sea air and wet grass wafts in through the camper's window, confirming that I have arrived in the British Isles. I'm at the start of a long loop through England, Scotland, Ireland and Wales in this group of islands steeped in history and culture and where unspoilt nature is never far away.

Disembarking at Dover after a ferry crossing from Calais, the journey begins by heading north, bypassing London on the M25 circular motorway – I prefer to avoid the British capital where I dread the traffic. My first stop, however, is no small one: Cambridge, the prestigious university town whose buildings exude a calm elegance, especially the chapel of King's College. A stroll along the banks of the Cam only adds to the city's many charms.

Though tempted to linger, I'm soon back on the road, heading north on the A1, which runs like a spine through the heart of England to Newcastle-upon-Tyne. Through the window is rolling countryside, as green as can be. There are countless spots to explore. Yorkshire beckons with its wild moorlands and tranquil valleys – the Yorkshire Dales and North York Moors National Park offer the opportunity for some splendid walks. Not far from the A1, you'll find a number of ancient towns including medieval York, Durham and its magnificent Romanesque cathedral (perhaps the most beautiful in England) and Newcastle-upon-Tyne, a former shipbuilding city turned cultural and culinary destination.

Beyond Hadrian's Wall, Scotland is not far away, and a stopover in capital Edinburgh ensues before crossing the Grampian Mountains, heading northwest. I reach the northernmost point of my road trip at Fort William, on Loch Linnhe. Many visitors climb nearby Ben Nevis, the UK's highest peak (1345m/4413ft), but I'm pushing on and after a look around the town I turn the vehicle southwards for the long drive to the port of Cairnryan, where the ferry leaves for Northern Ireland. The route takes me through glorious Loch Lomond and the Trossachs National Park, much to my delight – this part of the journey is idyllic.

Goodbye Scotland, hello Northern Ireland! Two and a quarter hours on the ferry and I'm in Belfast. After exploring this lively city, I set off on a highlights tour of the country: the Dark Hedges, a fantastic avenue of twisting beech trees, made famous by *Game of Thrones*; the rope bridge to the tiny island of Carrick-a-Rede; the coastal road to the Giant's Causeway, a geological marvel made up of columns of cooled lava.

I cross from Northern Ireland to the Republic of Ireland and County Donegal, where I immediately fall in love with Glenveagh National Park. The Glen Walk, a hike that winds its way through wild moorland punctuated by lakes and forests, allows me to soak up these landscapes. Another highlight of Donegal is an excursion to the cliffs of Slieve League, some 601m (1972ft) high. Their heather-covered slopes, plunging into the ocean, are spectacular at sunset. That night, I park the camper down by the beach near Kilcar.

On the way to Dublin, 270km (168 miles) from Slieve League, I cross back into Northern Ireland, through County Fermanagh. I follow the course of the River Erne, which forms a number of *loughs* (lakes) ideal for water sports. Dublin reached, I stay for several days, visiting museums and wandering around the city. Trinity College, in particular, is a haven of peace. Before leaving the country, I also savour the legendary warmth of the pubs.

Another ferry crossing, docking this time in Liverpool. I'm back in England and take advantage of a sunny day to visit The Beatles' hometown. This major port at the mouth of the River Mersey hides a number of surprises, including the Albert Dock, commercial warehouses converted into bars and museums.

Next stop on my itinerary is a little foray into Wales, the last country of the UK I want to visit. While it's not always easy to travel in a camper in Britain (many places are off-limits at night), I'm confident that it will be easier in the remote Welsh countryside. I'm planning to take in Eyri (Snowdonia) National Park. Its mountainous areas, full of rivers and lakes, is a hiker's delight, but the park is also home to many cute towns and villages, of which Portmeirion stands out for its bright colours and eccentric architecture.

THE CAUSEWAY COASTAL ROUTE

This 200km (124 miles) road, linking Belfast to Derry-Londonderry, runs along the wild coast of Northern Ireland. Highlights include Old Bushmills Distillery, Carrickfergus Castle and, most famously, the Giant's Causeway

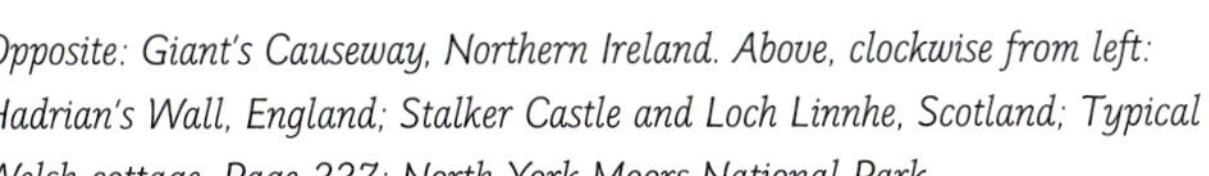

Opposite: Giant's Causeway, Northern Ireland. Above, clockwise from left: Hadrian's Wall, England; Stalker Castle and Loch Linnhe, Scotland; Typical Welsh cottage. Page 227: North York Moors National Park.

After this little Welsh side trip, I'm back on the road to England's West Midlands. The route takes in a number of Welsh lakes before crossing the border, with lovely picnic spots in prospect: Llyn Trawsfynydd, Afon Tryweryn and Lake Bala. Eventually, I reach Birmingham, where I spend a day strolling along its canals, lined with cafes and restaurants. This large conurbation is tinged with contrasts: ultramodern buildings stand side by side with edifices that bear witness to an era when manufacturing flourished here.

I finally let myself be carried along the M40 to Oxford, the final stop on my trip. Like Cambridge, this university city is home to both incredible architecture and some of the world's most brilliant minds. From famous museums to ancient streets, its historic centre is somewhere to explore with camera ready. I take a break in front of the Eagle and Child, JRR Tolkien's favourite pub, before leaving town.

I now have a rendezvous with Portsmouth, reached via the North Wessex Downs. The extraordinary beauty of these gentle hills and valleys would keep me here for a few more days, but the ferry home is waiting for me that evening so I have to bid farewell to this great British and Irish journey.

ROAD MAP

Start // Dover
Finish // Portsmouth
Distance // 2375km (1476 miles)
Recommended duration // Three weeks or more
When to go // Summer, for longer days and the best chance of sun
Culinary speciality // Haggis (stuffed sheep's stomach) is Scotland's most celebrated dish

THE PERFECT PICNIC SPOT

Description // Rest area on the shores of Lake Bala, Wales
GPS coordinates // 52.891726343947646, -3.6269314423010957
Access // Easy, via the A494 road
Facilities // None
Traffic // Busy in high season, quieter the rest of the time
Little extras // Direct access to the lake, the perfect opportunity to take the kayak out of the van for a few hours.

Opposite, from top: Lake Saimaa, Finland; Lake Skadar, Montenegro.

MORE LIKE THIS
INTO THE WILD

LA GARROTXA (SPAIN)

At the gateway to volcanic La Garrotxa Natural Park, the historic town of Besalú is well worth a visit, with its fortified bridge spanning the Fluvià River, the ancient stones of St Peter's monastery and the ruins of a synagogue. Move on to the hill-top village of Castellfollit de la Roca. You'll love the old-fashioned charm of the narrow streets and the panoramic view of the basalt cliffs and forest nearby. Back in the camper, enter La Garrotxa proper and visit Croscat volcano. A variety of trails allow you to immerse yourself in these rolling landscapes of ochre soil. Next stop, the Planes d'Hostoles Gorges whose magnificent waterfalls are set against a verdant natural backdrop. Explore on foot, after leaving the camper in the car park (where you also spend the night)

Start // Besalú
Finish // Planes d'Hostoles
Distance // 52km (32 miles)
More information // en.turismegarrotxa.com

LAKE SKADAR (MONTENEGRO)

South of Podgorica, the Montenegrin capital, visit the ruins of the Žabljak Crnojevíca Fortress – the panorama of the surrounding mountains and Lake Skadar glistening in the distance is spectacular. Further west, stop off in the fishing village of Karuč, whose scenery is among the most beautiful in the area. Take time to contemplate the green rocky massif, sprinkled with blue lakes, before getting back behind the wheel. From here, you can enjoy great views of the meandering Rijeka Crnojevíca River, which feeds Lake Skadar. You'll cross it over a centuries-old bridge, before descending southwards on a winding road to ancient Besac Fortress. From its heights, admire the mountain range reflected in the lake, then continue on the P16 road towards Livari. You'll find plenty of places to sleep in your van, with dazzling views of the lake.

Start // Žabljak Crnojevíca Fortress
Finish // Livari
Distance // 94km (58 miles)
More information // nparkovi.me

THE GREAT LAKES REGION (FINLAND)

Finland has thousands of lakes, the largest of which are concentrated in the southeast of the country. Start your blue tour on the shores of Lake Saimaa, the nation's biggest, near Mikkeli, a town surrounded by birch and spruce trees and the perfect place to stock up on supplies at the local market. Further east, nestled between two lakes, Savonlinna welcomes you with a boat trip around its castle built on a rocky island. Then head back to the camper for a night by the water – there's no shortage of spots here. Next day, continue to Linnansari National Park, an archipelago where you can observe seals (rent a kayak in Oravi). Finally, warm up with a moment of well-being in Kuopio's Saana Sauna – and cool off with a plunge into the calm waters of Lake Kallavesi.

Start // Mikkeli
Finish // Kuopio
Distance // 323km (201 miles)
More information // visitfinland.com

NORWAY'S SOUTHWEST COAST

Fjords as far as the eye can see, magnificent scenic roads and endless wilderness on a drive along the Norwegian coastline.

Leaving Oslo, my plan is simple. Follow the meandering coastal road to Kristiansund, enjoying a camper van circuit of southwestern Norway and stopping off in towns I imagine to be full of charm – veritable Scandinavian oases.

Walking through the capital, I travel from one architectural era to another: the Akershus Fortress, an imposing 14th-century castle of dark stone, offers a great view of the fjord. Further on, the Lutheran Cathedral is a colossal coral-toned brick building. From the Slottsparken, a huge expanse of grass where city dwellers like to soak up the sun, I admire the pale yellow Neoclassical Royal Palace. The Bjørvika neighbourhood's attractions are much more recent – its main draw is the striking opera house, inaugurated in 2008, whose strikingly sober white silhouette is reminiscent of a glacier.

The call of the road takes me back to the van, and I leave Oslo, taking the E18 and then the E134 westwards. From Notodden, feeling almost alone in the world, I drive through a mosaic of forests. In this green wilderness, speckled with small mist-covered lakes, I struggle to keep my eyes on the road, constantly distracted by the beauty. After more than 300km (186 miles) of uninterrupted spectacle, the town of Odda is on the horizon. The snow seems to have melted recently, and spring is in the air, making for a lovely atmosphere as I walk from the quiet streets of the town centre to the small fishing port. A few boats are docked at the end of the fjord and the mountain slopes are flecked with colourful houses – a postcard-perfect scene I relish for a few minutes before returning to the camper and setting off again. It's a bit of a detour, but I'm keen to go along the Hardangerfjord, Norway's second-largest fjord. My T4 threads its way under the cliffs, while a trickle of water runs along peacefully a few metres below the road. Numerous bridges and tunnels interrupt my advance towards the sunset, revealing one by one the rocky escarpments that follow the contours of the majestic fjord. In the midst of these great wild spaces, it's easy to feel infinitely small. I finally arrive in Bergen, a

'The steady stream of similarly astonished travellers doesn't detract from the magic . . . I savour the ballet of vehicles navigating this magnificent ode to the road.'

port on the North Sea and the capital of the fjords. The Bryggen neighbourhood, a UNESCO World Heritage Site, is extremely photogenic, its brightly painted warehouses with triangular roofs now converted into refined restaurants and art galleries. From the docks, you can see green valleys beyond the city, adorned with pretty houses. Closer to home, Bergen's streets – sometimes cobbled, sometimes decorated with street art – exude peace and tranquillity.

Since the start of this journey, I've had my sights set on the mythical *Atlanterhavsveien*, the Atlantic Ocean Road, an 8km (5 mile) carriageway between Vevang and Averøy that crosses eight bridges linking different islands, giving the driver the impression of flying over the water. I'm not so far away now, but getting there is an adventure in itself, first following the E16 and then the E13 along which the road plays hide-and-seek with various fjords. Arriving in Vangsnes, I buy a ferry ticket to take the camper across the Sognefjord to Dragsvik. From here, I continue my slow climb northwards and take a second ferry from Sykkylven to Magerholm, crossing a new inlet. I decide to stop in Ålesund, as the Atlantic Ocean Road is still 130km (81 miles) away.

Turns out stopping here was a good idea. Ålesund is a lovely place with, like any self-respecting Norwegian town, a picturesque port, a superb view of the fjords (from the top of Fjellstua Hill – after climbing 418 steps) and a few streets full of Art Nouveau buildings. I also make use of this stop to recharge my water reserves before, finally, setting off for the one destination that has attracted me for so long: the incredible *Atlanterhavsveien*.

It's in Møre og Romsdal county that this epic road unfolds. Of all the bridges along this drive that takes cars from one strip of land to another, the Storseisundet is the best known. This twisting grey bridge, nonchalantly tossed in the middle of the archipelago, has a rare elegance. I park nearby to better appreciate its wondeful design. Even the steady stream of similarly astonished travellers doesn't detract from the magic of the place, and I savour the ballet of vehicles navigating this magnificent ode to the road.

Daylight is fading though and I prefer to be closer to Kristiansund to spend the night. The town is relatively small, and its main attraction lies in its jagged coastline, which stretches for several kilometres. I aim to stay in a secluded spot by the water, and easily find a place to park as I head away from the town centre towards the marina, Dunkarsundet Småbåthavn. As I set up for the night, I consider one of the great luxuries of a life on the road – being able to end the day in a scenic location of your choosing, in this case, between sea and forest, with gulls as my only company. **AD**

THE FJORDS OF NORWAY

Fjords are deep, narrow indentations in the coast, whose walls sometimes sink several hundred metres below sea level. Norway boasts over a thousand, most on the jagged, spectacular west coast, including Sognefjord, the country's longest (204km/127 miles) and deepest (1308m/4291ft).

Opposite, from left: Ålesund; Bergen street; Hardangerfjord. Page 233, from top: Bergen; The Atlantic Route.

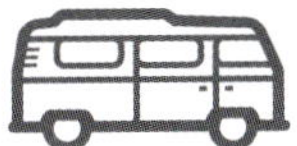

ROAD MAP

Start // Oslo
Finish // Kristiansund
Distance // 1511km (939 miles)
Recommended duration // 5-to-7 days
When to go // Summer, to avoid the rain
Culinary speciality // *Sild* (herring in a variety of sauces)

THE PERFECT PHOTO SPOT

Description // Skipsholmen car park, opposite Storseisundet Bridge
GPS coordinates // 63.01702719878612, 7.347088705323709
Access // Easy, via the Atlantic Ocean Road
Facilities // None
Visitor numbers // Quite a busy spot, and rightly so, as it's a fantastic place.
Little extras // Wait until the end of the day to enjoy the views with fewer cars and early evening light.

Opposite, from top: Transfăgărășan, Romania; Military Road, Isle of Wight, England.

MORE LIKE THIS
BREATHTAKING ROADS

THE TRANSFĂGĂRĂȘAN (ROMANIA)

Experiencing one of the most beautiful roads in the world has to be earned – you'll often need to be in second gear on the Transfăgărășan, built through the Carpathian Mountains. Open mid-June to mid-October, the road rises to 2000m (6562ft) above sea level from Curtea de Argeș, former capital of Wallachia. Allow plenty of time to take in its various stages and stops, including the ruins of Poenari Castle, linked to Vlad the Impaler, inspiration for Dracula. Just beyond, the route hugs Lake Vidraru, nestled in a mountainous setting. Do your best to keep your eyes on the road as you continue to the glacial lake of Bâlea. Not far away, the impressive waterfall (of the same name) is the ideal spot for a cool lunch break. Finish in the historic city of Sibiu, one of Transylvania's prettiest.

Start // Curtea de Argeș
Finish // Sibiu
Distance // 176km (109 miles)
More information // romaniatourism.com

ISLE OF WIGHT (ENGLAND)

In the south of England, the Isle of Wight is accessible by ferry from Portsmouth. Most of the island is classified as an Area of Outstanding Natural Beauty, and you can find out why on a weekend drive. Disembarking at Fishbourne, follow the east coast from lovely beach to quiet coastal town, all the way south to St Catherine's Point. The A3055 scenic route starts here, leading to Freshwater Bay, 17km (10 miles) west. Known as the Military Road, this route was part of the local defensive infrastructure in the 19th century. Today, it's frequented by visitors eager to follow this roadway, which offers a view of the sea on one side and green, rural landscapes on the other. Continue to the western tip of the island, where you can admire The Needles, three sharp chalk rocks overlooked by a red-and-white lighthouse. Finally, heading back to the start, visit Osborne House, former royal residence and home to splendid gardens.

Start/Finish // Fishbourne
Distance // 106km (66 miles)
More information // visitbritain.com

FAROE ISLANDS (DENMARK)

The remote Faroe archipelago can be reached by ferry, with a camper van, from the Danish port of Hirtshals – it's also an ideal stopover on a crossing between Denmark and Iceland. The attractions are many – basalt lava cliffs, immense waterfalls and lush green scenery await on these islands, linked by bridges and tunnels. The trip begins at the port of Tórshavn, capital of the Faroe Islands, on the island of Streymoy. The old town's wooden houses, with their grass-covered roofs and fjord views, are very photogenic. Further north, the village of Tjørnuvik offers magical landscapes worthy of the most beautiful postcards. Then head for Eiði and its famous football pitch, built between land and ocean, and on to the tip of the island of Viðoy, to visit the pretty village of Viðareiði, at the foot of snow-capped mountains. Return to Tórshavn to catch the ferry.

Start/Finish // Tórshavn
Distance // 202km (126 miles)
More information // visitfaroeislands.com

THE WILD SIDE OF SCOTLAND

Untamed, solitary spaces perfect for contemplation are the order of the day on this south-to-north Scottish tour.

Wilderness as far as the eye can see: that's what in store as I arrive in Scotland, continuing a road trip begun in England. The aim is to travel the length of the country, from Edinburgh to the mountains of the north, the famous Highlands. As it happens, I have Scottish cousins, some of whom I've never met – so it's with great emotion that I knock on my unknown family's door, on the outskirts of the Scottish capital.

Christiane, Anne, David and Tom welcome me with open arms, and over the next few days show me around the town. A perfect introduction to Scotland. We start with iconic Edinburgh Castle, an imposing fortress built on an extinct volcano. The Royal Mile, a street lined with pubs and restaurants, leads from the castle to the Gothic cathedral of St Giles with its distinctive spire. On the food side, I'm treated to a few specialities concocted by my cousins including *cullen skink*, a haddock and potato soup.

After this pleasant interlude of reunion and sharing, I'm back on the road. I can't wait to get to grips with the vast, wild expanses of the Highlands, so with my hands on the steering wheel, I take the M90 to Perth, then the A9 to the Grampians, crossing this mountain range from south to northwest. Through the camper's windows, spectacular scenes of alpine and lunar landscapes unfold. The road follows the curves of majestic glens (glacial valleys) through forests and past lochs. A few castles here and there add a postcard-perfect detail to the views.

Manoeuvering my old vehicle on such hilly roads is no mean feat but, fortunately, I live on the road, so have all the time in the world. The only downside? It's November, and in these high latitudes the days are short. Since I don't enjoy driving at night, and don't want to miss out on the views, I look for a spot to set up early every day.

A brief stopover in Inverness allows me to stock up on water and food. The port city is not devoid of charm. As in any self-respecting Scottish town, there's a splendid castle (made of red sandstone and dominating its surroundings), magnificent churches (including the Neogothic St Andrew's Cathedral) and, of course, lively pubs. But the town is also known as the gateway to one of the world's most mysterious lakes, famous Loch Ness, so I'm soon in the driver's seat again and cruising its shores, staring out over the tranquil waters. Is it the fog that prevents me from catching a glimpse of the celebrated monster?

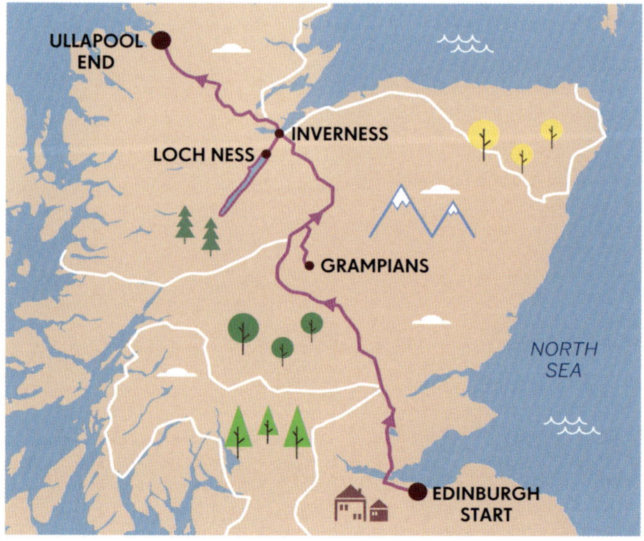

HIGHLANDS AND LOWLANDS

The Scottish Highlands make up the northern half of the country, beyond a geological fault line that runs from the Isle of Arran (in the southwest) to Stonehaven (in the northeast). This is a mountainous region of breathtaking scenery and undeniable tourist appeal on the edge of Europe. Further south, the Lowlands are home to most of the country's cities – including the biggest, Glasgow, and the capital, Edinburgh – and are where 80% of the population lives.

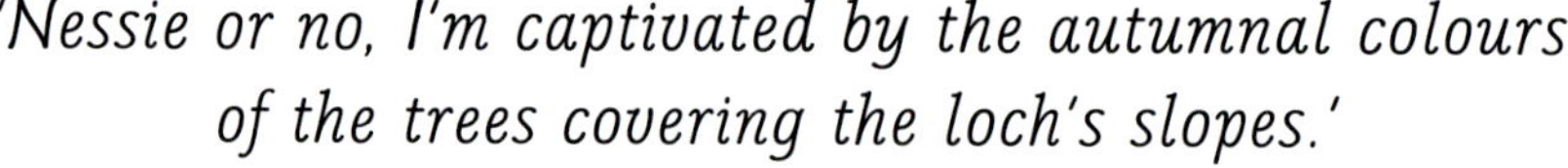

'Nessie or no, I'm captivated by the autumnal colours of the trees covering the loch's slopes.'

Nessie or no, I'm captivated by the autumnal colours of the trees covering the loch's slopes. A highlight of the area are the ruins of Urquhart Castle. Just outside the village of Drumnadrochit, they're exactly what I'd imagined Scotland to be – old ruins, a stretch of water, a few clouds and absolute silence.

Keen to keep going north, I set course for Ullapool, a town some 100km (62 miles) away. I don't think I've ever driven so slowly, but that's not really a surprise – I'm one of those unhurried people whose only watch is the sun and, it has to be said, that in addition to the twists and turns of the road keeping my speed down, I also allow myself I don't know how many stops just to pause and take everything in. It feels like a moment of grace, the likes of which are rare in a lifetime, so too good an opportunity to waste. The thin black ribbon of the A835 unrolls endlessly beneath my wheels, while my eyes are riveted by the scenery. Peaceful lochs, desolate expanses and dense deciduous and coniferous forests follow one after another for miles along the River Broom. When, on rare occasions, I come across another vehicle, I have to pull over into a *passing place*, a sort of roadside recess that allows me to give way on such a narrow lane. Apart from a few metal grids on the ground there's no 'passing place' provision made for the frequent flocks of sheep which graze brazenly on the edge of the road, sometimes blocking, albeit charmingly, my progress. Since it's better to look

Opposite: Urquhart Castle and Loch Ness. Left: Loch Broom. Below: Highland Road. Page 239: Highland landscapes.

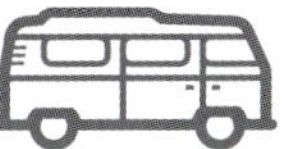

ROAD MAP

Start // Edinburgh
Finish // Ullapool
Distance // 432km (268 miles)
Recommended duration // 7-to-10 days
When to go // Summer, when the days are longer
Culinary speciality // Fish and chips

THE PERFECT SLEEP SPOT

Description // In the port of Ullapool
GPS coordinates // 57.89580766807917, -5.158917351524842
Access // Directly on the A893, Shore Street
Facilities // Public showers and toilets 200m (656ft) away
Traffic // Depends on road and port traffic
Little extras // Breathtaking views of Loch Broom (and seals, if you're lucky)

on the bright side, I grab a few sweets, slip a Bob Dylan CD into the player and wait patiently for my wooly roadmates to move on. In the distance, I can already see the Summer Isles, promising a pleasing coastal stretch on this drive.

More glorious moments follow until I finally reach Ullapool, a small town at the end of the world and the most northerly point of my Scottish road trip. After several days in the wilderness, it's good to have a few creature comforts again, so I park the camper near the fishing port, opposite Loch Broom which opens onto the Atlantic, and dive back into 'civilisation'. In this seaside town with its fresh sea air, I quickly feel at home and decide to extend my stay, falling in love with the peaceful place. The neat, white houses invite you to relax, while the colourful boats call you to the open sea. For the first time in my life, I'm seeing seals every morning as I drink my coffee on the beach. I might have found a place to grow old in peace when the time comes. **AD**

Opposite: Gran Sasso National Park, Italy.

MORE LIKE THIS
CLIMB EVERY MOUNTAIN

ABRUZZO (ITALY)

Travelling by camper is an excellent way to visit the mountainous region of Abruzzo, on the eastern side of the Italian Peninsula. Not far from the fortified town of L'Aquila, in the Gran Sasso e Monti della Laga National Park, the summit of the Corno Grande, the highest point in the Apennine Mountains at 2912m (9554ft), beckons the most athletic to hike its trails. From here, take the winding SS17 road to Sulmona, a pretty village from which it's easy to explore the surrounding rocky massif. After a detour to the splendid mountain village of Scanno, drive through the gorges of the Gole del Sagittario Natural Reserve. Retrace your steps to extend the adventure to Pescocostanzo, a delightful hilltop village. On the way back, enjoy the superb beaches around Pescara, on the Adriatic Coast.

Start // L'Aquila
Finish // Pescara
Distance // 324km (201 miles)
More information // abruzzoturismo.it

MARAMUREȘ (ROMANIA)

Get lost in the wilds of northern Romania, at the wheel of your camper van, in the Maramureș region. This land of folklore is renowned for its imposing wooden churches topped with spires, such as those at Budești and Desești. Not far from these two towns, a stopover on the heights of Breb, a traditional village as pretty as it is remote, will take you to the gateway to the Mara Valley. Now follow the river to Vadu Izei, a tranquil village in the heart of the mountains, also crossed by the course of the Iza. This second verdant valley is equally worth a look – set off on route 186 to Săcel, then rejoin route 18 to get to Borșa. In the surrounding area, a wide range of hikes allows you to get out and explore some fabulous rugged countryside.

Start //Budești
Finish //Borșa
Distance // 110km (68 miles)
More information // romaniatourism.com

LA SIERRA NEVADA (SPAIN)

Programme your GPS for Trevélez, the Andalusian town from which hikers can ascend the highest peak on the Iberian Peninsula, Mulhacén (3482m/11,424ft), in the heart of the Sierra Nevada. From the summit, you can even see Africa on a clear day. Explore the splendid white villages of the Alpujarras, such as Pampaneira, Bubión and Capileira, clinging to the southern slopes of the national park, and take a pleasant foray into the Poqueira Gorge. There are plenty of places to park your vehicle for beautiful, unobstructed views. Then head to sublime Granada, a must-visit city whose Alhambra palace makes the hearts of visitors from all over the world beat a little faster. In winter, enjoy snow sports at the Sierra Nevada ski resort, the southernmost in Europe.

Start // Trevélez
Finish // Sierra Nevada
Distance // 140km (87 miles)
More information // andalucia.org

SOUTHWEST FINLAND

Loop around southwest Finland discovering wonderful towns, picturesque roads, spectacular forests, serene lakes – and cakes.

Land ahoy! Pressing my face against the porthole, I can see terra firma – pink granite islands, fir trees, lawns and red houses. After a ten-and-a-half-hour crossing from Stockholm, the ferry is finally arriving in the Finnish city of Turku, the country's oldest. I gather my belongings and head down the stairs to the hold, where my LT35 is waiting. Arriving on the ferry the day before, it had seemed a pity that staying in the camper during this Baltic Sea crossing was prohibited, imagining that making the journey in my mobile home would be more comfortable. Back below deck, I realise I didn't miss anything when I smell the strong odour of exhaust fumes. I climb into my vehicle, dwarfed by the huge trucks around it, the bow doors finally open, and I disembark – southwest Finland is mine.

I park on the Aura River quay and walk along the flower-filled banks, where old sailing boats are moored. I continue through the city, my senses alert, savouring my first visit to this place. Lunchtime approaches and the sunny terraces fill up, but it's the red-brick covered market that catches my eye. As soon as I push open the doors, I'm overwhelmed by a wave of enticing smells. Along the huge aisles, stalls selling fresh local produce offer the chance to eat on the go. I start with a *karjalanpiirakka*, a rye-pastry tartlet filled with rice porridge and served with a mixture of butter and chopped eggs, followed by a dessert of *korvapuusti, a* cinnamon and cardamom brioche. Refuelled, I visit the colossal Gothic cathedral, Turku's castle and the open-air Luostarinmäki Crafts Museum.

The best way to round off the day is at the public sauna on Ispoinen Beach. I find a place in the large wooden hut, which seats 30 people, and try to endure as long as possible the hot steam coming from the stove, which contains lava stones. When the heat becomes unbearable, I imitate the locals, heading outside to dive from a pontoon into the cold sea – more pleasant and invigorating than I'd imagined. I repeat the experience several times before returning, relaxed, to my cabin on wheels.

That night, I stay in a car park at the entrance to the town of Rauma, 94km (58 miles) north, on the Gulf of Bothnia. The next day, I leave the camper where it is and visit the old historic centre, a UNESCO World Heritage Site where a maze of cobbled streets and brightly painted old wooden houses are home to artisan workshops. Sadly it's Sunday and everything's closed, making Rauma feel like a ghost town straight out of an old Western movie. I decide to move on, east towards Tampere.

Driving in Finland is very pleasant – the road surfaces are in good condition and the views encompass large expanses of wonderful nature with lakes and trees as far as the eye can see. I briefly leave Route 12 to reach the archaeological site of Sammallahdenmäki. Hidden in the middle of a forest, this Bronze Age burial site boasts 36 funerary cairns. The magnificent setting is a tempting place to overnight too – the parking area even has dry toilets.

Most of the time, sleeping alone in the middle of the forest guarantees a quiet night, lulled by the sounds of nature; sometimes I feel more anxious though, listening out for the slightest noise. What if a ferocious beast attacks the camper van? This time, fatigue silences my overactive imagination and sweeps me off into a deep sleep. It's nothing more ferocious than birdsong that wakes me up at first light the next morning.

Travelling by camper gives you the freedom to change itineraries and routes to suit your mood and interests. At the last minute, I decide not to take the excursion to the big city of Tampere, choosing instead to extend this dive into nature with a visit to Isojärvi National Park in the centre of the country. Captivated by the forests and lakes that flash by through the windows, I don't even notice I've notched up 213km (132 miles) on the clock. On arrival, to stretch my legs, I hike 6km (4 miles) through forests, ravines, lakes and beaver ponds, before setting up camp 25km (15.5 miles) to the south on the island of Papinsaari.

EXHIBITION CENTRE WEEGEE

Located in the town of Espoo, just 15km (9 miles) west of Helsinki, this former industrial printing works has been converted into four museums, offering a wealth of exhibition space: the Museum of Modern Art; the Toy Museum; the Watchmaking Museum; the Futuro House. The latter is a famous yellow building, shaped like a vintage flying saucer, designed by Finnish architect Matti Suuronen in the late 60s. There are fewer than 65 of these left in the world.

Bottom: Isojärvi National Park. Above: Forest landscape. Opposite: Porvoo. Page 245: Sammallahdenmäki forest.

Driving in Finland is very pleasant – the road surfaces are in good condition and the views encompass large expanses of wonderful nature with lakes and trees as far as the eye can see.

Next day, after a hearty breakfast facing Lake Vastiainen, a few photo stops along the way and a bit of a reading in the sun on Vääksy Beach, I finally arrive in Porvoo, on Finland's southern coast. This handsome medieval town is one of the oldest in the country, full of cute streets with cute houses, red warehouses by the river and an abandoned railway station. This is a place that takes you back to another era. I visit the old town hall, now a museum, continue past the antique shops and stop off at Helmi's to taste the famous *runebergintorttu*, an almond and rum cake topped with powdered sugar and raspberry jam. It's said to have been the favourite breakfast of great national poet Johan Runeberg, a native of the town.

All that's left to do now is head for Helsinki, where I have an appointment with a garage for a mundane but necessary vehicle service – taking good care of your trusty steed is essential when travelling long distances across Europe. The capital is easy to visit on foot and I'm seduced by this cutting-edge, dynamic city, a hub for design, where creativity is palpable everywhere – in the architecture, the boutiques and the trendy, offbeat bars. A contrasting but equally appealing side to Finland after the vast stretches of wilderness I've just crossed. **AL**

ROAD MAP

Start // Turku
Finish // Helsinki
Distance // 560km (348 miles)
Recommended duration // 7-to-10 days
When to go // Spring and summer for warm weather; autumn for forest colours
Culinary specialities // *Karjalanpiirakka* (traditional pasty), *korvapuusti* (cinnamon rolls), *grillimakkara* (grilled sausages), *silli ja uudet perunat* (new potato and herring salad)

THE PERFECT SLEEP SPOT

Description // Overnight option surrounded by nature
GPS coordinates // 60.840394, 21.290123
Light pollution // None
Access // Narrow gravel road for a few kilometres
Facilities // Barbecue area, dry toilets
Visitor numbers // Very low
Little extras // Very quiet location with a beautiful view of the water. Swimming is available.

Opposite, from top: Forest landscape, Sweden; Lofoten Islands, Norway.

MORE LIKE THIS
FAR NORTH FUN

NATIONAL PARKS OF NORTHERN SWEDEN

Northern Sweden lends itself to exploration by camper van, mixed with hiking and other outdoor activities. Abisko National Park is the starting point for the 440km (273 mile) Kungsleden (Royal Way) trail. In summer, explore the boreal forests, fjords, canyons and waterfalls, or sign up for one of the many activities from exploring caves to fly-fishing. In Kärkevagge valley, crystal-clear Lake Trollsjön makes for memorable photos. From November to March, take a chairlift up to Aurora Sky Station to watch the northern lights. Then head for Sarek National Park via the E10 and E45, which run alongside numerous lakes. This second park, with its peaks, massifs, glacial valleys and escarpments, appeals to experienced mountaineers and hikers.

Start // Abisko National Park
Finish // Sarek National Park
Distance // 414km (257 miles)
More information // visitsweden.com

FINNISH LAPLAND

For a winter trip in the camper van, start with Kemi, in northern Finland on the shores of the Gulf of Bothnia. Leave your vehicle here for a night to enjoy the icy decor of the SnowHotel (mid-December to end of March). Follow the fir-lined E75 along the Kemijoki River to Santa Claus Village in Rovaniemi. The capital of Finnish Lapland, this welcoming town, rebuilt after WWII, is surrounded by Arctic nature. Heading even further north, drive carefully along Route 79 – you're likely to come across wild reindeer – passing through beautiful countryside covered in a blanket of white. Next stop is the extraordinary snow village of Lainio, where a hotel, bar, chapel and numerous activities await, including snowmobile safaris and dog sled rides. If you're lucky you'll get to see the northern lights too.

Start // Kemi
Arrival // Lainio Snow Village
Distance // 284km (176 miles)
More information // visitrovaniemi.fi

THE LOFOTEN ISLANDS (NORWAY)

With its exceptionally scenic fjords and countless wilderness campsites on the Atlantic, the Lofoten Archipelago is one of Europe's most beautiful destinations, reached along the E10 road. The region boasts incredible white sandy beaches, such as Flakstad, Uttakleiv and Haukland, as well as dramatic coastlines, with lots of small red houses clinging to the mountainsides above deep blue waters. Take a trip out to sea to meet the orcas, hike the coastal paths or travel back in time with the reconstructions and activities at the Lofotr Viking Museum in Borg, including the replica *Vargfotr* ship and traditional houses. Once you've had your fill of *stockfisch* (dried, unsalted cod), take a walk through charming fishing villages such as Kabelvåg, Stamsund, Ballstad, Nusfjord, Reine and Å. Slow travel takes on its full meaning here.

Start // Fiskebøl
Finish // Å
Distance // 229km (142 miles)
More information // visitnorway.com

DISCOVERING WALES

Hit the road for a trip linking Wales' national parks with its Irish Sea coastline.

The sky is pouring its wrath onto the roof of the T4 and the storm is showing no signs of stopping. This sentence could sum up many moments of our Welsh road trip. Anastasia and I haven't had much luck with the weather, but we intend to make the most of our time in Wales regardless. I met my new friend three days ago, in Glasgow, through couchsurfing, a network for globetrotters. We quickly hit it off, and I offered her the chance to join me for a week, driving the camper across Wales from north to south, flanking the Irish Sea and exploring the country's three national parks.

There's no shortage of exceptional places to include on the itinerary and we have to choose between several great options. First choice is Snowdonia (Eyri in Welsh), in the northwest of the country, and we're immediately pleased with our decision: hilly landscapes, rocky outcrops, scattered lakes and panoramic views on either side of the A470. We travel through this mosaic of autumnal colours at a gentle speed, in no hurry to exit this glorious, mountainous region. There are many advantages to going slowly – it gives you time to spot things you might otherwise miss, stopping when something catches your eye. Among them is Dolwyddelan Castle, a fascinating ruined fortress built on a hill-top, whose stones have watched over Snowdonia since the 13th century.

The ribbon of tarmac we've been following for the past few days leads us to New Quay, a lovely coastal town of multicoloured houses. We wander along the beach, where small fishing boats are moored, and breathe in the Irish Sea air. In search of an overnight parking spot, we take to the road again and find what we're looking for 14km (9 miles) further south, at Llangrannog Beach, whose almost deserted car park has a direct view of the sea. We're delighted. The rain is now too heavy to set foot outside but my friend is from St Petersburg, so I have an idea. I grab my accordion and start playing *Katyusha*, a traditional Russian song, which Anastasia sings along to, accompanying herself on guitar. The hours fly by late into the night, with hazy moonlight making the occasional appearance, reflected in puddles between showers. If you're going to kill time, you might as well do it in style.

Next stop is Pembrokeshire National Park, one of the UK's smallest, but don't underestimate its appeal. A rugged coastline and grassy cliffs are accessible on foot via the awesome Pembrokeshire Coast Path. We park the van at Nolton Haven

and set off to hike up a steep, black rock face. Below us, St Brides Bay stretches out, with one cove after another creating a magical sight.

Back on board, we drive 140km (87 miles) along the south coast to Rhossili Bay on the Gower Peninsula, where more cliffs await. Crowned with lush grass, they enclose some real gems: small beaches protected by their rocky setting. A battalion of clouds followed by torrential rain force us back into the camper where we try to dry our clothes, a difficult operation in a vehicle with no heating and high humidity. Hanging from one end of the van to the other are lines on which a large part of our wet wardrobe can be found, making it laborious to move around. So we don't. Instead we opt for tea, followed by reading a good book under some blankets.

Brecon Beacons National Park has nothing to envy other parks in Wales. Along a misty, winding road, the park reveals itself to us, from lush valleys to peaceful lakes, and from high mountain plateaus to flat-topped hills. If years of nomadic life have taught me that the grass isn't greener elsewhere, it would seem that it is here – threading our way along the A4067 and then the A40, we are amazed by the patchwork of verdant hues around us. Along the way, we come across a few nuggets, including Llangorse Lake, home to a monster known as Gorsey. Much to our regret, we don't catch a glimpse of him. We do, however, spot a strange island featuring a circular thatched hut, later learning that this is the only *crannog* in the country, a lake dwelling built on stilts in Neolithic times.

It's impossible to take a road trip to Wales without stopping off at its capital Cardiff, a port on the south coast. After several days in the wilderness, we're happy to be back in the

THE PEMBROKESHIRE COAST PATH

The 299km (186 mile) Pembrokeshire Coast Path, inaugurated in 1970, is one of the most beautiful walks in Wales. From Poppit Sands in the north to Amroth in the south, one wonderful view follows another: sheer cliffs; volcanic rock; ancient glacial valleys. Not to mention 58 beaches and 14 ports where anyone hiking all or part of the path (allow 10 to 15 days in total) can refuel.

Above: Mount Tryfan, Snwodonia National Park. Opposite: Sheep in Brecon Beacons National Park. Below, from left: Pierhead, Cardiff; Llangrannog. Page 251, from top: Snowdonia National Park; Brecon Beacons National Park.

'If years of nomadic living have taught me that the grass isn't greener elsewhere, it would seem that it is here – threading our way along the A4067 and then the A40, we are stunned by the patchwork of verdant hues around us.'

city, but there's a tinge of sadness too as our arrival means the adventure is drawing to a close. The Welsh capital is very diverse. We start our tour in the area around the Millennium (or Principality) Stadium, famous to rugby and football fans the world over. We then cross the bustling city centre to Mermaid Quay for a completely different atmosphere. Among the modern buildings here, one stands out – the Pierhead, nicknamed 'Baby Big Ben' for its clock tower, houses a museum on Welsh history within its red brick walls. We sit on a bench outside for a while, and as other people speed past us, we remain quiet and still, trying to slow down time to savour the last moments of our journey together. **AD**

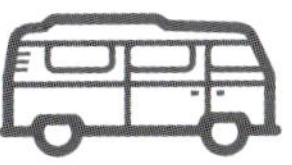

ROAD MAP

Start // Snowdonia (Eyri) National Park
Finish // Cardiff
Distance // 473km (294 miles)
Recommended duration // 5-to-7 days
When to go // Summer, when the weather is more inviting
Culinary speciality // *Welsh rarebit* (toasted bread with a melted cheddar, beer and mustard topping)

THE PERFECT SLEEP SPOT

Description // Splendid view of Llangrannog Beach
GPS coordinates // 52.15976594041786, -4.470239774319931
Access // Easy, by road (paid parking)
Facilities // Public showers and toilets
Visitor numbers // Very few in low season
Little extras // Nearby pubs for an evening drink

Opposite: Yorkshire Dales National Park, England.

MORE LIKE THIS
LITTLE-KNOWN WONDERS PARKS

THE YORKSHIRE DALES (ENGLAND)

This itinerary starts in Leeds, a dynamic city in the north of England, from where you drive north into the Yorkshire Dales National Park. Between wild hills and quiet valleys, you'll appreciate the absence of light pollution as you contemplate the Milky Way after dark. The national park is also famous for its caves, such as Stump Cross Caverns, where the magic of geology will fascinate you. Continue further north, past scenic villages, and discover the Cotter Force waterfalls, surrounded by a small wood – a delight for the eyes in every season. Other noteworthy waterfalls are those of Ingleton, to the south; a 6km (4 mile) trail leads to the Twiss and Doe rivers, with their rare flora. Before returning to Leeds, don't miss the Three Peaks (Whernside, Ingleborough and Pen-y-ghent), three mountains to climb for a privileged view of hills stretching to infinity.

Start/Finish // Leeds
Distance // 225km (140 miles)
More information // yorkshiredales.org.uk

THE BAVARIAN FOREST (GERMANY)

The Bavarian Forest National Park is Germany's oldest. This unspoilt area offers nature-loving travellers great walking opportunities and plenty of wildlife spotting (lynx, capercaillie, otters), as does the neighbouring Czech park of Šumava. Start the trip at the base of Grosser Arber, the highest peak in the region at 1456m (4477ft). You can walk to the summit to discover a sweeping view of the wooded mountain range below. For an overnight stay in a van, opt for the Lindberg paid car park, which has toilets and electricity. The next day, hike to the summit of Grosser Rachel and the glacial lake of the same name, watched over by a wooden church. After a 34km (21 mile) drive, be amazed by the Baumwipfelpfad footbridge near Neuschönau, an astonishing structure overlooking the forest canopy and with exceptional views.

Start // Grosser Arber
Finish // Neuschönau
Distance // 70km (43 miles)
More information // germany.travel

THE VALBONA VALLEY (ALBANIA)

In the heart of the Albanian Alps, the village of Bajram Curri marks the starting point for this trip to the furthest reaches of Albania. Get behind the wheel to discover the Valbona Valley National Park, near the border with Montenegro. Dragobi will be your first stop: admire its Alpine-style houses and the deep Valbona mountain stream, then hire a guide for a session in the nearby cave. If you're into mountain driving, take a round trip to Çerem, an attractive village in the middle of a forest. Set the GPS for Valbona, the most important – but still very quiet – village in the area. Its traditional dwellings, overlooked by high mountains, are very appealing. Before heading back to Bajram Curri, visit the hamlet of Rrogam. A crystal-clear river, sharp peaks and pretty waterfall make the valley here a place of rare beauty.

Start/Finish // Bajram Curri
Distance // 76km (47 miles)
More information // albania.al

WESTERN SCOTLAND'S SHORES

From port to port, escape along Scotland's coastline, with a stopover on the Isle of Skye.

I fell under the spell of Ullapool and its colourful harbour. After several weeks of road-tripping from the south of England to the north of Scotland, I've just made a long stopover in this quiet, welcoming Highland town. But after several days' rest, it's time for me to get back on course – I plan to drive to Glasgow along the country's west coast.

First though, Applecross. Only 140km (87 miles) separate me from my destination, and yet it's quite an adventure to reach this little corner of the world. Driving a camper van along the A835 and then the A890 requires as much patience as skill. Here, deer block my path; there, sheep pile up in front of my vehicle. On the Bealach na Bà pass, the last stretch of spectacular mountain scenery, I'm surprisingly slow. The gradient sometimes reaches 25% and my T4 struggles to keep up. Still, I arrive safely, as the sun sets, and settle down for a night on the edge of Loch a' Mhuilinn.

Early in the morning, I'm thrilled to discover a wild and grand place. I take my time driving around the Applecross Peninsula, so as to soak up all the sensational scenery. Rarely have I felt as isolated as I do in these desolate, mountainous lands. In places, lush green valleys fade into the immensity of the lochs, rock and water becoming one. People are scarce. Only the village of Applecross has a few inhabitants, most of whom seem to be on the pier.

After travelling back along the Bealach na Bà Pass, 70km (43 miles) further on I reach the coastal road leading to the Isle of Skye Bridge. The concrete structure spanning the inlet in no way foreshadows the beauty to come. The largest island in the Inner Hebrides Archipelago boasts plenty of highlights: medieval castles, fishing villages and iconic landscapes in abundance. Along the battered coastline, monumental cliffs and elongated lochs also offer superb places to pause.

I take the A87, dotted with ports, ruins, rivers and waterfalls, intending to tour the island without any specific destination in mind. The first night is spent in Portree, the largest town, very pretty with its elegant, tiered centre. The pastel houses that line

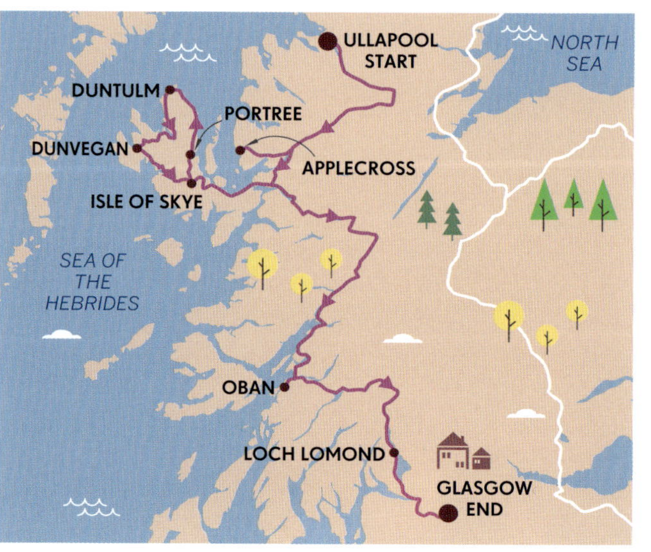

the harbour catch my eye as soon as I arrive and I park nearby. The air is stormy and it doesn't take long for heavy rain to fall on the sheet metal of the T4. The inside now smells of hot soup – a comforting meal I like to cook when the weather's bad. Darkness falls early, meaning it's only 6pm when I'm sipping my soup, in my pyjamas (keep that between us), absent-mindedly reading old travel magazines.

The next day, I stroll around Portree again before taking the A855 for 40km (25 miles) to the northern tip of the island. The scenic route takes in a number of viewpoints, including Kilt Rock, where a waterfall drops dramatically from a basalt cliff and plunges noisily into the Atlantic. Further afield, Duntulm is a pleasant stopping-off point. Black-headed sheep graze peacefully near the ruins of a castle overlooking the ocean. The very image of Scotland as I'd imagined it.

In fact, while I'm delighted with the Scottish landscape, one thing is weighing on my mind – after several weeks of solitude, I feel the need to meet new people and share my adventure with others. I'm used to travelling alone, and generally always find opportunities to make new friends, but few have presented themselves since the start of my British adventure. These are my thoughts as I drive towards the medieval castle of Dunvegan, a fortress of dull, massive walls built into the rock.

As luck would have it, a hitchhiker appears at just the right moment on the side of the road. As a frequent user of this mode of transport myself, I open the doors of the camper van to him and the ensuing hours pass quickly by his side as I take the opportunity to perfect my Scottish accent. Eventually, we find ourselves in Oban, his destination, which becomes mine too. I spend three days in this pretty, grey-stoned port in the county of Argyll. The main thoroughfare smells of chocolate, fish and chips and whisky (a distillery has been operating here since 1794), while sea spray wets the waterfront. After visiting the two brick cathedrals and inspecting the ruins of Dunollie Castle, I take the time to write a message on a couchsurfing site, which puts travellers in touch with each other. My little advert was enough to trigger numerous invitations, many of them from Glasgow, so I set off for Scotland's biggest city.

I pull up and park in front of the apartment of Thibaut, a young Frenchman living in Glasgow, with whom I plan to have a coffee. We hit it off immediately, and my trip takes a new turn as I spend several days with him discovering the city from his perspective. It's impossible to describe every one of my favourite experiences in this special place on either side of the River Clyde, but I'll single out a walk through the Victorian necropolis below medieval St Mungo's Cathedral: a collection of paths lined with tombs and mausoleums, from which the view over the Scottish metropolis is particularly beautiful.

I also make friends with other couchsurfers, some Glaswegians, others expatriates. Together, we set off on a

WALKS ON THE ISLE OF SKYE

The geology of the Isle of Skye makes for plenty of unforgettable hikes, including to the pointed summit of the Old Man of Storr, the Quiraing volcanic formation and the spectacular Cuillin Range. Other walking destinations include the turquoise Fairy Pools, beneath ebony mountains dotted with waterfalls, and the white sands of Coral Beach, a pristine paradise.

Below: Old Man of Storr, Isle of Skye. Above: On the shores of Loch Shieldaig. Opposite: Highland cattle. Page 257, from top: Views of Applecross from near Bealach na Bà pass; Near the ruins of Duntulm castle.

ROAD MAP

Start // Ullapool
Finish // Loch Lomond
Distance // 788km (490 miles)
Recommended duration // 7-to-10 days
When to go // May to September, for the best weather
Culinary speciality // Shortbread (traditional biscuits, often rectangular in shape)

THE PERFECT SLEEP SPOT

Description // Lookout on majestic Bealach Na Bà Pass, on the road to Applecross
GPS coordinates // 57.422149375874916, -5.693450049849343
Access // Via a steep road (take your time)
Facilities // None (but digital nomads will benefit from 4G)
Traffic // Large car park, busy during the day, but only a few vehicles stay overnight
Little extras // Magnificent views all the way to the Isle of Skye

'The scenic route takes in a number of viewpoints, including Kilt Rock, where a waterfall drops dramatically . . . into the Atlantic.'

camper tour around Loch Lomond, some 50km (31 miles) from the city. A sense of tranquillity emanates from this lake and spreads through its wooded shores. Surrounded by trees, the pebble beach at Firkin Point, near Luss on the western side, is the ideal place to bring out the thermos filled with hot tea and share a few shortbread biscuits in good company, gazing out at the loch at the end of a memorable trip. **AD**

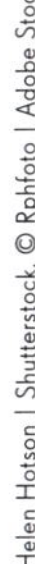

Opposite, from top: Peak District, England; Kirkjufell, Iceland.

MORE LIKE THIS
NORTH EUROPEAN LANDSCAPES

THE SNÆFELLSNES PENINSULA (ICELAND)

The 100km (62 mile) Snæfellsnes Peninsula is bordered by the 54, a loop of road offering impressive scenery and guaranteed driving pleasure. Explore the southern part of the island first, and park for a few hours at the Ytri Tunga Beach car park (no overnighting), where you can watch the seals without getting too close. A few kilometres further on, pose in front of the Malarrif Lighthouse, overlooking the wild Atlantic, before walking along the black sandy beach of Djúpalón and its rocky lagoon. Drive around the Snæfellsjökull glacier and continue your road trip on the northern side of the peninsula. Stop to be wowed at the cylindrical outline of Kirkjufell, an iconic mountain, then compose yourself over a hot chocolate in the charming village of Stykkishólmur.
Start // Ytri Tunga beach
Finish // Stykkishólmur
Distance // 150km (93 miles)
More information // visiticeland.com

SOUTHWEST DENMARK

Drive through the Wadden Sea National Park, a combination of lagoons, sandbanks, mudflats and salt marshes, in spring or autumn and witness the incredible 'black sun' – the murmuration of millions of starlings at the end of the day. Start your road trip in Ribe, Denmark's oldest town, with a visit to the Viking Museum and Viking Centre, as well as the Wadden Sea Centre to soak up the maritime atmosphere. Follow the coastline for around 30km (19 miles) to admire the *Man Meets The Sea* statues in Esbjerg, 9m (29.5ft) tall giants sitting facing out to sea. Continue north to Hvide Sande, a barrier between the North Sea and the Ringkøbing Fjord, known as a surfer's paradise. Vanlifers with a childlike spirit can then head inland to Legoland in Billund, an amusement park all about the famous little bricks.
Start // Ribe
Finish // Billund
Distance // 221km (137 miles)
More information // visitdenmark.com

THE PEAK DISTRICT (ENGLAND)

Sitting prettily between the northern English cities of Manchester and Sheffield, the Peak District is prime camper van territory, with its hills, moors and rock formations. Park near Blue John Cavern, Castleton, and treat yourself to an unforgettable spelunking experience in this limestone cave. Deep underground, you'll find a variety of fossils that bear witness to bygone eras. Wander the welcoming spa town of Buxton, then visit Chatsworth House, a stately home and one of the region's must-sees. Next, drive north to Stanage, where you'll discover a bleakly beautiful landscape of rocks and moorland. If you're interested in climbing, hiking, mountain biking or paragliding, you've come to the right place. All that's left to do is complete the loop by taking the A6187 along the River Derwent.
Start/Finish // Castleton
Distance // 74km (46 miles)
More information // peakdistrict.gov.uk

WEST COAST IRELAND WONDERS

Follow an itinerary through wonderfully unspoilt countryside along Ireland's western shores.

I quickly drive through the car park entrance while the barrier is up, leave the camper and race on foot to O'Brien's Tower, on the edge of the Cliffs of Moher, hoping to arrive just in time for sunset. No luck. The low clouds have decided to deny me the view of the sun sinking below the Atlantic I was hoping for. Instead I'm left contemplating the still impressive dark cliffs rising 214m (702ft) above the ocean. And anyway, I plan to devote the whole of the next day to this mythical site, the first stage of my western Ireland road trip through the counties of Clare, Connemara and Mayo.

As night falls, so does the temperature. Back at the van, I turn on the gas bottle but unfortunately my heater is acting up. I hold down the thermostat knob and turn it, but there's no spark. I check that the ground level is flat, the bottle and circuits are open, and the batteries are in good condition. All fine so I try again and again nothing happens. All I can do now is fill a hot water bottle and grab a cold-weather sleeping bag out of my cupboard.

At dawn, I'm back gazing at the cliffs, alone in this majestic landscape. I set off on foot along the rocky clifftop for 5.5km (3.5 miles), as far as Hag's Head. I'm not pressed for time, so take photos, walk around deep puddles, count cairns, look for the infernal cave where Dumbledore and Harry Potter sought a horcrux. When I return, the visitor centre has filled up in my absence. As I leave the car park, I realise I was supposed to pay for my stay but hadn't. Fortunately, the same barrier that let me in opens automatically and lets me leave without paying anything. '*Go raibh maith agat agus beannacht!*' ('Thank you and goodbye!')

East of the Cliffs of Moher, I cross the rocky plateau of the Burren National Park. Its vast, lunar-like expanses are a hymn to silence, and the immense crevasse-strewn karst zone at its heart is a delight for any geology enthusiast. At Leamaneh Castle, I turn north onto the R480, a church here and the ruins of a fort there marking out my route. I stop to visit the Poulnabrone dolmen, one of Ireland's oldest megaliths, topped by a vast

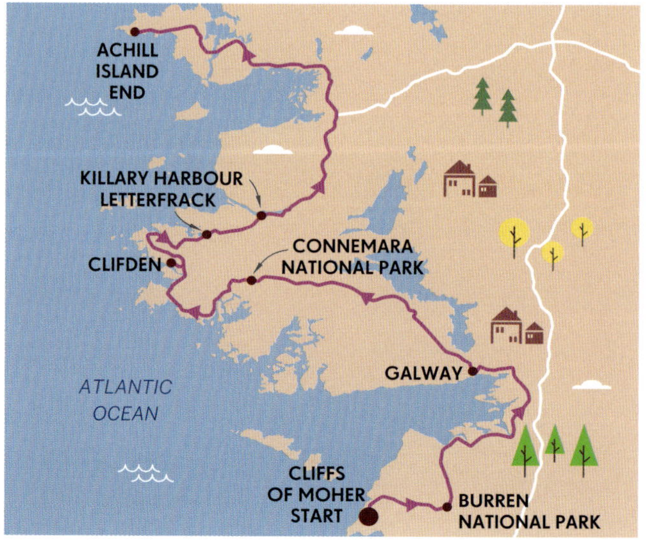

'After a feast of fresh oysters, I'm on the way to Clifden, the largest town in the Connemara region, crossing peat bog landscapes and skirting shimmering lakes.'

horizontal stone. Camp tonight is at Newton Castle, not far from Ballyvaughan and Galway Bay.

The next day, following the coast on the N67 for 50km (31 miles), I arrive in the city of Galway, in the middle of market day. On the church square are the colourful stalls of florists, artisans and takeaway food vendors. It's the perfect opportunity to sample local specialities – salmon, smoked mackerel and oysters – and to chat with local producers, who are often happy to offer advice to passing visitors. I return to the camper with a basket full of provisions.

After a feast of fresh oysters, I'm on my way to Clifden, the largest town in the Connemara region, crossing peat bog landscapes and skirting shimmering lakes. I recite out loud a few Gaelic words I learned in Galway: '*Dia duit*! *Conas atá tú?*' ('Hello! How are you?'). A stop at Pines Island Viewpoint – a small island planted with pine trees in Derryclare Lough, with the Twelve Bens range as a backdrop – marks my entry into Connemara National Park, one of Ireland's most beautiful nature reserves, with its bogs, moors, mountains and lakes. After practising my pebble skipping on the lough, I continue my exploration of the park and soon understand why this wild and bewitching terrain has inspired so many artists. I take refuge for the night in the campsite near Clifden Castle, west of the pretty Victorian town itself.

Next on the agenda the following morning are the sights and sounds of the Sky Road. This short 10km (6 mile) circuit winds through craggy landscapes dotted with heather, offering lovely views of the ocean, Inishbofin and other smaller islands. I then join the N59 towards Letterfrack, park at the visitor centre and set off to climb Diamond Hill, a loop of around three to four hours. The summit offers a 360° view of Connemara National Park – weather permitting, because, yet again, I've got my head in the clouds today.

Just past Letterfrack lies Kylemore Abbey, a splendid Gothic Revival castle with extravagant gardens, commissioned by Mitchell Henry, a successful businessman, for his wife Margaret Vaughan. In 1920, the house was bought by the community of the Irish Benedictine Ladies of Ypres. It's a sublime spot on the shores of Pollacapall Lough and definitely worth a visit.

Penultimate stop before end of the road Achill Island is Killary Harbour, 10km to the northeast (6 miles). This fjord separating County Galway from County Mayo is the longest in the country (14km/9 miles). A food truck, Misunderstood Heron, is perfectly positioned to provide a spectacular view with the opportunity to sample the excellent local mussels. After this break, I head north on the N59 to end this trip in style on Achill Island, linked to the mainland by a bridge. I instantly have a crush on this mountainous place, its wild moors, heavenly beaches and striking cliffs a fitting full stop to this west coast drive. **AL**

GOLF IN IRELAND

Ireland is renowned as a golfing paradise, with almost 400 links and parkland courses. Many international golf competitions are held here. Located in a grand natural setting, the Galway and Ballyconneely links offer exceptional windswept rounds.

Opposite, from left: Pines Island viewpoint; Achill Island; Connemara Mountains. Page 263, from top: Cliffs of Moher; On Achill Island.

ROAD MAP

Start // Cliffs of Moher
Finish // Achill Island
Distance // 341km (212 miles)
Recommended duration // 5-to-7 days
When to go // The region is beautiful year-round
Culinary specialities // Chowder (fish and seafood soup), shepherd's pie (minced lamb topped with mashed potato), Irish coffee

THE PERFECT SURF SPOT

Description // Magnificent meadow by the ocean
GPS coordinates // 53.721687, -9.899625
Light pollution // None
Access // Easy, by road
Facilities // Public toilets
Visitor numbers // The spot is very spacious.
Little extras // A great place for beach walks, swimming, surfing and kitesurfing.

Opposite, clockwise from top: Highlands near Glencoe, Scotland; The Dark Hedges, Northern Ireland; Statue of the Bremen Musicians, Germany.

MORE LIKE THIS LEGENDARY LANDSCAPES

THE FAIRY TALE ROUTE (GERMANY)

Follow in the footsteps of the Brothers Grimm on the 600km (373 mile) German Fairy Tale Road. Between Hanau, the brothers' hometown, and Bremen, enchanted forests, mythical castles, nature parks and cultural highlights follow one after another. Leave Hanau and head into the lovely countryside of the Spessart Mountains. Further afield, don't miss Alsfeld, a gorgeous medieval town leading to Little Red Riding Hood country. Visit Snow White in Hesse's most beautiful gardens at Bad Wildungen. Discover Sleeping Beauty's castle in Sababurg. And don't forget Rapunzel's Tower at Trendelburg Castle. Once past the Weser River, take a side trip to the Steinhuder Meer, the largest lake in northwest Germany. Along its way, the route has plenty of country campsites and parking areas.

Start // Hanau
Finish // Bremen
Distance // 600km (373 miles)
More information // deutsche-maerchenstrasse.com

IN THE LAND OF GAME OF THRONES, (NORTHERN IRELAND)

You don't have to be a die-hard fan of *Game of Thrones* to marvel at the Northern Irish landscapes that served as backdrops for its filming: the rocky coastline, the sandy and shingle beaches, the moors, the green valleys and the churches, chapels and castles that dot them. This route starts at Tollymore Forest Park, joins the coast north of Belfast, then follows it to Downhill Beach. Between these two destinations, you'll discover a wide variety of places and get to gaze on the Giant's Causeway, over whose famous basalt columns a legendary giant walked to reach Scotland. The GOT scouting team did a remarkable job unearthing stunning locations such as Castle Ward, Cushendun Caves and the Dark Hedges, a twisted tree-lined avenue.

Start // Tollymore Forest Park
Finish // Downhill Beach
Distance // 277km (172 miles)
More information // discovernorthernireland.com

IN SEARCH OF HARRY POTTER (UNITED KINGDOM)

A Harry Potter-themed road trip is a great way to explore the UK. After a visit to Warner Bros Studios near London, take the M40 to Oxford where Christ Church College and other university buildings stood in for Hogwarts school. Continue west to Gloucester's Gothic cathedral, another Hogwarts set. As you make your way to the North Sea coast, discover at your own pace other places that served as filming locations, such as Durham Cathedral and Alnwick Castle, before crossing into Scotland. In Edinburgh, George Heriot's School is said to have been JK Rowling's inspiration for the wizarding school. Continue on to Glencoe in the Highlands, where the quidditch matches were filmed, and then to Glenfinnan Viaduct, crossed by the Hogwarts Express (aka the Jacobite Steam Train). You can camp on the Ardnamurchan Peninsula, but beware of the narrow road.

Start // Warner Bros Studios
Finish // Ardnamurchan Peninsula
Distance // 1168km (726 miles)
More information // visitbritain.com

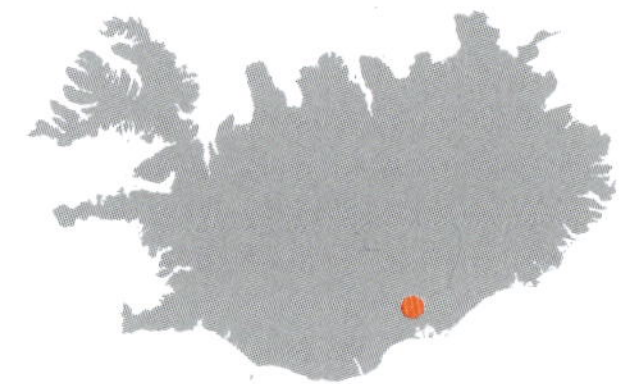

JEWELS OF SOUTHERN ICELAND

On your checklist: exceptional waterfalls; a magnificent glacial lagoon; sometimes frozen, often lunar landscapes; and a few wildlife encounters.

The wind whips my face relentlessly, and snowflakes pile up on my backpack. Winter might not be the best time of year to explore Iceland, but I wanted to experience the extreme cold once in my life. I've just spent a month alone, on foot, in this land of ice and fire, and am now looking forward to meeting up with two friends for a week, to cross the country with them from east to west.

In Seyðisfjörður, the port where ferries arrive from Denmark, I meet up with Clara and Eva. Our plan is to travel to Reykjavík, following the famous Ring Road, aka Route 1, taking in fjords, waterfalls, glacial lagoons and 'diamond' beaches.

First, we take a quick tour of the small village of Seyðisfjörður, admiring its elegant pale-blue church, before turning south and beginning our drive. This adventure across Iceland gets off to the best possible start. Along a road that is half-covered in snow we're treated to one awesome fjord after another. The coastline, rocky and covered in a great white blanket, is so rugged that we'd soon lose all sense of direction if the sun didn't light up the sky, pointing us towards the sunset. Time to apply the handbrake and settle in for the night. The cabin is cramped for three people, but that has at least one advantage – combined body warmth helps win our first battle against sub-zero temperatures.

Waking up next morning, hot cups of coffee are the first item on the day's agenda. Caffeine consumed, we tidy up the vehicle and set off again along Route 1. A herd of twenty or so reindeer, their coats a mix of grey and white, treads the frozen expanse bordering the Atlantic Ocean. We pull over to contemplate them in silence. A timeless moment.

Some 350km (217 miles) after leaving Seyðisfjörður, we reach the Jökulsárlón Lagoon, this time greeted not by reindeer but by seals. On the edge of Vatnajökull National Park – and its namesake glacier, Iceland's largest – the lagoon is home to these marine mammals who swim peacefully in its waters between blue-tinged icebergs. On the other side of the lagoon,

the famous ice rocks that give Diamond Beach its name glisten on a long black sandbank. Nature never ceases to surprise.

Another unforgettable black-sand beach, that of Vík, awaits us 190km (118 miles) further on. If this dark stretch resembles the previous one at Diamond Beach, its setting is entirely unique. A handful of sharp rocks jut out of the ocean. Behind us, basalt columns line up in perfect harmony. The vision is hypnotic, but we're still mindful of the rising tide, an all-too-often fatal trap for visitors. We head into Vík village, dominated by a charming white church with a red roof. With the panorama of the open ocean as a backdrop, the whole place is worthy of the most beautiful postcards.

Some 35km (22 miles) after this tiny town, we reach the site of the famous Skógafoss waterfall at dusk. It's not always easy finding a place to sleep in Iceland as many of the country's natural sites are protected. Here, however, a sign indicates that overnighting is possible for a fee. We're delighted to have stumbled across an authorised spot. What's more, at this late hour, we're the only ones at the foot of the falls, feeling its presence despite the darkness, hearing it splashing continuously. Mistresses of all we survey, we pull out all the stops: gas bottle, dented saucepan and packet of spaghetti. What a pleasure to eat hot food in such cold temperatures.

After a few hours' sleep, we head out to see the wide, milky veil of tumbling water before the influx of visitors, continuing our hike to where more modest waterfalls can be found. The scene is exceptional: numerous gulls nest in the nooks and

HALLGRÍMSKIRKJA CHURCH

Impressive Hallgrímskirkja, built between 1945 and 1986, is the capital's iconic Lutheran church and the country's largest. This bold, rocket-like concrete structure, with its stark interior, evokes the basalt organs, mountains and glaciers found throughout Iceland. A 74.5m (244ft) spire makes it one of Iceland's tallest buildings. Accessible to the public, the tower offers a wonderful view of the capital, which the church dominates.

Above: Eva's converted vehicle. Opposite: Seljalandsfoss waterfall. Below, from left: Seyðisfjörður church; Mountainous landscape on Route 1. Page 269: Vík.

'A herd of twenty or so reindeer, their coats a mix of grey and white, treads the frozen expanse bordering the Atlantic Ocean.'

crannies on the cliffs and we catch a glimpse of the ocean in the distance.

Our next stop is 30km (19 miles) further on, at Seljalandsfoss, one the country's best-known waterfalls. The car park is full – and understandably so as this place is breathtaking. The torrent falls from a height of 65m (213ft) into a pool underneath, and a bonus feature of this cascade is that you can walk behind the sheet of water for an extra special encounter.

At the southwestern tip of Iceland, the Reykjanes Peninsula is less popular with visitors. Attracted by the promise of wide open spaces and fewer fellow travellers, we decide to explore this desolate land and, the only time we're unfaithful to Route 1 on this trip, we drive 170km (106 miles) along Route 427 to the Selvogur Campsite. The strip of land we're now surveying was worth the detour. We discover lunar, almost apocalyptic landscapes. Here more than anywhere else, surrounded by intensely geothermal lava fields, mineral lakes and jagged mountains, we feel that nature, all-powerful, will always have the last word.

The week is drawing to a close and we need to reach Reykjavík. Reluctantly giving up dreams of more side trips, the last leg of our journey is on the straight Highway 41. Soon, the world's most northerly capital, nestled between two magnificent fjords, welcomes us. After a tour of the museums and galleries, we take a long stroll along its shopping streets, including the famous, multicoloured Laugavegur, before heading to the seafront for one last deep breath of sea air. **AD**

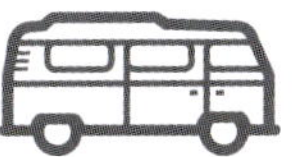

ROAD MAP

Start // Seyðisfjörður
Finish // Reykjavík
Distance // 844km (524 miles)
Recommended duration // 7-to-10 days
When to go // Summer has endless days; winter is a snowy wonderland
Culinary speciality // *Skyr* (traditional, creamy, thick yoghurt)

THE PERFECT SLEEP SPOT

Description // Skógafoss waterfall car park
GPS coordinates // 63.529681081237584, -19.5119793407158
Access // Easy, via Route 1
Activities // Plenty for hikers and amateur photographers alike
Visitor numbers // Well-known site very busy during the day; try to come early
Little extras // Follow the path up to the top of the waterfall for a view out to the Atlantic.

Opposite, clockwise from top: Seyðisfjörður; Around Lake Mývatn; A fissure in Þingvellir National Park.

MORE LIKE THIS ICELAND IN DEPTH

ROUTE 1'S NORTHERN REACHES

A thousand natural gems line Iceland's Route 1, the Ring Road, a legendary itinerary that circumnavigates the island. In a camper, you'll disembark the ferry at Seyðisfjörður. Drive 200km (124 miles) northwest and stretch your legs climbing Hverfjall, an ebony-colored volcanic crater (2-hour hike). Nearby, marvel at the geological wonders on the shores of Lake Mývatn and get up close – but not too close – to the boiling mud pools at Hverir. Continue west to spectacular Goðafoss waterfall, one of the most beautiful in the country, before taking a well-deserved break in the fishing village of Húsavík. Finally, back behind the wheel, head for Varmahlíð, near which you can visit the Glaumbœr Museum, featuring fascinating traditional turf-roofed buildings.

Start // Seyðisfjörður
Finish // Varmahlíð
Distance // 475km (295 miles)
More information // visiticeland.com

THE WESTFJORDS

Located at the northwestern tip of Iceland, the Vestfirðir (Westfjords) region experiences extreme winters, but can be explored in a camper from May to September. Start in Ísafjörður, the most important town in the area, a pleasant place to spend a few hours. Continue on to the Dynjandi Waterfalls, accessible on foot along a short trail, along which you can admire several exceptional cascades. Then head south along Route 60 to Hellulaug for a soak in a hot spring right on the beach – a classic experience on any trip to Iceland. You can then take the 62 and 612 westwards to stop off at the incredible red sandy beach of Rauðasandur. Finally, head for the Látrabjarg cliff at the tip of the peninsula, a favourite with birdwatchers for the puffins, guillemots and razorbills that can be seen there in summer.

Start // Ísafjörður
Finish // Látrabjarg
Distance // 204km (127 miles)
More information // visiticeland.com

THE GOLDEN CIRCLE

Iceland's flagship tour, the Golden Circle, will leave no vanlifer disappointed. Begin in Þingvellir National Park, gazing out over the natural lake of Þingvallavatn. You're at the junction of the Eurasian and North American tectonic plates. Walk through the impressive Almannagjá fault along a path that leads to stunning Öxaráfoss waterfall, set in basalt rock. Just 60km (37 miles) away, Geysir is another treat for the eyes, with its Strokkur geyser's jet of boiling water shooting 30m (98ft) skywards every ten minutes or so. Nearby, it's the turn of popular Gullfoss waterfall to fill you with wonder – this huge, multilevel cascade, steeped in legend, is particularly photogenic. Last stop on the trip is the purple volcanic crater of Kerið and its emerald lake, a place that will leave you with unforgettable memories.

Start // Þingvellir National Park
Finish // Kerið
Distance // 125km (78 miles)
More information // visiticeland.com

ESCAPE TO THE NORTH OF ENGLAND

Venture into the north of England to enjoy a scenic coastline, expanses of wilderness and charming towns.

The central part of Great Britain has a thousand and one destinations that I can't wait to explore, from the coastline that stretches as far as the eye can see, to the rolling countryside inland. I'm also planning to visit a few must-see cities, including Liverpool, famous home of the Beatles.

Right now, I'm in the middle of York, on the ridiculously cute medieval street called the Shambles, which is said to have been the inspiration for Diagon Alley in the *Harry Potter books*. All around me, elegant half-timbered houses display their well-presented shop windows. Christmas is fast approaching, and retailers are vying with each other to catch the eye of potential seasonal customers. Not far away, the limestone towers of York Minster, northern Europe's most important Gothic building, fascinate me. The interior is no less impressive, the stained-glass-lined nave leaving me open mouthed.

I'm planning to visit the coast further north, around Whitby, and I see on the map that the North York Moors National Park lies halfway between York and the sea. Seizing this chance to kill two birds with one stone, I set off without hesitation on the A169, which crosses the park. In these sparsely populated heather moors, sprinkled with pockets of forest, I relish the cloudless skies, taking short walks on either side of the small country road wherever I fancy. Sheep often block the way, forcing me to take further short breaks. I also make a longer stop at the scenic Goathland car park to enjoy the lush green scenery without worrying about keeping my eyes on the road .

Having imagined Whitby as a quiet seaside town, I'm surprised to find so many holidaymakers there. Although the resort is very busy, it's nonetheless attractive. The cliff-top ruined medieval abbey is incredibly photogenic – and featured prominently in Bram Stoker's novel *Dracula*. However, it's at the foot of the James Cook statue (the illustrious British explorer cut his sailing teeth in Whitby), at the mouth of the River Esk, that you can enjoy the best view of the town and its tiered brick houses.

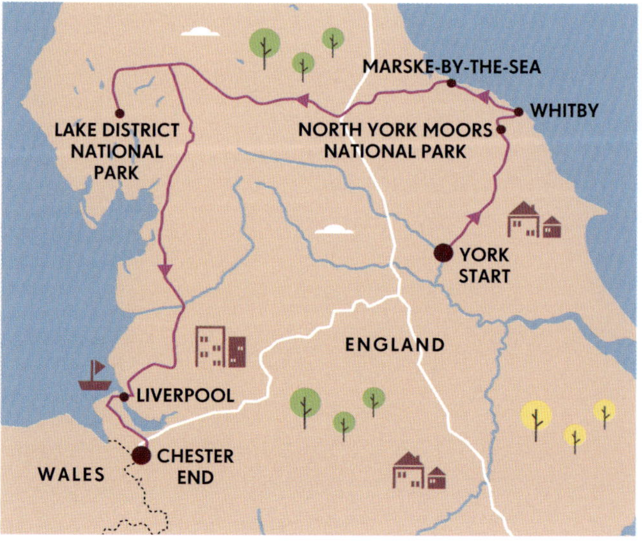

'I relish the cloudless skies, taking short walks on either side of the small country road wherever I fancy. Sheep often block the way, forcing me to take further short breaks.'

I'd like to sleep somewhere quieter though, so take the wheel again, heading for Marske-by-the-Sea, 35km (22 miles) away, following the coastal road northwards. I find a spot facing the sea and take advantage of the last rays of sunshine to walk along the long stretch of fine sand. The shore is so vast that, despite the few fellow strollers, I'm largely alone with my thoughts until the night catches up with me.

In these latitudes, autumn envelops my sleep with an icy breath, and I have to cover up warmly to avoid freezing once I've slipped under the duvet. I experience this even more when I cross the country from east to west (via the A66, for 165km/103 miles) and reach the Lake District National Park, near Keswick. Here, the mercury on my thermometer has dropped again and I'm disappearing more and more beneath my woolly hat, ski socks and thick fleece jacket. That doesn't stop me from succumbing to the joys of Cumbria though, a mesmerising patchwork of lakes and mountains that has nothing to envy the landscapes of neighbouring Scotland. The soft curves of the hills, colours of the changing leaves and infinite bodies of water are a delight to behold. A feeling of satisfaction washes over me as I realise that, at this very moment, there's nowhere else I'd rather be.

But I've got to get a move on if I don't want to spend the winter here, so I turn the vehicle south, following the A591 and then the M6 to Liverpool. I have an appointment with Carola, an

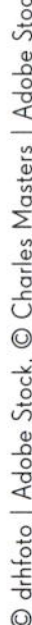

IN THE FOOTSTEPS OF THE BEATLES

Liverpool offers many celebrated venues for Fab Four fans. St Peter's Church in Woolton, where John Lennon and Paul McCartney met; the Cavern Club where the group first performed; the house where John Lennon grew up; and several places that inspired their songs, such as Penny Lane and Strawberry Field. Don't miss The Beatles Story Museum either.

Opposite, clockwise from left: Whitby Abbey; Lake Ullswater; County Cumbria. Above: North York Moors National Park. Page 275, from top: North York Moors National Park; Lake District National Park.

English friend who welcomes me to her flat. The first thing to do before visiting the city – take a shower. After so much time on the road, and despite a daily wash, feeling the warm water running over my skin is highly welcome. Now I'm ready for a night out in the footsteps of the Beatles. We take a walk through the lively streets of the city centre and have a pint at the Cavern Club, the intimate venue where the legendary quartet first performed. After a good night's sleep, we wander along Albert Dock, a lively cafe-lined quarter next to the River Mersey. Finally, Carola recommends that I visit the city's two cathedrals. The first is the world's largest Anglican church, an architectural masterpiece by Sir George Gilbert Scott (designer of the famous red British telephone box) which is home to England's largest working organ. A complete change of style comes with the second, the Catholic Metropolitan Cathedral: this modern building, made of concrete, glass and metal, features a surprising conical structure, crowned by a round tower.

On the other side of the Mersey lies Chester, 45km (28 miles) away, a medieval city rich in history. I take in the view from the ramparts, a legacy of Roman times. During this festive season, the entire centre is lit up. I join the crowds window-shopping, head under the famous Eastgate Clock, and set off to discover the city with the reputation of being the most haunted in England. **AD**

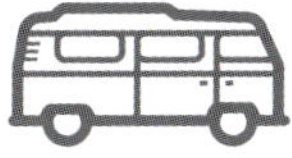

ROAD MAP

Start // York
Finish // Chester
Distance // 500km (311 miles)
Recommended duration // 5-to-7 days
When to go // Summer, for mild temperatures and longer days
Culinary speciality // Full English breakfast (toast, bacon, eggs, sausages, baked beans, mushrooms and tomatoes)

THE PERFECT SLEEP SPOT

Description // Panoramic view of the North York Moors National Park
GPS coordinates // 54.378515473830674, -0.6744826066278977
Light pollution // None
Access // Easy, via the A169
Facilities // None, but the view makes it worthwhile.
Traffic // Some during the day, but very little at night
Little extras // The ability to photograph the stars after dark.

Opposite: A view over the verdant Dordogne valley, just south of Sarlat-la-Canéda

MORE LIKE THIS
ROLLING LANDSCAPES

SOUTHERN SARDINIA (ITALY)

Driving to Costa Rei, in southeastern Sardinia, takes you on scenic roads through the Sarrabus region, past a parade of wooded hills. Once in the port, explore its centre, from where you can easily reach a long beach lapped by turquoise waters. Move on to Cagliari, Sardinia's unmissable capital. The Castello district, high up in the hills, offers the best views of the sea. The rest of this Italian island holds so many heavenly beaches that it's hard to choose. One notable nearby option is Spiaggia Su Giudeu and its crystal-clear water, at the island's southern tip. Next day, follow the curving SP71 west to the Arenas Biancas dunes, then take it easy en route to the island of Sant'Antioco, accessible by a bridge. It's the ideal place to take a boat out into the rivers, with the mountains always in the background.

Start // Costa Rei
Finish // Sant'Antioco
Distance // 192km (119 miles)
More information // sardegnaturismo.it

DORDOGNE RIVER VALLEY (FRANCE)

Plot a meandering journey along the Dordogne River valley, toasting the upcoming drive the evening before you depart with a glass of local Monbazillac wine in Bergerac. Head east along the river to Lalinde, stopping to explore the English heritage of the town's historic *bastide* (fortified town), or negotiating walking trails along the river's traditional towpaths. Every Thursday morning, there's an excellent food market crammed with local treats. Follow the river's northern bank around a gentle loop, stopping for sky-high views at Trémolat and to spot canoeists and kayakers during the summer. Further upstream, La Roque-Gageac's cliffside location and the mighty châteaux at Beynac and Castelnaud-la-Chapelle are some of the Dordogne's most memorable sights. End this riverside adventure amid the traffic-free cobblestoned squares and lanes of Sarlat-la-Canéda, one of southwestern France's best preserved medieval towns.

Start // Bergerac
Finish // Sarlat-la-Canéda
Distance // 100km (62 miles)
More information // visit-dordogne-valley.co.uk

LAKE KERKINI (GREECE)

Northern Greece's Lake Kerkini has an idyllic natural setting, and the national park of the same name is home to a rich biodiversity of birds – including cormorants, herons and Dalmatian curled pelicans – and water buffalo, wallowing in a sea of water lilies. Start your loop at Kerkini town, and take the opportunity to get out your binoculars at the birdwatching site. Then head north to the port of Mandraki, where, surrounded by mountains, the banks of the lake are great for walking or cycling. Don't miss a visit to the monastery of Timios Prodromos, close to the charming village of Akritochori, before heading south to shoreline Lithotopos, set amongst trees. For overnighting in the camper, you'll have no trouble finding a spot on the southern stretch of lakefront, leading back to Kerkini.

Start/Finish // Kerkini
Distance // 62km (38.5 miles)
More information // discovergreece.com

THE RING OF KERRY AND THE DINGLE PENINSULA

Road trip through the wild landscapes of County Kerry's peninsulas.

Kerry. This county in southwest Ireland, nicknamed 'the Kingdom', conjures up images of green meadows dotted with sheep, untamed coastlines, ruined castles and mysterious lakes. I reach this dream land from France via Cork, having to adapt to driving on the left as soon as I get off the ferry. Despite initial concerns, it's easier than I imagined, and the 100km (62 miles) or so that separate me from my destination, the Iveragh Peninsula, allow me to familiarise myself with this unfamiliar side of the road. My plan is to travel clockwise around the famous Ring of Kerry, a 180km (112 mile) circuit that loops around the Iveragh Peninsula, before continuing on to the Dingle Peninsula.

First stop is Killarney National Park, a UNESCO World Heritage Biosphere Reserve which, at 10,000 hectares, is the largest tract of wilderness in Ireland. I pick up a map at the visitor centre and make my way to the car park and the trailhead for hikes to the Gap of Dunloe. This magnificent valley is accessible only to pedestrians, cyclists and horse-drawn

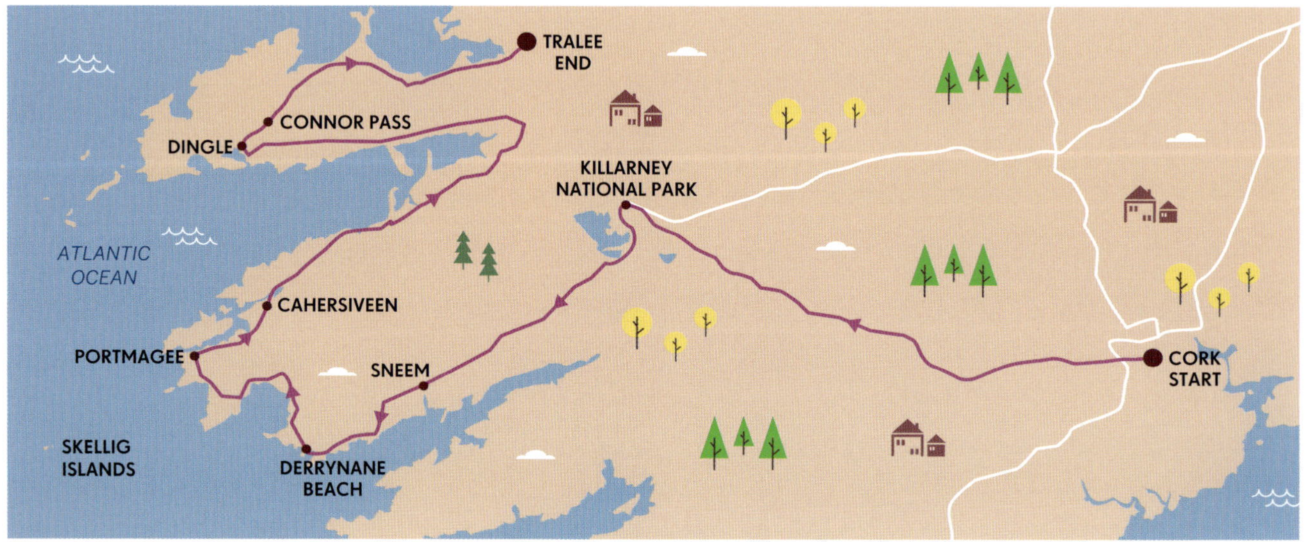

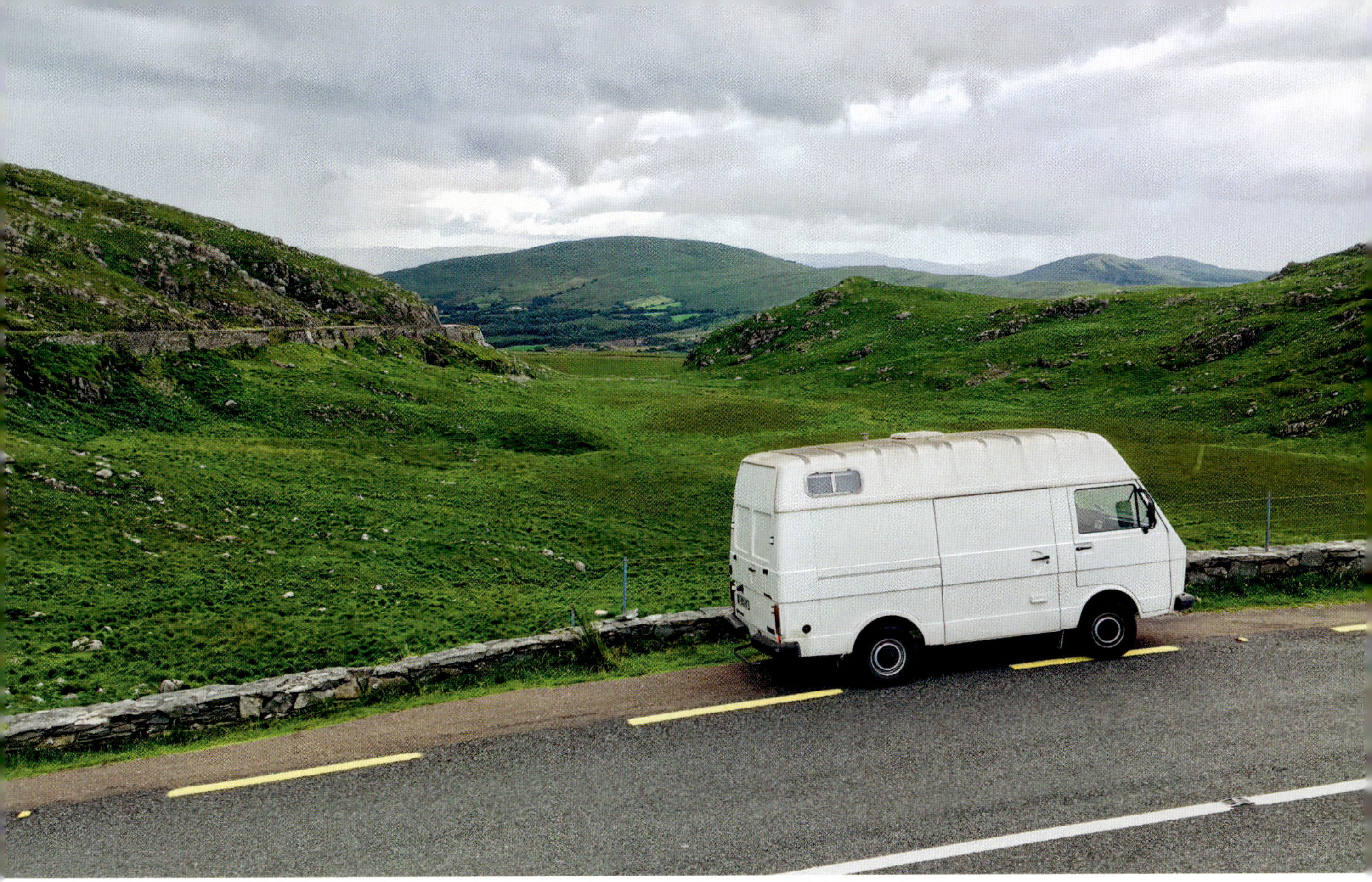

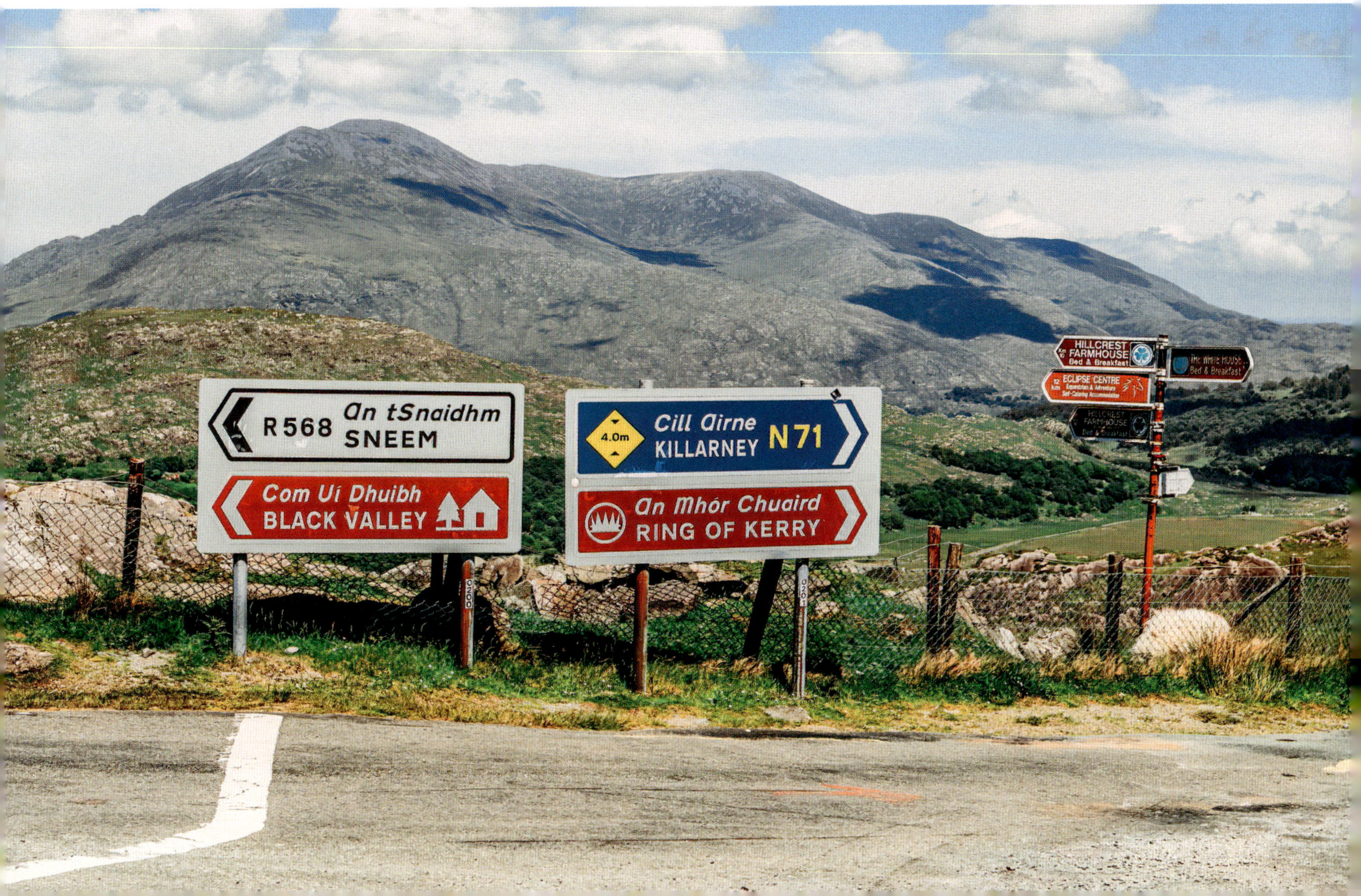
R568 An tSnaidhm
SNEEM
Com Uí Dhuibh
BLACK VALLEY
4.0m
Cill Airne
KILLARNEY N71
An Mhór Chuaird
RING OF KERRY
HILLCREST FARMHOUSE
Bed & Breakfast
12 km
ECLIPSE CENTRE

carriages. A narrow path runs alongside a succession of lakes, sometimes crossing them with small stone bridges, such as the pretty Wishing Bridge. Beyond Augher Lake, the valley narrows. I follow the zigzagging path up to the pass, surrounded by sheep bleating as if to encourage us hikers on. At the top, a beautiful view unfolds, encompassing the Black Valley and Carrauntoohil (1040m/3412ft), Ireland's highest peak.

Back in the camper, it's on to Ross Castle, a 15th-century fortress on the banks of Lough Leane, then Torc Waterfall, hidden in lush vegetation – I expect to come across elves at any moment. Passing Derrycunihy Church, I reach Ladies' View, looking out over peat bogs and Upper Lake. At Moll's Gap crossroads, I choose to turn right onto the R568 and stop just a few hundred metres later in a car park on the banks of Lough Barfinnihy. The silence is total, the surface of the water sparkles – a perfect place for lunch. Taking your time and getting off the beaten track often leads to the discovery of breathtaking landscapes like this.

The drive continues on the Iveragh Peninsula, a place where you can't help but drive slowly to appreciate the natural wonders around you – and because the roads are rather narrow. Sneem, a typical Irish village with colourful houses and pubs, is where I rejoin the N70 and go southwest for 23km (14 miles). Out in the Atlantic are the islands of Scariff and Deenish. I park at Derrynane Beach whose white sand, turquoise water and green hills combine to make a heavenly setting. The ruins of an abbey on a small island are accessible at low tide.

Shortly after Waterville, I momentarily leave the Ring of Kerry for the Ring of Skellig, a beautiful 18km (11 mile) circuit that follows rough cliffs and is known as a *Gaeltacht* stronghold, where Irish Gaelic is spoken. You can see the Skellig Islands, two rocky peaks, one of which is home to an abbey. Boat trips are available to get there, usually from Portmagee, but as the day is drawing to a close, I opt to head back to the Ring of Kerry and a campsite I've reserved at Cahersiveen. I lie on my bed and read a book facing the ocean.

When I wake up, drops of water are beading on the windows. The insulating curtains I use aren't enough to stop night-time condensation caused by high humidity and the temperature difference between inside and outside. So, as always, I make sure to air out the van before setting off for the day.

My last stops on the Ring of Kerry are the Rossbeigh lookout, a sandy outcrop in Dingle Bay, and the Kerry Bog Village Museum, a reconstruction of a 19th-century village typical of this peat bog environment. I'm now heading for the Dingle Peninsula. Also in County Kerry, it marks Ireland's most westerly point. The R561 runs along its southern coast, taking me to the immense golden sands of Inch Beach, stretching 5km (3 miles) into the bay. From here, I continue west to the charming coastal town of Dingle. A statue has been erected in tribute to the local mascot, Fungie, a wild dolphin who lived in the bay for almost 40 years.

SKELLIG ISLANDS

This archipelago off the Iveragh Peninsula comprises the islands of Skellig Michael and Little Skellig. As the latter is a bird sanctuary, only the island of Skellig Michael is open to visitors. No fewer than 660 steps carved into the rock lead up to an abandoned monastery, dating back to the 7th century. Its dry-stone structures are a UNESCO World Heritage Site. This striking location had a starring role in *Star Wars* episodes 7 and 8.

Below: Torc waterfall. Above: Lough Barfinnihy. Opposite: Inch Beach. Page 281: On the Ring of Kerry.

ROAD MAP

Start // Cork
Finish // Tralee
Distance // 458km (285 miles)
Recommended duration // 7-to-10 days
When to go // The scenery is sublime year round
Culinary specialities // Fish and chips, Irish stew (mutton stew), Gubbeen cheese (cow's milk cheese)

THE PERFECT PHOTO SPOT

Description // Cé Dhún Chaoin/Dunquin Pier
GPS coordinates // 52.1243, -10.46067
Access // Easy, small car park on Slea Head Drive
Visitor numbers // Busy at sunset
Little extras // Superb views over the twists and turns of this steep pier.

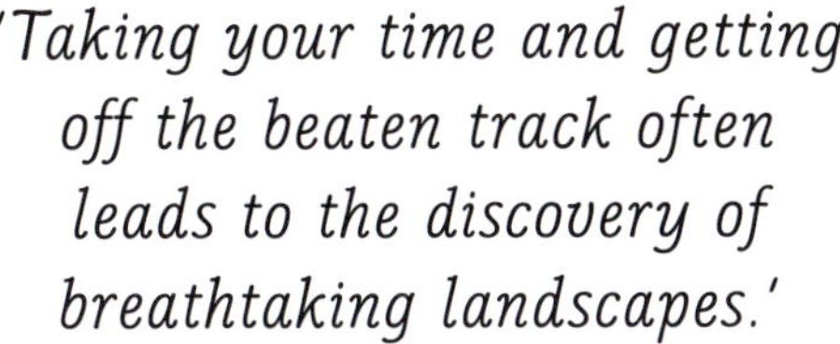

'Taking your time and getting off the beaten track often leads to the discovery of breathtaking landscapes.'

I start the Slea Head Drive, a 50km (31 mile) circuit that crosses empty valleys, skirts sea-worn cliffs and reveals *beehive huts*, the Gallarus Oratory (looking like the upturned hull of a ship) and so many other beauties.

Aboard my home on wheels, I extend this wonderful trip at Conor Pass to admire the view of lakes, moors, bays and Mt Brandon. Very quickly, the narrowness of the road means there's no turning back or overtaking. Hands gripping the steering wheel, I break out into a cold sweat, hugging the edge of the vertiginous precipice and waiting on the left-hand side of the road as soon as I spot an oncoming car. Fortunately, traffic is light and the driver behind me is patient. I'm so focused that I'm not even enjoying the glorious panorama. It's not until I reach Peddler's Lake car park that I relax – before spotting a road sign stating that this stretch of road is not authorised for vehicles weighing over 2 tons or wider than 1.80m (6ft). Oops. Luckily, the final push to my ultimate destination, Tralee, is less traumatic. **AL**

Opposite: Lake Masuria, Poland.

MORE LIKE THIS
NATURAL HIGHS

THE THOUSAND LAKES (POLAND)

Poland's northeastern Warmian-Masurian Province is covered with rivers, canals and lakes. Iława, in particular, is a popular resort for water sports enthusiasts. Park near Lake Jeziorak for a day of swimming or kayaking. Follow Route 16 through the woods to Olsztyn, a colourful historic town with a planetarium and observatory. To sleep in a camper, just pick one of the many lakes in the area, such as nearby Wadąg. Further east, still following Route 16, stop at Sorkwity for its marvellous red-brick castle, nestled between two stretches of water. The next day, discover the Masurian Landscape Park, a green lung whose wetlands are home to wild animals including boar, deer and beavers. Finish your Polish tour on the shores of the great glacial lake of Śniardwy, easily reached by camper from the village of Zdory.

Start // Iława
Finish // Zdory
Distance // 213km (132 miles)
More information // poland.travel

LA ROUTE FAGNES ET LACS (BELGIUM)

Head to Belgium and enter the world of the Hautes Fagnes (High Fens), a wild land of marshes and moors. The starting point for this green drive is Malmedy, where you can discover the richness of the local heritage at the Malmundarium. Leave town and head through the fields to visit the medieval Reinhardstein Castle, built on a rocky outcrop, before calling at the Botrange Park House to learn more about the flora and fauna of the region. Enter the Hautes Fagnes-Eifel Nature Park (via the N68 and then the N67) and stride out on the hiking trails winding through fascinating peat bogs and forests. After crossing the German enclave of Mützenich, make a final stopover in the town of Bütgenbach, whose large lake has several car parks where you can overnight.

Start/Finish // Malmedy
Distance // 109km (68 miles)
More information // ostbelgien.eu

NORTH KARELIA (FINLAND)

In eastern Finland, the village of Koli, near huge Lake Pielinen, welcomes vanlifers venturing to the furthest reaches of Europe. After a soothing night on the water's edge, enter Koli National Park for an unforgettable trek featuring a succession of breathtaking views over the taiga. Then drive along the wooded road to Patvinsuo National Park. The wetlands of this other natural treasure are home to a remarkable array of wildlife, including lynxes, bears and wolverines. Here, walkers can make their way to Lake Koitere to admire the reflection of trees shimmering in the water. Back in the camper, return to Uimaharju and head southeast, still deep in the forest, towards Petkeljärvi National Park. Get ready for wow-inducing scenery, featuring eskers (flat-topped glacial mounds) above a multitude of deep-blue lakes.

Start // Koli
Finish // Petkeljärvi National Park
Distance // 183km (114 miles)
More information // visitfinland.com

HEADING NORTH IN NORWAY

Embark on an adventure that takes you to the north of Norway and the Lofoten Islands, one of the most beautiful archipelagos in Europe.

Life can be full of surprises and this trip is no exception. I'm in Norway, in the converted vehicle of Vladimir, a globetrotter I recently met on the road, and I have only one idea in mind – getting to the Lofoten Islands, a spectacular archipelago located beyond the Arctic Circle and reached via the towns of Trondheim, Mo i Rana and Bodø. From one adventure to the next, this itinerary will take us to far distant destinations.

Sitting in the last bend of the Nidelva River, Trondheim opens its doors to us under a sparkling sun. The town is relatively sprawling, and we take a long walk from the marina to the town centre, where the Gothic cathedral of Nidaros stands, the largest medieval building in Scandinavia. Within its grey soapstone walls, it houses the tomb of St Olav, a Viking king who converted to Christianity; many pilgrims come here to pay their respects. Nearby, the river banks are adorned with houses on stilts, painted in a palette of bright colours.

We leave the town to begin our expedition northwards. The immense Trondheimsfjord accompanies us along the E6. Known as the Arctic Highway, this route is more direct than the famous Kystriksveien coastal road, and is said to be almost as beautiful. Postcard landscapes, wild, hilly and wooded, follow one another, leaving no room for boredom. We leapfrog from fjord to fjord, landing in the town of Mo i Rana after a day's drive. The rain has suddenly started pouring down and we don't dare go outside for the time being – coming home soaking wet is out of the question when you're travelling in a converted vehicle as it's hard to get

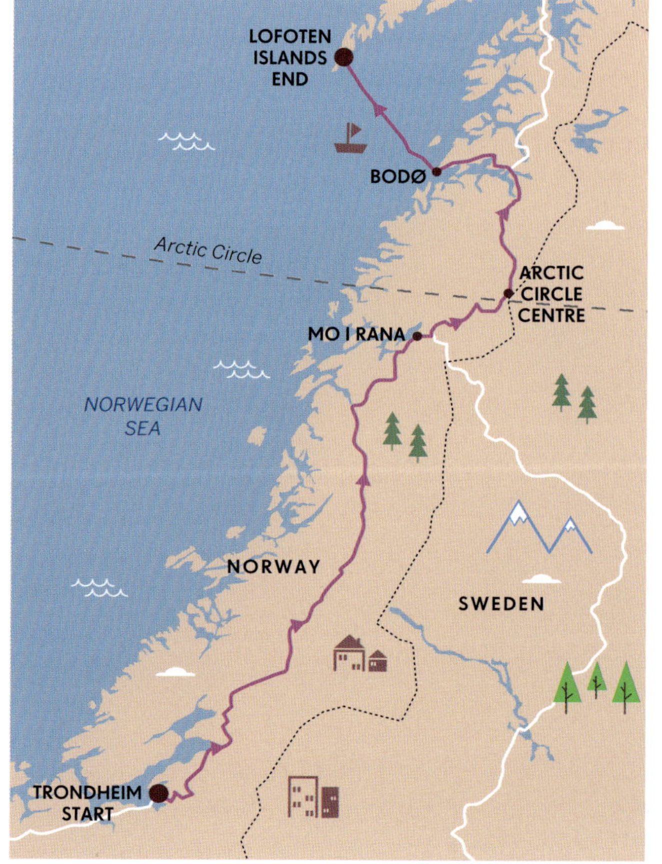

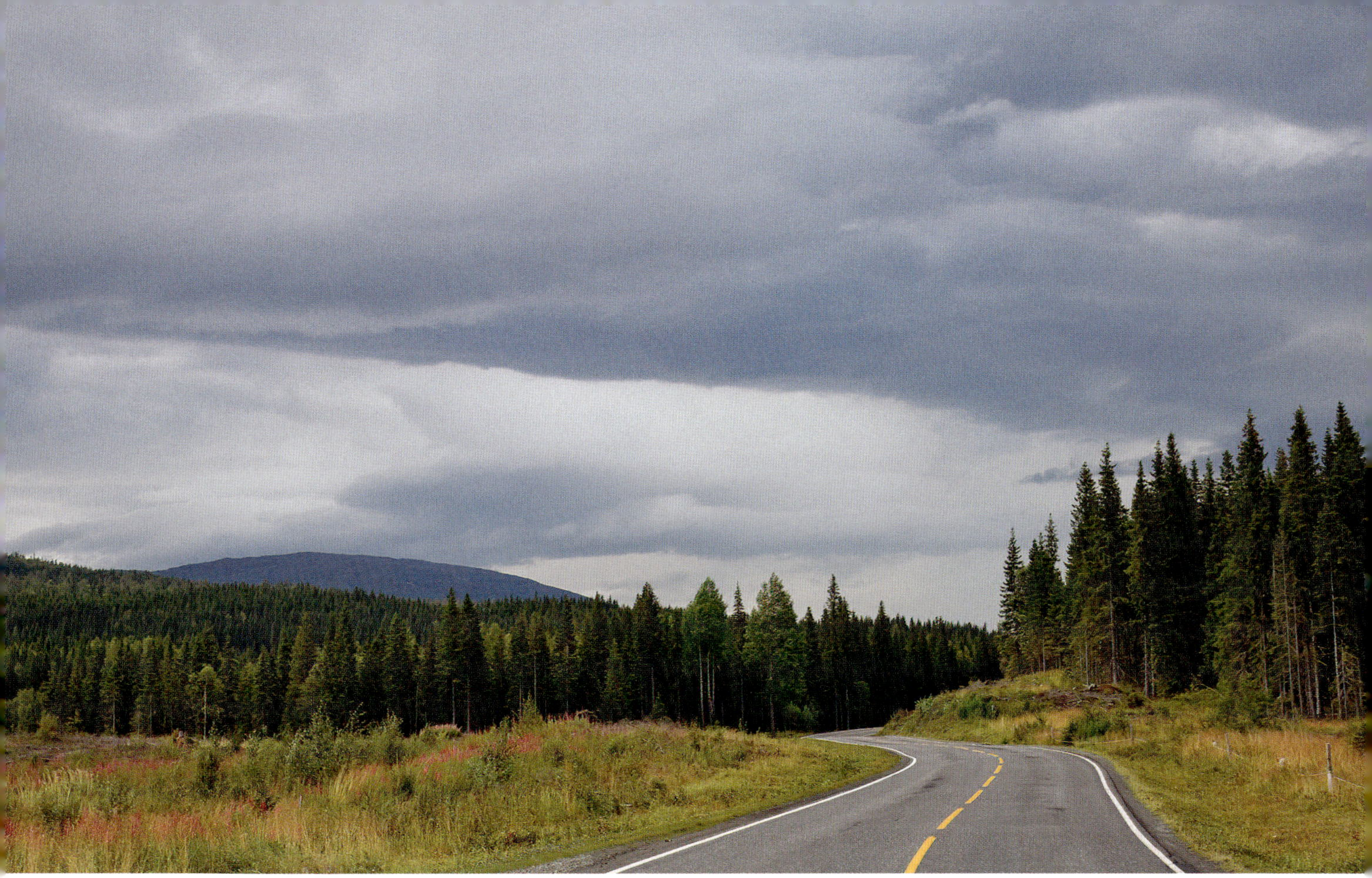

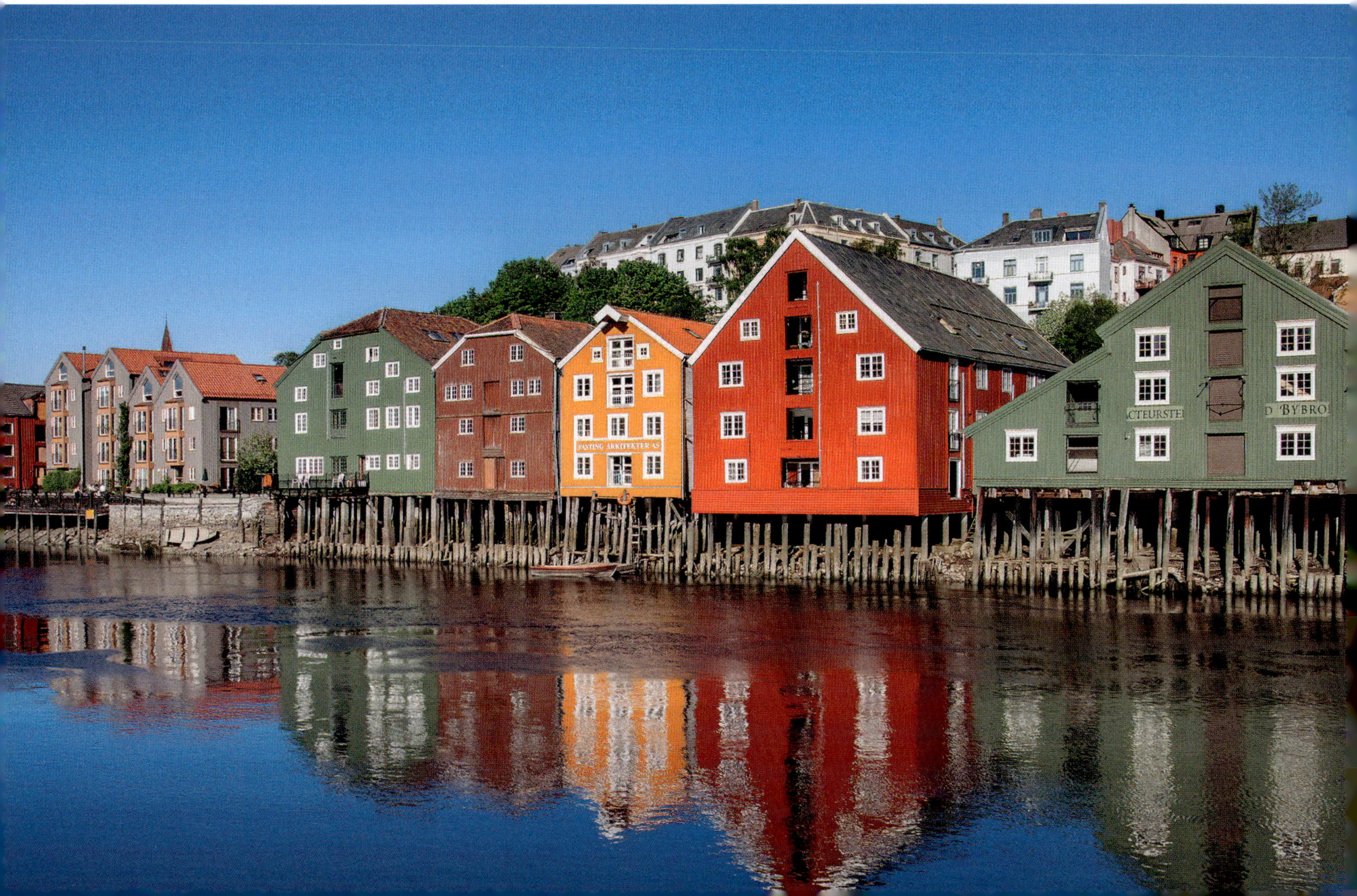

THE LOFOTEN ISLANDS

Located between the Norwegian Sea and Vestfjorden, the Lofoten Archipelago is accessible by ferry from Bodø, or road via the E10. Its chiselled landscapes, with sharp peaks and beautiful bays, make it unique in the world, popular with travellers, photographers and hikers. In addition to tourism, the inhabitants of these far northern islands make a living from fishing, especially for cod.

'At the foot of the menacing mountains, the deep-red houses are beautifully scattered across the Vestfjorden.'

dry and keep the humidity levels down in the camper. So we stay in and have a simple dinner: a sandwich made with *brunost*, a Norwegian brown cheese with a sweet, caramelised flavour.

This far north, night is absent for part of the summer – the the polar day – and our biological clocks are not used to it, meaning every morning we get up at a time when night owls would hesitate to go to bed. This has the advantage of giving us plenty of free time though, and we make the most of a ray of sunshine to briefly visit Mo i Rana, located at the end of a fjord. Below brightly painted houses, a marina proudly displays its flotilla of pretty boats. This tiny town is an ideal base for visiting the Arctic Circle region, 85km (53 miles) away.

The E6 is embedded between two walls of ice and many adventurous travellers follow this route to discover what the Polarsirkelen, the mythical invisible frontier with the Far North, is like. We park near the Arctic Circle Centre, an enormous black dome in the middle of a high valley offering magnificent scenery. Walking around the area, each of us takes souvenir photos, our faces beaming with happiness in this symbolic but special place.

And then we're off for a closer look at the Far North. Our road trip to the top of the map continues through the Saltfjellet-Svartisen National Park towards Bodø, where the ferries to Lofoten depart. For 150km (93 miles), we drive along the E6 and then Route 80, from fjord to fjord, through increasingly desolate landscapes. The swift waters of the Luonosjåhkå River, which we flank for most of the way, end up flowing into the peaceful Saltdalsfjorden – an ideal place to stop and appreciate nature's spectacle. Two elks, their antlers just beginning to regrow, seem to be enjoying the show as much as we are.

We arrive late in Bodø and look for a place to spend the night, picking a park away from residential areas which hugs the shoreline of the Norwegian Sea. Early in the morning, I'm off to the harbour to buy a ticket for the Lofoten Islands. Vladimir prefers to stay in town for a while, and we bid each other an emotional farewell after sharing such a long journey. So it's on foot that I board the boat, which will drop me off four hours later in Moskenes. It's a dream come true to set foot on one of the world's most beautiful archipelagos. I walk 5km (3 miles) to Å, a

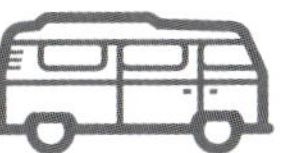

ROAD MAP

Start // Trondheim
Finish // Lofoten Islands
Distance // 840km (522 miles)
Recommended duration // 7-to-10 days
When to go // Summer, for warmer temperatures and midnight sun
Culinary speciality // Smoked salmon, usually served on bread with eggs and dill

THE PERFECT PHOTO SPOT

Description // The postcard-pretty landscape of Reine
GPS coordinates // 67.92909091126745, 13.08769732755557
Access // By road (short-term parking) or on foot
Activities // Hike along the fjord to the lighthouse on the other side of town
Visitor numbers // Well-known for offering one of the best views in Lofoten
Little extras // To enjoy this extraordinary view in solitude, get up (very) early

Above: village of Reine, Lofoten Islands. Below: In front of the Polar Circle Centre. Page 286, from top: E6 road; Trondheim.

fishing village with vermilion huts, protected by a rocky outcrop. The surrounding cliffs are immense, and in places covered with thick grass. A sudden storm forces me to seek shelter. I quickly find a place to pitch my tent away from the trees, and try in vain to sleep under a leaden sky.

The vagaries of the weather are part and parcel of the trip, they even give it a special flavour. I take full advantage of the next day's calm by walking 10km (6 miles) to Reine, a village renowned for its incredible scenery. Many tourists, like me, come here in search of a touch of enchantment. At the foot of the menacing mountains, the deep-red houses are beautifully scattered across the Vestfjorden. Amazed, I savour this haven of peace, a place that contradicts Philippe Pollet-Villard's quote: 'On a journey it's not the destination that counts, but always the road travelled, and especially the detours.' There are always exceptions though, and the Lofoten Islands are definitely one. **AD**

Opposite: Waterfall in Geirangerfjord.

MORE LIKE THIS
NORWAY'S BEST OF THE REST

THE EAGLE ROAD

Breathtakingly beautiful, Geirangerfjord is a Norwegian landmark. Start your tour in the town of Billingen, followed by a stop nearby at the Breiddalen Valley viewpoint, overlooking Djupvatnet, a deep-blue lake often encrusted in ice. Then drive to the summit of Dalsnibba (1476m/4843ft), accessible by van, to enjoy the sensational panorama of this rocky terrain studded with lakes. Set off on the Eagle Road (Ørnevegen; closed in winter) to take on its hairpin bends and take in its majestic views of the fjord. Stop off at Geiranger to admire its many waterfalls on foot. If you're travelling with a kayak, put it in the water to approach the Seven Sisters – seven waterfalls lined up on the cliffside. Finally, head north along the beautiful Eidsvatnet lake for the ferry from Eidsdal leading to the start of the Troll Road.
Start // Billingen
Finish // Eidsdal
Distance // 80km (50 miles)
More information // visitnorway.com

THE TROLL ROAD

This route, one of the most beautiful in the country, follows on from the Eagle Road – your Norwegian adventure continues on Route 63, nicknamed Trollstingen (Troll Road) in this second part. Closed in winter, this spectacular stretch starts in Valldal, where you can take one last look at the Geirangerfjord before pushing north on an incredible series of switchbacks. Guided by the lovely Valldøla stream, drive up to the Troll Road pass, where you'll find a steel footbridge, a window onto an awe-inspiring landscape that is worth the journey on its own. Nearby, follow the path to Bispevatnet glacial lake (easy), while other (more difficult) trails can be found further on, around the summit of Trollveggen. Finish this captivating circuit in Åndalsnes, and climb the Rampestreken platform for a gasp-provoking view of Romsdalsfjord.
Start // Valldal
Finish // Åndalsnes
Distance // 54km (34 miles)
More information // visitnorway.com

THE KYSTRIKSVEIEN

A coastal road between Trondheim and Bodø, the FV17, or Kystriksveien, is a slower alternative to the E6 – but arguable more spectacular. By camper van, allow three days and extra money to cover the route and its succession of bridges and ferries. From this winding road, you can admire 14,000 islands lost in the open sea, occupied by fishers for generations. Along the way, you'll find pretty little towns where you can grab a bite to eat, like Brønnøysund, surrounded by agricultural hills and several islands, or Sandnessjøen, a small port at the foot of the Syv Søstre Mountains. The most beautiful part of the road trip is yet to come, stretching along the coast to Storvik. On this exceptional section, prepare to flirt with the water along a causeway and to contemplate fjords and glacier tongues. Beyond the Arctic Circle, you'll reach Bodø and, if you're up for it, the Lofoten Islands.
Start // Trondheim
Finish // Bodø
Distance // 851km (529 miles)
More information // visitnorway.com

DISCOVERING THE BALTIC STATES

Cross the Baltic States visiting UNESCO-listed capitals, iconic sights and nature reserves.

For the start of this drive through the Baltic States from north to south, the ferry drops me off in Tallinn, the capital of Estonia. I've just arrived from Finland, and my first instinct, given the lower price of fuel here, is to quench the thirst of my VW LT35 at a service station. Cacou, my non-human travelling companion, is often dehydrated so I take the opportunity to fill up my water tank too and spend a quiet night in a large car park on Kalasadama Street.

The next day, my footsteps echo on the cobblestones of the medieval old town, protected by its ramparts and home to many pretty churches, as well as the multicoloured houses typical of Hanseatic towns. After a hearty elk broth at III Draakon, a tavern with an olde worlde ambience, I visit the gloomy KGB prison cells, a reminder of the Soviet era, and the monuments on Toompea Hill – the old citadel here enjoys a beautiful view over the lower town. To the northwest of the old town, I'm seduced by the liveliness of the alternative Telliskivi Loomelinnak district, housed in disused factories.

I leave Tallinn for Jägala Falls, nicknamed 'Estonia's Niagara'. It's a charming spot on the edge of the forest, but the 8m (26ft) high waterfall is probably more spectacular in winter, when the water is more abundant and icy cold. Continuing eastwards, I take the E20 road to Lahemaa National Park, a concentration of Estonian nature including bays, peninsulas, peat bogs, lakes and forests.

From the Viru peat bog car park, a boardwalk traces a 6km (4 mile) loop around the marshes. Binoculars in hand, I climb the

RUMMU KARJÄÄR

The Rummu quarry is located in Lääne-Harju, 45km (28 miles) southwest of Tallinn. It was first mined in 1938, when inmates of nearby Murru Prison extracted Vasalemma limestone and marble. The spoil from the quarrying turned into a hill of dust, and when mining operations ceased, the quarry and its facilities became flooded. Today, the site attracts many visitors, who explore the prison or swim in the strange azure lagoon among the ruins.

Right: Riga street. Opposite, from top: Lahemaa national park; Saulkrasti. Page 293: Village of Altja; Lithuanian countryside.

'Binoculars in hand, I climb the watchtower. It's a beautiful slice of Nordic nature, wild and peaceful'

watchtower to survey this beautiful slice of Nordic nature, wild and peaceful. Driving deeper into the park along Route 85, I find wonderful walks in Käsmu, taking you through the forest and along the rocky beach. To the east lies the village of Altja, where fishing net sheds have been restored using old photos and memories of the villagers. I sleep in the car park near the Oandu information centre, where I aim to follow the nature trail tomorrow.

I wake up with a start. A storm is rumbling outside. I open the curtain to find heavy rain, forcing me to reconsider my plans. I decide to take the long way down to Piusa, in the southeast of the country. Highlights of this stretch of road include a rainbow at Rakvere Castle, a picnic on the pretty shores of Lake Peipus, which separates Estonia from Russia, and a stroll through the university town of Tartu, which boasts the beautiful ruins of a Gothic cathedral. At nightfall I arrive at the Piusa sandstone cave museum. The place is deserted and there are no signs prohibiting overnight stays, so I park and visit the museum before settling down for the night.

It's time to move on to Latvia, heading southwest towards the Baltic Sea along roads which are wide but in poor condition. After 200km (124 miles) on the E77, through landscapes of meadows bordered by forests, I visit the rock formations of the Gauja River and the medieval red-brick castle of Turaida. Then it's back to the Baltic at Saulkrasti, the 'Sun Coast' in Latvian,

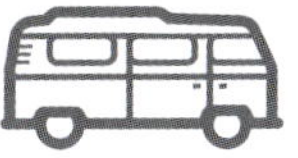

ROAD MAP

Start // Tallinn
Finish // Vilnius
Distance // 1066km (662 miles)
Recommended duration // 12-to-15 days
When to go // Late summer, outside school holidays
Culinary specialities // *Kringle* (braided brioche with butter and cinnamon), *biešu zupa* (beetroot soup), *kibinai* (meat pastry)

THE PERFECT SLEEP SPOT

Description // Camping Daina on the banks of Latvia's Gauja River
GPS coordinates // 57.178908, 24.85099
Light pollution // Low
Access // Dirt track and lawn
Facilities // Showers, toilets, picnic tables and electricity
Parking // 20 pitches
Little extras // This campsite has a huge wood-fired cauldron that can be reserved for an outdoor hot tub.

arriving in time to enjoy an exceptional sunset from the White Dune, a pine-covered sandy beach.

The next day, I'm off to Riga, 46km (28.5 miles) away, to explore the Latvian capital's historic centre, listed by UNESCO for its high concentration of Art Nouveau buildings. I admire the House of the Black Heads (an identical replica of a guild house from 1344), look for the House of the Cat (1909), walk along the Daugava River, feast on local specialities at the Central Market (located in former Zeppelin hangars) and finish with a drink, surrounded by hipsters, on Tallinas Square.

After a night in the city's Eksporta neighbourhood, I'm back behind the wheel, driving past the astonishing Latvian National Library, the famous 'castle of light, to pick up the E67. My last stop in Latvia will be the 18th-century Baroque Rundāle Palace, 80km (50 miles) south of Riga, looking like a miniature Versailles.

I'm now entering Lithuania. My first destination, in the north of the country, is the surprising Hill of Crosses, north of Šiauliai. This legendary pilgrimage site and symbol of patriotic resistance has no fewer than 100,000 crosses. During the Soviet era, between 1944 and 1990, placing crosses here defied the ban on practising a religion, but repeated bulldozing by the Soviets had little effect – locals would just replace the crosses overnight.

A few hours' drive across the plains would get me to Kaunas, but it's raining so I take the A1 to Trakai instead, an imposing brick castle built on an island in Lake Galvė. After a night in the countryside, I'm just leaving in the morning when my tyre slides into a dip, hidden under some grass. I try to manoeuvre the camper free but without success, so I resign myself to seeking help. Luckily, a lovely farmer at the wheel of his tractor is on hand and rescues both the vehicle and me from this predicament. After a thousand thanks, I finally continue my road trip, finishing in Vilnius, the Lithuanian capital. **AL**

Opposite: The village of Juodkrantė, Lithuania.

MORE LIKE THIS
BEST OF THE BALTIC STATES

SETOMAA REGION (ESTONIA)

On the borders of Estonia and Russia, enter the remote, wooded lands of Setomaa, a region with its own cultural identity. From the peaceful village of Räpina, where you can admire the magnificent yellow Sillapää manor house, take the road to Värska, a small lakeside village perfect for a night on the water's edge (pay for parking at the Reegi Museum, which has its own facilities). Detour to the Seto Museum in Saatse, some 20km (12 miles) away, via a road through the taiga-like Mustoja Conservation Area. Learn more about the ancestral culture of the Seto, a fascinating people. Further on, the village of Obinitsa, set in a forest and featuring a plain but pretty white church, is an interesting stopover, before finishing in the middle of the woods near Lake Kirikumäe – fires are permitted in a dedicated area along Route 164.

Start // Räpina
Finish // Lake Kirikumäe
Distance // 102km (63 miles)
More information // visitsetomaa.ee

KURZEME DISTRICT (LATVIA)

At the western end of the Gulf of Riga, Cape Kolka is the perfect place to start this adventure – a long stretch of fine sand surrounded by forest. Drive along the water following route P214 for 5km (3 miles) and enter Slītere National Park, a paradise of dunes, hardwood trees and peat bogs that's home to numerous birds. Continue southwest along the Baltic to the coastal town of Ventspils and inspect the sand-coloured castle built near the Venta Estuary. Further south, the splendid cliffs of Jūrkalne are a great spot for a night by the sea, before continuing to the pretty town of Liepāja, still on the coast. Finish the drive on the shores of Lake Pape, 15km (9 miles) further south, to discover the rich ecosystem that makes up this marshy area.

Start // Cap Kolka
Finish // Lake Pape
Distance // 240km (149 miles)
More information // latvia.travel

THE CURONIAN SPIT (LITHUANIA)

The Curonian Spit is a Lithuanian must-see accessible from Klaipėda, a coastal town with a historic port, a castle with imposing ramparts and a pedestrian-friendly old town. After a few hours in the town, set out to conquer the narrow strip of sand separating the Baltic Sea from the Curonian Lagoon, and head for Juodkrantė where you'll find several authorised spots for spending the night in your camper, close to the sea on the western side of the isthmus. Next day, take Route 167, which literally cuts through the woods, and stop off at the pretty hamlet of Pervalka – look out for its thatched-roof houses. Visit Preila, further south, another charming village dotted with traditional wooden houses. Push on to the seaside resort of Nida and its marina, where you can spend another night before turning back north and returning to the start.

Start/Finish // Klaipėda
Distance // 102km (63 miles)
More information // nerija.lrv.lt

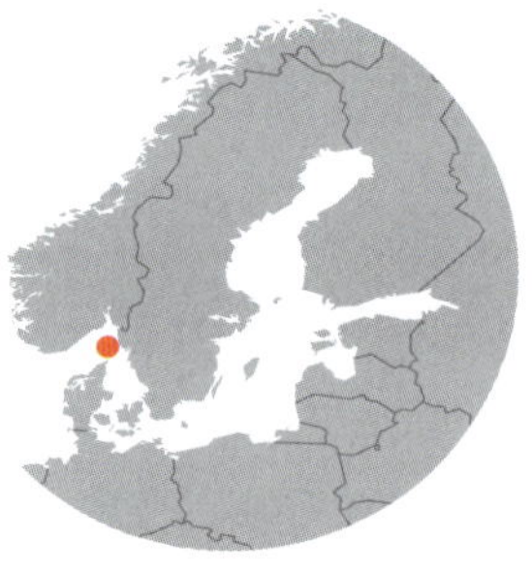

SAMPLING SCANDINAVIA

Enjoy a taste of Scandinavia on a Denmark-to-Norway drive through landscapes where water and handsome towns are never far away.

How can you resist the call of the north when you love wilderness more than anything else? From the first to the last day of my road trip through Scandinavia, I was thrilled to come into contact with an admirably preserved, often surprising, always breathtaking natural environment. What's more, I had the chance to visit some attractive villages in Denmark, Sweden and Norway. From Odense to Trondheim, there were 1300km (808 miles) of protected coastline, captivating roads and cute little towns.

Urban focus of the island of Funen, Odense is the ideal starting point for this tour. The city where Hans Christian Andersen was born contains a number of interesting historical and cultural sights, including an interactive museum that presents the illustrious author's work to perfection. Storms Pakhus, a street food market where world cuisines meet, is also worth a stop, before leaving this city of quaint streets lined with yellow-walled houses and restaurants.

At the wheel of the camper van, I cross the gigantic Storebælt Bridge (18km/11 miles) to reach the island of Zealand, Denmark's largest, where the capital is located. The only advantage of taking the E20 is that it takes me quickly to Copenhagen, 165km (102.5 miles) away, along a straight stretch of road. As always, to get the most out of the city, I park on the outskirts and do my sightseeing on foot, beginning with the Tivoli Gardens amusement park. After wandering its wooded avenues, from attraction to attraction, I make my way to the port of Nyhavn, long a home for sailors and writers. Its flamboyantly coloured buildings, under which magnificent boats are moored, make it a must-see in the capital. I enjoy a plate of *sild*, herring served in three marinades (capers, mustard and cinnamon), accompanied by rye bread. It's a delicious snack that gives me enough energy to continue my walk along the water's edge to the famous *Little Mermaid* statue. Finally, I make a brief incursion into Christiania neighbourhood, the highly touristy 'freetown', which is nonetheless pleasant to explore.

Heading from Copenhagen to Elsinore, coastal route 152 offers an opportunity to stop at the Louisiana Museum of Modern Art, a superb gallery of contemporary pieces, with its sculpture garden overlooking the sea. Just 10km (6 miles) further north, a ferry line departs for Helsingborg – my adventure continues in Sweden. The country's southwest coastline is an alluring combination of wild seascapes, colourful fishing villages

'The country's southwest coastline is an alluring combination of wild seascapes, colourful fishing villages and offshore granite islands.'

and offshore granite islands. Then, 165km (103 miles) north of Gothenburg, Kosterhavet National Park appeals to even the most nature-averse vanlifers. It's possible to reach this marine park by boat from Strömstad – look out for a large colony of seals on the way. Once there, diving and hiking are common in this idyllic slice of nature – as is just lounging on one of its magnificent beaches.

After leaving the Koster Archipelago, I set course for Oslo. I'm still following the E6 and, 115km (71.5 miles) after crossing the border, I enter the Norwegian capital, easily finding a place to park. The city might be packed with galleries and museums, but it still manages to keep an eye on nature, surrounded by mountains, forests and lakes, and facing a fjord. The tone is set for the rest of the trip – from here on, the scenery is as untamed as it is magical.

While the Norwegian coast is well known, less celebrated is the interior of the country, so I'm delighted to discover its calling cards, racing along the E6 for over 200km (124 miles). I find several stretches of water, all offering exceptional locations for an overnight stay – Lake Mjøsa, on whose northern edge the town of Lillehammer lies, is truly stunning. I stop to briefly visit this quiet winter sports resort which hosted the 1994 Olympic Games – you can explore the Olympic Park facilities, including the lofty ski jump.

From Ringebu, whose remarkable wooden church is well worth a look, I turn off the main road to follow the Glomma Valley to Røros, a former mining town. Arriving in this UNESCO World Heritage Site, I'm overwhelmed by the beauty of the colourful houses, full of character. In the middle of the village, an octagonal church, with a whitewashed facade and tower lined with dark grey edges, is clearly the pride and joy of the locals.

There are now only 150km (93 miles) to go before I reach my goal, Trondheim, on the coast. The road follows the Gaula River for almost its entire length, and this final stretch is as bucolic as it gets. Happy to have the chance to experience such moments, I head for the coastal town with a smile on my

VISITING GOTHENBURG

Sweden's second largest city is the perfect destination for an urban getaway. Its many assets include Scandinavian architecture, rich cultural life and a warm atmosphere. Gourmets will be happy too in this coastal town, with various specialities including lobster and craft beer. Finally, it's the ideal starting point for an excursion to the Bohuslän Archipelago, a rocky heaven made up of 8000 islands.

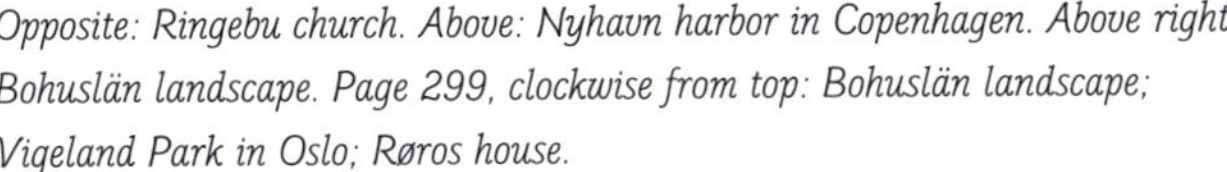

Opposite: Ringebu church. Above: Nyhavn harbor in Copenhagen. Above right: Bohuslän landscape. Page 299, clockwise from top: Bohuslän landscape; Vigeland Park in Oslo; Røros house.

face. In the wide pedestrian streets of this picturesque city with its spectacular Gothic cathedral, friendly cafes and restaurants welcome visitors. For my part, I stop for a long time on the old bridge, the Gamle Bybro, topped with red wooden gables, to contemplate the brightly painted buildings that line the banks of the Nidelva River.

Here I am at the end of this memorable adventure, between land and sea. I open a road atlas that's been gathering dust in the corner of the van and retrace the miles already covered. But rather than focusing on the route already taken from Denmark through Sweden and into Norway, my gaze is constantly drawn to the thousand other possibilities still open to me. One of them really catches my eye. At the top of the map, the Far North has an irresistible appeal. **AD**

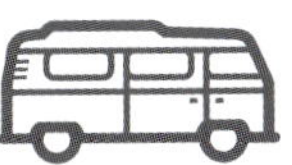

ROAD MAP

Start // Odense
Finish // Trondheim
Distance // 1318km (819 miles)
Recommended duration // Three weeks or more
When to go // In summer for long, warm days; in winter to try see the northern lights around Trondheim
Culinary speciality // *Smørrebrød* (Denmark), *smørbrød* (Norway) or *smörgåsbord* (Sweden): slices of buttered rye bread served with fish, cold meats, eggs, cheese or raw vegetables

THE PERFECT PICNIC SPOT

Description // Paid parking with view of Marstrand and its archipelago
GPS coordinates // 57.887130921216965, 11.603788782830142
Access // Located 50km (31 miles) north of Gothenburg, easy access via the E6 and Route 168 with its many bridges
Activities // Stroll around the marina, taste the local cinnamon buns and take some pictures
Visitor numbers // Quieter outside high tourist season
Little extras // Enjoy a walk in the nearby nature reserve (Marstrands Naturreservat) before getting back behind the wheel

Opposite: Lyngenfjord landscape, Norway.

MORE LIKE THIS
SCANDINAVIAN JEWELS

NORTHERN DENMARK

At the gateway to the North Sea, get ready to rub shoulders with some of Denmark's most beautiful wilderness spots. In the far north of Jutland, along the Limfjord, discover the pretty town of Aalborg, a cultural centre not to be missed, before heading northwest to the coast on the 55. The beaches seem endless – stop at Løkken's, a popular spot with photographers for its perfectly aligned white huts. Only 10km (6 miles) separate you from the Rubjerg Knude Lighthouse, destined to be swallowed up by the waters. Then it's a one-hour drive to Tversted Lakes car park to overnight in the heart of the woods (with toilet and picnic area) and scale the nearby Råbjerg Mile dunes, the largest in Europe – they move 15m (49ft) per year. Now you've reached the northern tip of the country, all that's left to do is visit Skagen, a fishing village that's a good spot to hang out for a few days.

Start // Aalborg
Finish // Skagen
Distance // 131km (81 miles)
More information // visitdenmark.com

BOHUSLÄN ARCHIPELAGO (SWEDEN)

Between Gothenburg and the Norwegian border, Bohuslän is home to the very best of Sweden. Enjoy a walk around the island of Tjörn (reached by a bridge), and soak up the maritime atmosphere of the various fishing hamlets. Drive your van to the Orust Peninsula along Route 160 then take the back roads and discover some truly stunning scenery. Continuing northwards, stop off at Lysekil, a handsome town where you can wander for a few hours and stock up on provisions. But it's definitely Smögen that will win you over the most, 50km (31 miles) further on. This village of multicoloured huts, nestled in an magical natural setting, is rightly one of the country's most visited sites. For even more peace and quiet, end your road trip in Fjällbacka, a picturesque resort of pretty red wooden houses.

Start // Tjörn
Finish // Fjällbacka
Distance // 161km (100 miles)
More information // visitsweden.com

FROM SENJA TO THE NORTH CAPE (NORWAY)

In the north of Norway, on the island of Senja, fjords and fairy-tale landscapes follow one after another, offering a particularly exhilarating setting for a drive. In winter, the northern lights are a common sight in the region. After Senja, head for the university town of Tromsø and enjoy breathtaking views on the cable car up to Storsteinen. Then head for Lyngenfjorden and gaze into its deep blue waters. Here you're in the Norwegian Alps, a favourite spot for winter sports. Stay on the E6 until you reach Olderfjord, then follow the E69 along Porsangerfjorden to Skarsvåg, the world's northernmost fishing village. A handful of kilometres away, bring the adventure to a splendid conclusion at the North Cape, which, from its rocky promontory, offers unrivalled views of the neighbouring cliffs and Arctic waters.

Start // Senja Island
Finish // The North Cape
Distance // 658km (409 miles)
More information // visitnorway.com

ALL THE WAY AROUND SOUTHERN ENGLAND

Characterful towns and villages, a dramatic coastline and a sense of the end of the world: there's no doubt that the south of England has plenty to tempt travellers.

The gleaming cliffs of Dover are ahead and I can't wait for the ferry from Calais to arrive. For months now, I've been imagining the adventure that awaits me: campervanning across the south of England, all the way to the tip of Cornwall, between green hills, rolling landscapes and picturesque towns.

After the short Channel crossing, I land in Kent and get into the left-hand lane of traffic. It will take me several days to really feel at ease with this way of driving. Fortunately, I have an appointment with my sister in Deal, only 15km (9 miles) away. An expat in Britain for many years, she and her English husband welcome me and after an eternity without seeing each other, our reunion is a warm one. We tread the pier of this fishing town, to the lively cries of the gulls. The waterfront is lined with cube-shaped houses, some white, others pastel, several home to restaurants. We push open the door of one of them and I choose a cottage pie, a delicious dish that immediately shatters my prejudices about British cuisine.

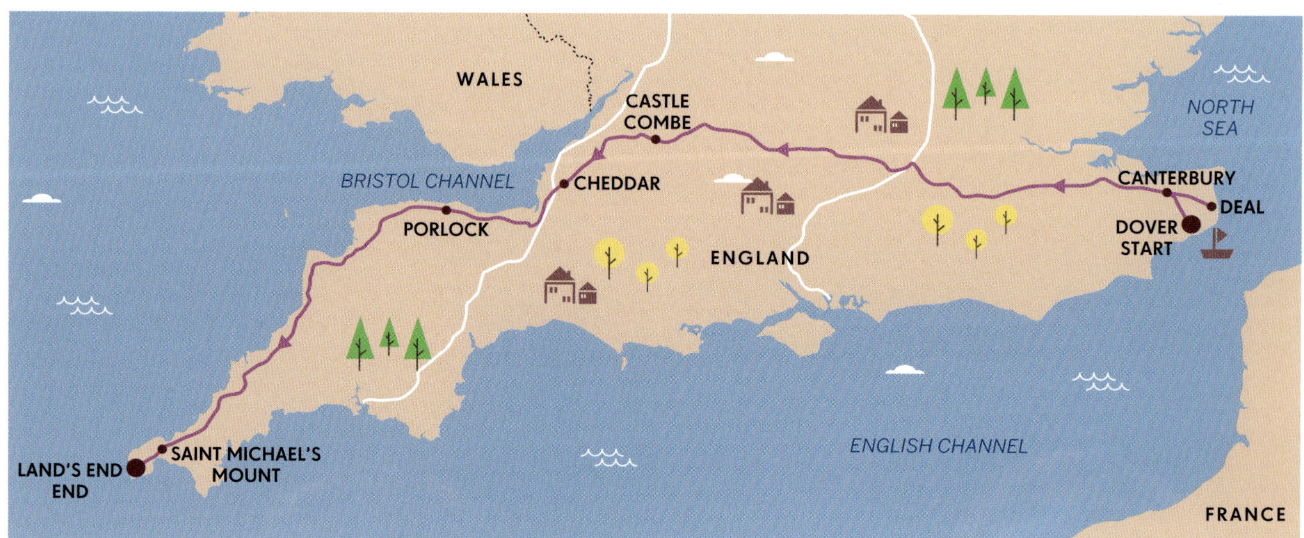

Following my family's recommendations, I then travel to the medieval town of Canterbury, some 30km (19 miles) away. As parking spaces are relatively expensive, I leave the camper on the outskirts and climb on my BMX, the perfect way to visit urban areas for free (another advantage is that it doesn't take up too much space in the passenger compartment). Surrounded by ramparts, the town features numerous half-timbered houses along picturesque cobbled streets. I gaze in admiration at the Gothic cathedral, the spiritual home of the Anglican Church; its stained-glass windows, some dating back to the 12th century, are a marvellous way to brighten up the building. I then explore the castle ruins, away from the centre but with the advantage of offering a privileged view of the city.

Having decided to make a big leap westwards, I bypass London via the M25 ring road. I don't want to venture into the streets of the capital at all, preferring first to get to grips with left-hand driving.

The 250km (155 miles) that separate me from the Cotswolds and their chocolate-box landscapes feel like a long way, so when I arrive at my destination, I'm delighted to park at last, far from civilisation, by some random pastures interspersed with low stone walls. These bucolic hills are classified as an Area of Outstanding Natural Beauty (AONB) by the British authorities, and it's an understatement to say that they exude a real sense of enchantment. Of all the gorgeous villages that adorn this verdant land, Castle Combe is a highlight. The singular architecture of its honey-coloured houses and the peaceful banks of the Bybrook River have a lot to do with it.

Somerset is my next stop and I set my GPS for Cheddar, 58km (36 miles) away. To reach this place famed for its namesake cheese, I have to navigate huge limestone gorges along the B3135 road. The small town doesn't disappoint. In the touristy centre, cheese sellers compete with each other in inviting customers to sample their products – I don't need asking twice. Aged in local cellars, the famous yellow cheese is very tasty, adding more points to my British cuisine scorecard.

Back at the wheel, I soon cross the untamed landscape of the Quantock Hills (another AONB area) and then head into Exmoor National Park, 80km (50 miles) further west. Straddling the border between Somerset and Devon, this mountainous region is covered in forest, moorland and farmland, giving me plenty of opportunities to get out and enjoy the pleasures of hiking. The A38 and then the A39 bring me to Porlock, a coastal village with a pretty marina. I take a long walk and, one step leading to another, I find myself exploring the coastline all

'Straddling Somerset and Devon, this mountainous region is covered in forest, moorland and farmland'.

ST MICHAEL'S SITES

Throughout Europe, several major locations are dedicated to St Michael. Along with Mont-Saint-Michel in Normandy and St Michael's Mount in Cornwall, others include the ancient monastery of Skellig Michael in Ireland, the rock of Saint-Michel d'Aiguilhe in Le Puy-en-Velay, France, the Sacra di San Michele near Turin and Monte Gargano in Puglia.

Above: Saint Michael's Mount. Opposite, from left: Canterbury Cathedral; Land's End. Page 305, clockwise from top: Sheep in the Cotswolds; Land's End, Cheddar Gorge.

the way to Hurlstone Point, a natural lookout over the Bristol Channel. The sun weakens and its rays soften, enveloping the bay in a golden light. The moment seems timeless, but I have to hurry back to the van before night falls.

In a wind so strong that I have to grip the steering wheel firmly, I enter the home stretch of my road trip – the southwestern tip of England, Cornwall. The name evokes a promise of the end of the world. Barnstaple, Bude, Newquay – for over 200km (124 miles), I follow the coast on the A39 towards Sennen. Along the way, the Channel is lined with pretty bays and small fishing ports. Some beaches are white sand, others are dotted with ebony rock. Not far from Penzance, I'm astonished to see the silhouette of St Michael's Mount, a granite island with an imposing castle at the end of a tidal causeway. This ancient place is reminiscent of its French cousin, Mont-Saint-Michel.

Pleasantly surprised, I get back on the road and realise I'm very close to Sennen. The tourist village itself doesn't hold my attention, but I'm keen to hike its steep coastline on one final walk between waves and cliffs. The geographical feature known as Land's End marks the southwestern tip of England. Beyond it, the Atlantic. A sign indicates that New York is 5064km (3147 miles) away. This isn't the end of the world but the start of another one. **AD**

ROAD MAP

Start // Dover
Finish // Land's End
Distance // 708km (440 miles)
Recommended duration // 5-to-7 days
When to go // Summer, for warmer temperatures (June or September if you don't like crowds)
Culinary speciality // Cream tea (a cup of tea accompanied by scones with cream and jam)

THE PERFECT PICNIC SPOT

Description // Paid parking with direct view of Porlock harbour
GPS coordinates // 51.218893884902414, -3.6270171036317973
Access // Via Anchor Rd
Facilities // Free public toilets
Visitor numbers // Very quiet (overnight stays are prohibited)
Little extras // Nearby bars and restaurants

Opposite: Dunstanburgh Castle, England.

MORE LIKE THIS
NORTH EUROPEAN COASTLINES

NORTH COAST 500 (SCOTLAND)

The north of Scotland hides some of the most beautiful scenery in Britain. At the very edge of Europe, you'll be driving your camper along very small roads, so take your time. Ruined castles, mountain ranges speckled with lochs and a rugged coastline mark out your itinerary, not to mention a few flocks of sheep. From Inverness, the capital of the Highlands, head inland towards the west coast, to climb slowly towards Applecross and Ullapool, then the Kyle of Durness, a superb secluded cove. You'll be riding along a spectacular panoramic roadway. Then follow the northern edge of the country, staying on the A836 all the way to John O'Groats, where a small row of painted houses overlooks a rough sea. Finally, return to Inverness, via quiet coastal ports and the pretty historic town of Dingwall.

Start/Finish // Inverness
Distance // 800km (500 miles)
More information // northcoast500.com

THY NATIONAL PARK (DENMARK)

Limestone cliffs, sandy meadows, moorlands – these form the backdrop for a camper van trip in northern Denmark's Thy National Park. Start off in Agger, a village rich in biodiversity (birds, seals), from where you'll follow the coastline to the Lyngby Dunes and the chance to come face to face with lots of deer on a beautiful walk. Nearby, take a few photos of Stenbjerg and its shoreline fringed with white houses with painted shutters. Further north, the windy Klitmøller Beach is a favourite destination for surfers, windsurfers and kitesurfers. Continue on to Hanstholm, where you can sample local specialities in a fish restaurant. To get back to Agger, you can take Route 26, which leads to the Vester Vandet lake and Thisted's Limfjord.

Start/Finish // Agger
Distance // 139km (86 miles)
More information // eng.nationalparkthy.dk

THE NORTHUMBERLAND COAST (ENGLAND)

Among England's areas of outstanding natural beauty (AONB), Northumberland stands out for its wilderness, punctuated by peaceful market towns. Slip a pair of good shoes, a bike and a kayak into your van to enjoy this jewel. From Warkworth and its castle, head north to the ruins of Dunstanburgh Castle, then on to the historic port of Beadnell. Nearby, leave your camper at the tiny port of Seahouses for a boat trip to the Farne Islands to spy puffins and cetaceans. Next stop is the dramatically situated Bamburgh Castle, dominating the local area from its cliff-top home. Drive carefully to Holy Island on a causeway accessible only at low tide. In this birdwatcher's paradise, the remains of a medieval priory are fascinating. End of the road is Berwick-upon-Tweed, with the opportunity to enjoy some beautiful walks along the river.

Start // Warkworth
Finish // Berwick-upon-Tweed
Distance // 88km (55 miles)
More information // northumberlandcoast-nl.org.uk

SOUTHERN SWEDEN

A loop around Skåne, along the Baltic Sea and the Öresund Strait.

I arrive in Sweden on the ferry from Rostock (in Germany) to Trelleborg. I can't wait to begin this trip around Skåne, a little-known region of Scandinavia that I've already had a small taste of by living for a while in Malmö, its main city. As soon as I disembark, I head west to the town of Skanör on the Falsterbo Peninsula in the far southwest of Sweden. At the top of a dune bordering a sandy beach, small wooden huts inevitably attract visitors. I follow in their footsteps and slalom between these colourful, picturesque shacks, before heading for Malmö, 30km (19 miles) further north.

Skåne's capital is well worth a day. Criss-crossed by canals and famous for its Turning Torso (at 190m/623ft, it's Scandinavia's tallest skyscraper), the country's third-largest conurbation has everything to offer visitors passing through – it's astonishing that it attracts so few tourists. Among the attractions of this city of parks, its central square, Stortorget, and little sister, Lilla Torg, will delight fans of brightly painted facades, while others will prefer to sample the joys of the Ribersborgs sauna, set up near the beach on a wooden pontoon. I stop off in Malmö to refuel, then head for Landskrona, 45km (28 miles) away on the west coast. An inspection of its brick castle surrounded by a moat is a must. Along the marina, other buildings are much more contemporary, achieving that subtle balance between tradition and modernity done so well in Scandinavian countries.

Still following the Baltic shore, new adventures await me 25km (15.5 miles) further on. Some places have the power to touch us more than others, without us necessarily knowing why, and, for me, Helsingborg is one of them. The town hall and medieval Kärnan Tower lend undeniable charm to the ancient walled city, while the coast, just a stone's throw away, offers a special view of the Öresund Strait. From the beach, you can see Denmark, only 4km (2.5 miles) away. Gradually, the light fades and I leave the city. I want to sleep alone, facing the sea, lulled by the bewitching sound of the waves. I reach the Margreteberg foreshore, north of Höganäs, as the sun is dropping below the horizon. Overnighting is allowed and the site has its own toilet facilities: a rare find. Barefoot, I pace the sand, watching the last rays of daylight. To my right, in the distance, the rocky outcrop of the Kullaberg piques my curiosity. It's decided: I'll go there tomorrow.

I leave my van before dawn in Mölle, on the south coast of the Kullaberg Peninsula, with an irresistible urge to make the most of

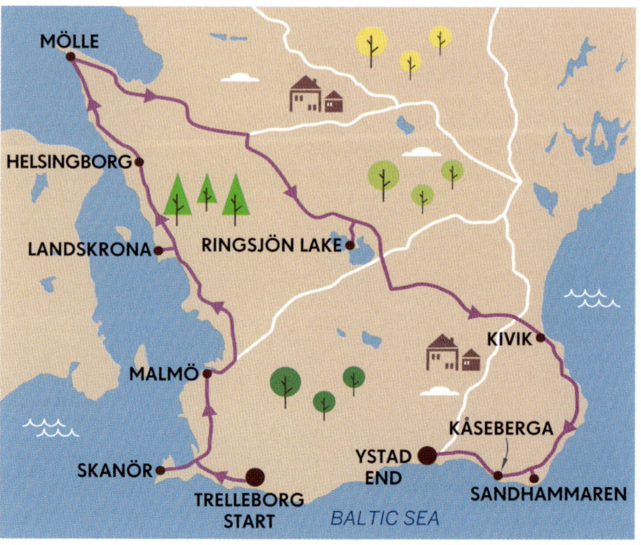

TRELLEBORGS KOMMU
TRYGG-HANSA

'I leave my van before dawn in Mölle, on the south coast of the Kullaberg Peninsula, with an irresistible urge to make the most of the day.'

the day. The place is popular, but at this hour there's no chance of meeting a crowd of hikers. With the Kullen Lighthouse in my sights, I make my way through the undergrowth as day breaks. In this granite empire, there are many caves to explore, as well as a less expected place: the micronation of Ladonia. Cautiously descending the steep path leading to the shore, I discover *Nimis*, a gigantic wooden structure, the fruit of artist Lars Vilks' fertile imagination, as was the creation of this micronation. Intrigued, I stand there for a long moment before heading back. Two hours later, sitting by the lighthouse, I take an apple out of my backpack. Devouring it, I watch from the top of the cliff the perpetual battle between sea and rock.

The second part of my road trip in southern Sweden takes place on the east coast, which I reach after crossing Skåne and passing by Ringsjön Lake, as beautiful as it is wild. On small country roads lined with forests and rapeseed fields, it's a peaceful drive to the fishing village of Kivik. Near the garnet-coloured huts in the harbour, children play and laugh their hearts out. Their good humor is contagious. I sit for a while facing Hanö Bay, *kanelbullar* (cinnamon bun) in hand, savouring this sweet treat as I contemplate the still expanse of water stretching out before me.

Route 9 takes me some 40km (25 miles) south, to a beach reputed to be the most beautiful in the country Sandhammaren is indeed a breathtaking place. On this immense white shore, time seems suspended. The only reality is the immaculate beach, glistening in the sun's strong rays. I meditate facing the sea until my shadow lengthens, then retreat to the forest. After a long search for an authorised parking area for the night, I fall asleep listening to the rustle of the trees, sand in the cabin and a smile on my face.

Arriving in Kåseberga, 9km (6 miles) away, I fall under the spell of Ales Stenar, a megalithic site that awakens memories of Stonehenge. Scandinavia's largest group of menhirs comprises 59 age-old tombs in granite, sandstone and gneiss. Cleverly arranged in the shape of a ship, these stones have watched over the Baltic since the Bronze Age. A long walk along the top of the cliffs where the stones stand ends with a spectacular sunset

Final call, 18km (11 miles) west of Kåseberga, is a visit to Ystad, a lovely little town with a pink-brick abbey and dapper half-timbered houses. A fitting end to my southern Sweden circuit. **AD**

THE ROYAL REPUBLIC OF LADONIA

The wooden sculptures of *Nimis* and *Arx* form an unusual ensemble in the Kullaberg Nature Reserve. The authorities brought several lawsuits against Lars Vilks for installing his work here – so in 1996 he proclaimed an independent micronation and called it the 'Royal Republic of Ladonia'.

Opposite, clockwise from left: Mölle; Ystad; Kullaberg nature reserve. Page 311, clockwise from top: Kivik harbour; Skanör beach; Trelleborg.

ROAD MAP

Start // Trelleborg
Finish // Ystad
Distance // 397km (247 miles)
Recommended duration // 7-to-10 days
When to go // Summer, for swimming in the sea (although Swedes swim year round)
Culinary speciality // *Kanelbullara* (tasty cinnamon buns)

THE PERFECT SLEEP SPOT

Description // Facing the sea
GPS coordinates // 56.21535791480702, 12.545722625356762
Access // Easy, by road
Facilities // Toilets, cold shower (beach) and drinking water
Visitor numbers // High in summer, low otherwise
Little extras // Great view of the sea and the Kullen Peninsula

Opposite, clockwise from top: Sõrve lighthouse on Saaremaa Island, Estonia; Stockholm street, Sweden Panga cliffs, Estonia.

MORE LIKE THIS ON BALTIC SHORES

EASTERN GULF OF BOTHNIA (FINLAND)

The Gulf of Bothnia's eastern, Finnish side has all the Scandinavian wilderness you could ask for. Vaasa, capital of Ostrobothnia, is a place where life seems resolutely peaceful, but the town opens onto the Kvarken Archipelago, recognised by UNESCO for its unspoilt nature. Connected to the mainland by various bridges, it's the ideal place to explore by camper, travelling from port to port. Shifting northeast on the E8, Jakobstad makes an appearance after 100km (62 miles). Park your vehicle to visit the old quarter, then take the wonderful coastal road to Oulu, a small town where you can enjoy a pleasant stroll along the Baltic shoreline. To make the most of the area's sandy beaches, take the ferry to reach the region's largest island, Hailuoto, inhabited by fishers almost cut off from the rest of the world.

Start // Vaasa
Finish // Hailuoto
Distance // 319km (198 miles)
More information // visitfinland.com

SAAREMAA ISLAND (ESTONIA)

It's impossible to resist the appeal of Saaremaa, Estonia's largest island. Take the Virtsu-Kuivastu ferry to reach an intermediate island, which you can then cross along National Route 10. The Saaremaa Bridge, an extraordinary sight stretching across the water, then leads you to Saaremaa itself. Stop at the Kaali Craters, carved out by a falling meteorite and now occupied by lakes surrounded by vegetation. Further afield, Kuressaare welcomes wellness enthusiasts with its spas, saunas and mud treatments. Others opt for a saunter around the medieval castle. Whatever your preference, just don't miss this town. In the northwest of the island, Kiipsaare Lighthouse, looking over the Baltic, entices lovers of wide-open spaces – if you're lucky, you'll spot seals. Complete the loop by following Route 129 to the north, stopping at the spectacular Panga Cliff.

Start // Virtsu
Finish // Panga
Distance // 200km (124 miles)
More information // visitestonia.com

SOUTHEAST SWEDEN

While Sweden is a great place in general for camper vans, capital Stockholm is an exception. Park outside and take a leisurely walk around the capital, built on an archipelago, enjoying its pretty streets and grand architecture. Back at the wheel, follow the straight E4 to Norrköping, a medium-sized town opening onto a bay into which the Motala Ström River flows. In Gamla Staden, the old town, beautiful multicoloured buildings catch the eye. Afterwards, stop as you please at the various coastal towns along the road to Kalmar, one of the country's oldest cities – its castle is home to 800 years of history. From here, cross the bridge over the island of Öland to find a discreet spot in the heart of nature, ideal for an unforgettable night. Finish in Karlskrona, a city jutting out into the Baltic Sea and famous for its epic offshore fort.

Start //Stockholm
Finish // Karlskrona
Distance // 774km (481 miles)
More information // visitsweden.com

INDEX BY COUNTRY

Authors: Astrid Duvillard and Alexandra Lam
Project Editor: Becca Hunt
Editor: Cliff Wilkinson
Maps: Caroline Sahanouk
Designer: Originally designed by Caroline Donadieu; changes to this edition Hillary Caudle
Publishing Director: Piers Pickard
Publisher: Becca Hunt
Art Director: Emily Dubin
Print Production: Nigel Longuet

Published in March 2025 by Lonely Planet Global Limited
ISBN: 9781837583119

10 9 8 7 6 5 4 3 2 1
Printed in China

Originally published by édi8 in France as *Van en Europe*, 2022.

Photographers as indicated. **Cover illustration** Ross Murray (www.rossmurray.com) **Photo credits** p. 8-9 : © Jonathan Friebel/ Adobe Stock; p. 112-113: © luengo_ua/Adobe Stock; p. 180-181: © reisegraf.ch/Shutterstock; p. 224-225: © Michael Charles/Adobe Stock; credit for images of tire tracks used in the sidebars of this book: © My Portfolio/Shutterstock

STAY IN TOUCH
lonelyplanet.com/contact

Lonely Planet Office:
IRELAND
Digital Depot, Roe Lane (off Thomas St), Digital Hub, Dublin 8, D08 TCV4, Ireland

Paper in this book is certified against the Forest Stewardship Council™ standards. FSC™ promotes environmentally responsible, socially beneficial and economically viable management of the world's forests.